Advocate for American Enterprise

William Buck Dana (1829–1910) at eighty. Photograph courtesy of William Floyd Estate/National Park Service, Fire Island National Seashore, Long Island, New York.

Advocate for American Enterprise

William Buck Dana and the
Commercial and Financial Chronicle,
1865–1910

Douglas Steeples

Contributions in Economics and Economic History
Number 226
David O. Whitten, Series Adviser

Greenwood Press
Westport, Connecticut • London

Library of Congress Cataloging-in-Publication Data

Steeples, Douglas W.
    Advocate for American enterprise : William Buck Dana and the Commercial and
financial chronicle, 1865–1910 / Douglas Steeples ; foreword by David O. Whitten.
        p.   cm.—(Contributions in economics and economic history, ISSN 0084–9235 ; no. 226)
    Includes bibliographical references and index.
    ISBN 0–313–32102–7 (alk. paper)
    1. Dana, William B. (William Buck), 1829–1910   2. Commercial and financial chronicle
3. Finance—United States—History.   4. United States—Commerce—History.   5.
Journalists—United States.   6. Journalism, Commercial—United States—History.
7. United States—Economic conditions.   I. Title.   II. Series.
HG181.S796   2002
070.92—dc21
[B]   2001033725

British Library Cataloguing in Publication Data is available.

Library of Congress Catalog Card Number: 2001033725
ISBN: 0–313–32102–7
ISSN: 0084–9235

First published in 2002

Greenwood Press, 88 Post Road West, Westport, CT 06881
An imprint of Greenwood Publishing Group, Inc.
www.greenwood.com

Printed in the United States of America

The paper used in this book complies with the
Permanent Paper Standard issued by the National
Information Standards Organization (Z39.48–1984).

10 9 8 7 6 5 4 3 2 1

With deep gratitude to my wife and best friend, Christine Steeples,
and all of my children

Contents

Illustrations

Foreword

During the five decades of William Buck Dana's editorship of the *Commercial and Financial Chronicle* the American cathedral of market-driven capitalism was only a dream, an image visible to few in the United States and still fewer abroad. Dana, like the faceless medieval craftsmen who laid down foundations for vast structures they would never see completed, devoted himself to shaping what he knew instinctively would one day astonish all who beheld it. As the 100th anniversary of Dana's death approaches, his legacy is lost in the overwhelming events that forged the United States and her business machinery into the model for a global economy beyond the imagination of the nineteenth-century mind. As disruptive and distressing as the war with Mexico, the American Civil War, and the Spanish-American War were for Dana and his fellow citizens, who could have anticipated the harrowing world wars of the twentieth century? the Nazi atrocities against humanity? the atomic bomb and the nuclear overtones of a half century of international political and military conflict that threatened to destroy the planet?

Dana was more than the founder of a business weekly or the formulator of a philosophy compatible with the mind-set of a brash young agrarian nation in the act of becoming an industrial and commercial power. Through his paper and the editorials he published in it, Dana helped forge an American philosophy of business that would withstand rigors beyond his imagining and prevail in a twenty-first century that is increasingly American, not by military expansion, but by commercial and cultural exchange.

Shortly after Dana's death, the monetary system that had weakened the economy in a society loath to be "crucified on a cross of gold" was shored up by a new financial structure erected in 1914 after passage of the Federal Reserve Act in December 1913. The years of Dana's life (1829–1910) encapsulated a monetary era without an American central bank. When he was born, seven years remained on the twenty-year charter for the second Bank of the United States, but conflict between bank president Nicholas Biddle and U.S. president Andrew Jackson had sealed the fate of that institution. Dana was destined to grow up in the era of the Independent Treasury and the financial difficulties associated with it. Business panics punctuated those years. Some historians argue that the depression of 1837 was the worst in American history; twenty years beyond that downturn, the panic of 1857 set the stage for the bloody and expensive Civil War. In 1873 and again in 1893, the United States suffered panics and depressions. For most of Dana's life the United States was heading toward panic, suffering depression, or reconstructing a broken economy. His response was to devote himself and much of his editorial space to the problems of money, banking, finance, and the business cycle. The Great Depression of the 1930s, twenty years after Dana's death, was the culmination of the cycle of panic and depression that had dominated his life and was more severe than any downturn Dana experienced as an adult. Yet the economic collapses and monetary affairs of his day—the Crime of '73, Greenbacks, the National Banking Act, national banknotes, the Bland-Allison Act, the Sherman Silver Purchase Act—were probably far more perplexing and frustrating than any since his passing.

Dana tried to rationalize a volatile business and financial world, but like everyone else then and now, he could only guess where its oscillations would take business, government, America, and the world. The future was as hazy for Dana in 1901 as it is for Americans in 2001. The nineteenth and twentieth centuries were beset with fantastic change. Dana was born before the telegraph and the great expansion of railroads, and he died early in the telephone era as automobiles began to replace trains and men took to the air in machines. In 2001, it is easy enough to see how radio, television, and the electronic revolution grew out of the telegraph and telephone or how powered flight gave rise to airlines and the rapid movement of people around the globe. But it is no easier for observers in 2001 to see where today's technology will take society by 2101 than it was for Dana to see in 1901 where his nation would be in 2001. Nonetheless, he sought a moral paradigm suitable for commercial interests as they met the unknown much like today's editors at *Business Week, Newsweek, Time, U.S. News & World Report*, and the *Wall Street Journal* seek the same holy grail for a global economy in a world harried by a deteriorating and dangerous Russia, political unrest in a dozen hot spots, and epidemics (HIV and AIDS) and epizootics (foot and mouth) that threaten life on earth in 2001 as much as nuclear war had threatened it in 1950.

Dana was caught between Adam Smith's *Wealth of Nations* (1776) and John Maynard Keynes's *General Theory of Employment, Interest, and Money* (1936). Smith described an economy in the throes of industrialization, an economy whose markets were just beginning to show their capacity to determine what was produced, how it was produced, and for whom it was produced; most of the economy, however, functioned without markets and was dominated by tradition and command (mercantilism). The world Dana knew was vastly different from the one Smith had written about. By the time Dana reached adulthood, the market segment was growing faster than the total economy and dominating an ever-increasing portion of it. At Dana's death, markets dominated the lives of nearly all citizens.

In the United States of 1776, perhaps 10 percent of the population was dependent on employment and an income for survival; in 2001, nearly all Americans are directly or indirectly dependent on employment and income for their livelihood. The change from a tiny market presence to an overwhelming market economy is the story of Dana's lifetime, the experience he tried to isolate, identify, codify, and rationalize. As many Americans do in 2001, Dana insisted on extrapolating Smith's teachings to the contemporary economy. Indeed Smith addressed some truths that transcend the size of the market in an economy. The working of supply and demand, which is the essence of market operation, continues to be the mainstay of any market, large or small, for it is a theoretical rendering of the interplay between the potential buyers and sellers of goods or services.

The market's function in society in Smith's day and Dana's was quite different. It was of little consequence if economists or politicians assured the public that markets, if left alone, would return to a working equilibrium when these markets played a small part in determining how people secured their food, clothing, and shelter. But the public today is poorly advised if encouraged to protest intervention in market operation when the exchange of money for goods and services is the lifeblood of society. In a nutshell, that is the difference between the economy Adam Smith observed and generalized and the one John Maynard Keynes hoped to resuscitate in the 1930s. Dana looked to Smithian and classical prescriptions to interpret the economy of his era. (The classical economists were followers of Smith and include Thomas Robert Malthus, David Ricardo, James Mill, John Stuart Mill, and Alfred Marshall.) He refused recourse to the writings of Karl Marx, a compelling contemporary interpreter of society and the economy. Dana was an advocate of business and himself an entrepreneur vested with an interest in a thriving capitalist society. The Marxian commitment to the demise of capitalism was not an option Dana and his audience endorsed.

Every social observer struggles with an unknown future while trying to make sense of the confusing complexity of the present. And therein lies Dana's value in the twenty-first century. In *Advocate for American Enterprise*, Douglas Steeples brings together his long experience in studying, teaching, and writing history to illuminate the life and work of a preeminent commentator on the American milieu in the late nineteenth and early twentieth centuries. Steeples has done yeoman service in merging biography and analysis. Had Dana written a philosophical tract setting out his views on life, labor, capital, finance, and general business he could not have presented better insights into his reasoning and how it evolved. But that tract would have been a static paradigm for American business. Steeples' gleanings constitute a year-by-year appraisal of Dana's thinking as it materialized in response to the stimuli—the money panics, labor strife, the public's demand for free coinage of silver, debates over tariff policy, immigration laws and immigrants, antitrust laws—that shaped his day and ours.

The *Commercial and Financial Chronicle* has, like Dana, its founder and creator, disappeared into history. Perhaps a thousand men and women in 2001 can identify Dana and a slightly larger number recollect his paper. Steeples' work will not return Dana to center stage, nothing can; but it secures Dana's place in American history and makes his life and work accessible to anyone interested in the development of business thinking in nineteenth-century America and, more importantly, how that thinking influenced the progress of a great nation.

David O. Whitten, series adviser
Contributions in Economics and Economic History

Preface

There are moments in history when powerful currents of change seem to threaten the foundations of society. The United States, from the mid-nineteenth century through the first decade of the twentieth century, underwent such a profound transition. It suppressed an armed resistance by the Confederate States of America that challenged the very survival of the federal union. It experienced revolutionary advances in communication and transportation. It entered into the epoch of heavy industrialization and the formation of corporations of unprecedented, immense scale and power. Waves of settlement washed across the remaining habitable portions of the interior. The country's population quadrupled to more than 92 million, as a result of natural increase and of foreign immigration. Urbanization became a dominant feature of the national landscape: population of places of more than 2,500 inhabitants grew from 3.54 million to 41.99 million, while that of rural areas rose only from 19.65 million to 49.97 million. New and often baffling problems posed themselves with bewildering frequency.

Over a span of two generations the nation saw the political bonds that united it tested to the utmost, and restored. The United States endured one of the bloodiest civil wars of modern times. Afterward, it struggled with the task of reconstructing its federal system. The abolition of Negro slavery necessitated wrenching adjustments in relations between Blacks and Whites. The destruction of the slave-based antebellum plantation system brought into being widespread resort in the South to sharecropping and crop liens as means to finance agricultural production. Reconciliation of the northern and southern states required a generation.

Innovation in communication and transportation reshaped national life. In 1866 Western Union and American Telegraph combined, forming the basis of a national network. Soon after, the laying of an undersea cable from North America to Europe introduced transatlantic telegraphy. So rapidly did use of the telegraph grow that in 1892 Western Union's 21,000 offices sent 62.4 million messages. Meanwhile, Postal Telegraph entered the scene in 1881. And shortly before, in May 1876, Alexander Graham Bell had perfected the first practical magnetoelectric telephone. Prefiguring even greater impact to come, as an instrument that expedited commerce, facilitated social exchanges, and interrupted daily routines, use of the new device grew explosively. Within fifteen years, 8,000 employees served 788 exchanges operating 266,000 miles of line. Transcontinental railroads furnished the transportation counterpart to these new means of transmitting information. Within a quarter century of the joining of the Central Pacific and the Union Pacific (at Promontory Point, Utah, on May 10, 1869), a half dozen systems connected the West to the East Coast. The new railroads affected the movement of people and goods as fundamentally as telegraphy and telephony had the dispatch of information. Formerly isolated local communities and businesses, where relative freedom from competition had existed, suddenly found themselves bound more and more tightly to a national, and then an international, market and economy.

A turn to new sources of power to serve machines and manufacturing, and then daily life, was no less far-reaching in impact. The introduction of incandescent electric lighting illuminated even mines and stamp mills in locations as remote as California's Mojave Desert by 1888, only nine years after Thomas Alva Edison had developed the lightbulb. Two years after his invention, the advent of the steam-powered dynamo drove a rushing expansion of the commercial generation of electricity. Construction of the first power grids occurred apace. It became possible for industry to begin a shift from reliance on steam-powered machines to electric motors for production. The 1890s saw the internal combustion gasoline engine come into increasing use, first as a mechanism to assist in industrial activity and then as the source of motive power for the machine that reshaped urban America during the twentieth century—the automobile.

As these events unfolded, relentless land-hungry pioneers cleared the West of the last of the great herds of bison that had once ranged from Virginia to Idaho. With the bison went the remaining free-roaming bands of Indians. The process of settlement was far from the pretty one that long ago entered into our national myth of inexorable, benign progress. The elimination of the bison was but one step in a profligate consumption of resources anticipated earlier by the near extinction of beaver to satisfy the demands of the fur trade. It accompanied a comparable extravagance with mineral and timber resources, and the western soil itself. Savage episodes of war, sometimes aimed at exterminating rather than simply relocating Indians, punctuated the advance of settlement. No matter. Almost always there was a prodigal faith that occupation of new regions to mine, log, and farm would prosper settlers and advance civilization.

The swelling population, especially as it clustered in growing urban centers, brought urgent new problems. Congestion, construction of adequate streets and roads, creation of means of mass transit, provision of a safe domestic water supply, treatment and disposal of sewage, design of adequate means of protection from fire and from lawlessness, and prevention of the spread of disease were only the most obvious of these. Expanding ranks of industrial laborers found themselves at the mercy of changing business conditions no less than of the new circumstances of life. Structural unemployment averaged 7 to 10 percent during the entire period. Periodic business recessions and depressions—no fewer than seven between 1850 and 1907—thrust increasing and far greater numbers temporarily out of work. The scale of need outstripped the capacity of private charity, while public means of assistance had scarcely begun to evolve.

The very shape of the economy underwent a sea change. The sheer size of the task of building transcontinental railroads required amassing huge amounts of capital. The corporate form of organization was an ideal instrument for raising this capital, through sales of securities. As a result, the roads emerged as our first truly large corporations, their arrival announced by a cacophony of thundering locomotives, clattering cars, and a flood of issues of stocks and bonds. By 1890 the growth of railroads and the advance of manufacturing had struck a new balance. Capital invested in railroads and manufacturing for the first time surpassed that in agriculture. Between roughly 1890 and 1910, after the end of the great era of railroad building, the advance of manufacturing brought the creation of immense industrial corporations. Expanding enterprise subjected the country to an ever-growing need for credit. Fluctuations in foreign economies joined seasonal variations here in demand for cash and credit, associated with building construction and with planting and then harvesting and marketing corn, wheat, and cotton, to add to this need. Central reserve banks, where member institutions of the national banking system placed a portion of their deposits, assumed growing importance. Often these same banks consolidated their positions at the apex of the new economy by underwriting the stock and bond issues of the emergent giant corporations and placing their own officers on their boards of directors.

Frightening challenges accompanied the growing scale of enterprise. Many people wondered what was to become of the opportunity for the individual workingman to become a small businessman, or the latter to succeed competitively in the new business environment. Given the disparity of power between the large employer and the individual laborer, what chance had the latter to bargain successfully for improved wages and working conditions? In broad farming regions similar problems loomed. Growers of wheat and corn on the great plains, and southern cotton farmers, often found themselves obliged to deal with a single local grain elevator or cotton gin, ship over a single railroad, and purchase seed and necessities from one or a small handful of suppliers. How could they hope to prosper? In towns and cities, citizens and consumers faced comparable problems. Too often, local streetcar, electrical, water, and other public utilities shamelessly corrupted municipal officials in pursuit of exclusive long-term franchises and other privileges, including tax advantages and exemption from regulation.

Bribery and kickbacks not infrequently accompanied the award of municipal street paving and sewer construction contracts. The influence of corporate beneficiaries of such arrangements reached even into state legislatures, which were too often unresponsive to the complaints of angry urban residents. In short, and all things considered, monopolistic corporate power seemed to cast a deepening shadow over the country.

At the end of the century the United States dramatically thrust itself into a newly prominent role on the stage of world affairs. As early as 1867 it added its first significant noncontiguous territory, with the purchase of Alaska. The 1890s brought, in quick succession and by a variety of means, a series of acquisitions through which the country came into ownership of an overseas empire. American planting and commercial interests, with the connivance of this country's minister to Hawaii, engineered a rebellion that ousted the last queen of the islands. The coup paved the way for annexation by a joint resolution of Congress five years later, in 1898, while this country was at war with Spain. The brief but decisive Spanish-American War transferred to the United States Guam, the Philippines, Puerto Rico, and, for a time, Cuba. The United States claimed Wake Island and Midway the same year, and in 1899 took American Samoa through an international agreement dividing the Samoan Islands. A republic born in a revolt against British colonial control was now, ironically, an imperial power. Unimpressed by the benefits of American control and bent on winning their own independence, ungrateful Filipinos turned from rebellion against their Spanish former masters to insurrection against their new American overlords. The resulting conflict lasted three years, forced the United States to commit a force of 70,000 to action that was often savage and brutal, and cost the Filipinos hundreds of thousands of lives. The turn of the century era of overseas expansion ended when the United States helped rebels detach Panama from Colombia as a precursor to negotiating a treaty through which it won from the new republic a swath of land across which to cut an interoceanic canal. Work began at once and was completed eleven years later in 1914.

So much is familiar to people knowledgeable about American history. A summary as compressed and incomplete as this will nevertheless serve to make an important point: it was no easy task to make sense of such far-reaching, rapid, even turbulent change. Many people tried to do so, with radically differing results. Labor sociologist John Rogers Commons, historian and social theoretician Henry Brooks Adams, novelist William

Dean Howells, Utopian writer Edward Bellamy, critics of big business Ida Tarbell and William Zebina Ripley, evangelist Josiah Strong, advocate of the free coinage of silver William Hope "Coin" Harvey, naval captain Alfred Thayer Mahan, and a corps of others joined local, state, and national politicians of every stripe in attempting to fashion understandings of the new order. There were, of course, daily newspapers, but they scarcely resembled those with which modern readers are familiar. They trafficked in fiction, local affairs, crime and society news, partisan political messages, sensational reports, advertising, public announcements, and, in Charles Adams Dana's *New York Sun*, a new genre, the human interest series.

Not until late in the century were there technological means for rapid mechanical typesetting and large daily press runs, permitting the rise of the penny press. The absence of mass electronic media allowing for instantaneous communication of even the most essential information added to the difficulty to adjust. Before the Civil War the most substantial efforts to chronicle events in the national and international economy resided in monthly publications. Of these the most prominent were *Hunt's Merchants' Magazine* and *DeBow's Review*. Before the great conflict between the states hastened the pace of events, they were sufficient. As the struggle ground on, monthly news about military, national political, and business matters came to be no news at all. It was simply not current enough to meet the needs of government, business, or society.

People living on the cusp between the twentieth and the twenty-first centuries have come to regard their era as the age of the "new information economy." Computers, multiplex fiber optical telephonic cables, wireless microwave transmission, communication satellites, and the like permit around-the-clock worldwide transaction of business. The new electronic technology increasingly drives robotized methods of production, manages inventories, enables customizing of products, and allows for "just-in-time" delivery. It may come as a surprise, then, to learn that about 130 years ago an earlier, simpler "information economy" took form in the United States. We have already alluded to elements of it previously. It relied at first on telegraphic communication, then telephony. The former gave rise to the Associated Press, organized as early as 1848. As undersea cabling was extended, and improved steamship transoceanic mail delivery improved, they also contributed their share. So did railroad mail dispatch. The telephone added its own impact during the final quarter of the century. Together these were latent resources for commerce. They could be bent toward furnishing intelligence on output in all of the major lines of manufacturing. They could be employed to disseminate reports about the inventories of major products throughout the commercial world and the movements of demand and price. They could be conduits through which to inform about the status of crops and probable harvests worldwide, the production of crucial new materials, shipping and postal costs, and monetary exchange rates. They could communicate the condition of capital markets and of banks, how war and the threat of war might affect the credit and trade of nations, and the likely commercial impact of political trends. All of this information and more—provided accurately, comprehensively, and in the most timely possible manner—became, as the nineteenth century merged into the twentieth, essential for successful competition in the developing national and global marketplaces that were eclipsing local markets and economies.

The first American with the acumen to exploit the telegraph and improved overseas communications in order to meet the burgeoning needs of business for ample and high-quality current information was William Buck Dana (1829–1910). His contribution was the United States' first business weekly, the *Commercial and Financial Chronicle*. He established it in 1865 in the country's commercial nerve center, New York City. For as long as he lived and beyond, his paper was unequaled as a comprehensive and accurate source for all aspects of domestic and many aspects of world business. It was also, because of its authoritative character and its influential readership, a unique lens through which to view important tendencies in economic thought. Journalistically, it was as significant as the railroad and the telegraph and telephone were in their ways in creating a national and an international economy.

Dana was long an obscure figure. He led a singularly unobtrusive life. Its most important record was found in his ideas, which dominated his paper until his death. Discovery and subsequent preservation of his personal papers added materially to this record. They yielded information and clues essential for researching toward a fuller understanding of him. Readers will quickly come to appreciate just how important Dana and the *Chronicle* were. One can scarcely reconstruct the business history of the United States between the Civil War and 1910 without immersing oneself in his paper. Even the most important series of business statistics for the period published by the U.S. government, *Historical Statistics of the United States* (three editions since 1945), depends heavily on his work and that of the correspondents worldwide who contributed to the *Chronicle*. The ideas and motives that allowed for such comprehensiveness and accuracy will become evident as we explore Dana's education and his conduct as a businessman and journalist.

This book is not a conventional biography, nor is it a "life and times" study. It is, rather, a study of a man, his ideas, and their importance. Chapter 1 considers the formative experiences that prepared Dana for his career as an editor-publisher, real estate developer, and spokesman-advocate for business. The second chapter covers his career and later life. The following four chapters turn to the main themes conveyed in the editorial (and relevant news) content of the *Chronicle*. With the first, they allow us imaginatively to reconstruct and enter into Dana's "mental world." The concluding chapter is a brief essay commenting on Dana's, and his paper's, importance and influence. In many respects this section seeks the elusive answers to the most significant questions that a close reading of Dana's life and the *Chronicle* pose. Few things are more difficult to pin down than "influence" and "representativeness." Yet this book would be incomplete without some attempt to treat them. It will have served its purpose well if, in enlarging our understanding of Dana, the *Chronicle*, and economic thought of his time, it stimulates further exploration of business attitudes of his era and achievement of an even better grasp of this critically important time.

Acknowledgments

Every work of scholarship depends for its success on the contributions of many individuals and institutions. This book is no exception. It originated with questions asked many years ago by the eminent southern historian Fletcher Green at the University of North Carolina at Chapel Hill. On one memorable occasion Professor Green wondered, in particular, about certain little-known aspects of national economic development from the 1850s onward. He was especially interested in the influence, and then the obscure demise, of the country's foremost pre–Civil War business publication. This was *Hunt's Merchants' Magazine.*

The curiosity that Dr. Green piqued freshened when, working on a study of the depression of 1893 with Auburn University economist David Whitten, it struck me forcefully that it was significant that the *Commercial and Financial Chronicle* was the successor publication to the *Magazine.* How had the one given way to the other? Ongoing research answered that, and many other interesting questions. It also resulted in a further debt to the *Chronicle* and its founding editor-publisher William Buck Dana, who guided it for a half century. We discovered that it is practically impossible to reconstruct the story of American business for the period without relying heavily on Dana's publication. As I wrote in the preface, it is *the* source for inquiry into this field and into contemporary business thought.

My obligations extend to many others as well. Through the staff of the Genealogy Room of the New York City Public Library I was led to Dana's grandson–adoptive son's widow Ella Lindley Dana. Her generosity in inviting me to the old Dana summer residence. Moss Lots at Mastic, Long Island, New York, bore more fruit than I could have imagined. Given the run of the house I was able to photograph it extensively, inventory Dana's library and office, and discover his personal papers. Financial support from

Earlham College and the Johnson Fund of the American Philosophical Society enabled me to photocopy Dana's papers. Fortunately, Ms. Dana's generosity resulted in the deposit of these papers with the William Floyd Estate unit of the Fire Island National Seashore shortly after I worked with them. In 1968 Moss Lots burned to the ground, but Dana's papers remain available to scholars in the archives of the Floyd Estate.

In 1989 David Whitten placed me in touch with Lester Ewell, who had just purchased the William A. Dana Company and wished to commission an article commemorating the sesquicentennial of the founding of *Hunt's Merchants' Magazine–Commercial and Financial Chronicle*. This contact reactivated my research about Dana and his paper. Dr. Whitten has been a constant source of encouragement and a willing reader and critic of many drafts of this manuscript during the following years. Assistance from Aurora University and Mercer University made possible research trips back to Long Island, to Yale University, to Hackensack and Englewood Cliffs in New Jersey, and to Utica and Vernon, New York. Archivist Janet Schiff of the Yale University Archives offered valuable assistance. The clerks of the Surrogate Courts of Oneida and Suffolk Counties, New York, at Utica and Riverhead, helped with location of wills and other items relating to Dana estates and bequests. Personnel in the office of the clerk of Bergen County, New Jersey, guided me to records of various Dana real estate transactions. Staff members at the Utica Library, Englewood Public Library, and Johnson Free Library in Hackensack directed me to rare and valuable items in their special local history collections. Patricia Dixon, librarian at Vernon, New York, where Dana studied at a local academy, was helpful in locating material bearing on his schooling.

Rayonia Babel, reference librarian at Aurora University's Charles Phillips Library, was indefatigable at tracking down rare source materials and securing them through interlibrary loan. The staffs of the Newberry Library in Chicago and of the Manuscripts Division of the Library of Congress provided help at critical moments. My colleague at Aurora, Dr. Michael Sawdey, made excellent reproductions of old, sometimes damaged, photographs, which were made available from the archives of the William Floyd Estate. Jean Coco, Susan Duncan, Richard Stavdal, and Steve Czarniecki, all of the Floyd Estate, made working in the archives there a joy. The National Park Service has generously permitted use of most of the photographs that appear between the covers of this volume. Eric Nelsen of the New Jersey Unit of the Palisades Interstate Park tracked down additional photographs and information. Doris Dana, William Buck Dana's great granddaughter, graciously granted permission to quote from the Dana Papers.

Virginia Cairns, David Bunnell, David Greenebaum, and Karen Harrell at the Mercer University Library have gone far beyond the call of duty in finding and borrowing through interlibrary loan volumes of the

Chronicle, as well as numerous other materials. The reference librarians at the Baker Library, Graduate School of Business, Harvard University, have guided me to key materials in their collection of the records of R. G. Dun & Company, who were the foremost creators of credit records in Dana's day. Mercer University has, meanwhile, maintained an environment in which a dean can function and publish as an historian while discharging decanal responsibilities. This rare circumstance is a tribute to the university and its leadership, as well as to a faculty in the College of Liberal Arts who encourage their dean in such activity. Colleagues in the Economic and Business and Historical Society have been generous in listening to and commenting on papers presented treating aspects of Dana's career and thought. I am grateful to the *Long Island Forum* for permission to use material that it published in greatly condensed form. Anonymous referees, and professors Edwin Perkins of the History Department at the University of Southern California and William Childs of the History Department of The Ohio State University furnished useful critical suggestions. Drs. Perkins and Childs, as successive editors of *Essays in Economic and Business History* (*EEBH*), published much-abbreviated versions of some of the content of chapters 1 and 2 in *EEBH*. They have generously consented to use of this matter in the present volume. Professors H. Roger Grant at Clemson University, Michael Namorato at the University of Mississippi, and Gloria Ricci Lothrop of California State University-Northridge have enriched the book with perceptive readings of the manuscript.

Senior Editor Cynthia Harris, Production Editor Liz Leiba, and my copy editor at Greenwood deserve special recognition for their fine work. My deepest thanks must be reserved for the one who has persisted with me through all of the drafts of this book, captured infelicities of style, and proposed innumerable improvements. That is my wife, Christine Steeples, without whose partnership this book could not have come into being.

Douglas Steeples
Mercer University

1

The Education of an Entrepreneur

... the impossibility of our setting up in business with so small a capital.

—William Buck Dana, September 27, 1854

On February 1, 1861, William Buck Dana purchased *Hunt's Merchants' Magazine* for $7,000.[1] The transaction was an uncharacteristically bold departure for Dana, who was a temperamentally cautious thirty-one-year-old attorney from Utica, New York. He had foreseen that it would radically change his own life, removing him from Utica and plunging him into the unfamiliar world of publishing and editing in New York City, where *Hunt's* was produced. But neither he nor anyone else foresaw the momentous national consequences that would follow the purchase. Within a very few years Dana mastered his new profession and worked a bold new departure in American journalism. Building on his success with the monthly *Merchants' Magazine*, in 1865 he introduced the country's first business weekly, the *Commercial and Financial Chronicle*. He soon after emerged as our most respected reporter and commentator on business and finance. His paper stood preeminent among business publications, and he was the authoritative exponent of the dominant business ideology until his death in 1910.

The purchase of the *Merchants' Magazine* was itself one of the chief sources of Dana's rapid ascent to prominence. Launched with borrowed capital in July 1839, the *Magazine* was the creation of one of the United States' best-known journalists, Freeman Hunt. The Massachusetts-born Hunt had entered the publishing industry at the age of twelve, after the death of his father. His first job was as a printer's devil, at the *Boston Evening Gazette*. He quickly rose, becoming a compositor, then a writer, then an editor, and, finally, a publisher, individually, in partnership, and in management for a corporation. In Boston and New York he shared in the publication of a number of successful books and periodicals. Known as an advocate of the abolition of slavery and as a champion of persons struggling against adversity, he was described as a man of kindly disposition, of above-medium height, with light brown hair, blue eyes, and a florid complexion. He was by turns a superb editor and a hopeless drunk. From its inception until his death, the *Magazine* was his consuming interest. He managed it from his sick bed during his final illness, succumbing in 1858, at the age of fifty-four, to "disease of the liver."

The *Magazine* was a distinguished success and the country's leading business periodical under Hunt's direction. Hunt conceived it to fill a void, which it did without competition before 1850. As he later recalled, he could find at the time of its introduction many books and newspapers that dealt with commercial topics, but "not a single magazine, of high or low pretensions, either in America or, to the best of our knowledge, in Europe, to represent and to advocate the claims of commerce." Believing that improved knowledge and increasing ties of trade would prosper humanity and advance civilization, he took a very broad view of commerce. The *Merchants' Magazine* provided reports on agriculture, manufacturing, commodities, and merchandise trade; banking; insurance; currency; navigation; and legislation and court decisions affecting the conduct of business. It offered profiles of successful merchants, and, initially, articles by leading writers of the day, including Charles Francis Adams, Horace Greeley, George S. Boutwell, and Francis Wharton. An "encyclopedia of commercial subjects, remarkable for its orderly arrangement of masses of material," it sought to provide merchants with guidance for the conduct of business.

Hunt's set the standard for accuracy and for comprehensiveness, while functioning also as an expression of growing American nationalism and of a consciousness of expanding national economic prospects and power. By the 1850s, each issue averaged some 150 octavo pages and included four to six signed articles and a mass of statistical information gleaned from newspapers and other magazines, reports of public officials and court decisions, and other sources. Regular monthly departments on each of the leading lines of business, on mercantile law and commercial regulations, and chronicling commerce conveyed this material. At the time of Freeman Hunt's death, the *Merchants' Magazine* commanded a readership throughout the United States, in Canada, and in Europe.[2]

William Dana's own abilities, character, and knowledge constituted the second source of his striking success. In this chapter I trace his circuitous path to the purchase of *Hunt's*. In doing so, I shall emphasize the experiences that prepared him to embark on a career in journalism through which he assumed a pivotal position and amassed a fortune. The most important of these are to be found in the nature of the community in which he grew up and later practiced law, in his family, in his formal education, in his law practice, and in his courtship and marriage. Each played a role in his education. All helped to shape him.

The history of Utica until 1860 compressed in the span of scarcely more than two generations the experiences transforming the contemporary United States. The fascinating story of the city's development has generated a rich body of historical writing. Our discussion here depends heavily on Robert Frederick Berkhofer, Jr's. "The Industrial History of Oneida County, New York, to 1850," and Mary P. Ryan's superb *Cradle of the Middle Class*. Ryan's book is particularly valuable for its penetrating treatment of economic and social change and the evolution of family life and religious practices.[3]

Utica grew on a fertile plain lying on the south bank of the Mohawk River, close to the geographic center of New York. The site held great strategic importance. It lay at the crossing of a system of historic Iroquois trails. One of the most important of these ran up the Susquehanna River from Pennsylvania and then along the Black River toward Canada. Another extended west from the Hudson River to the Great Lakes, connecting the council fires of the great Iroquois confederacy, and forded the Mohawk. Utica thus developed astride the key transportation routes of central New York and could aspire to become a major hub of commerce and industry. The first local settlement accompanied the construction of Fort Schuyler in 1758, to protect the route from Fort Stanwix (now Rome) during the French and Indian War. The full-scale peopling of the area began a quarter century later, after the end of the American War of Independence in 1783 opened the way. Between 1785 and 1797 New York eliminated any threat from the few thousand Iroquois who had not fled to Canada, negotiating the cession of their lands. It also settled a dispute with Massachusetts, establishing jurisdiction over the lands between Albany and the Great Lakes. The thin stream of people drifting in to found towns along the Mohawk soon swelled to a great flood of migrants.[4]

Hugh White, a Connecticut veteran of the New York campaign during the Revolutionary War, was at the head of a mass of settlers who arrived in the Utica area in the 1780s and 1790s. Expelled from Connecticut, Massachusetts, and Rhode Island by a scarcity of good farmlands, immigrants poured into western New York. White in 1784 bought 1,500 acres on Sauquoit Creek, near its junction with the Mohawk. Within a year, he settled five sons, two daughters, and three daughters-in-law on pieces of the tract surrounding his homestead, anticipating a pattern of land distribution that many other heads of family followed. Soon after, Whitestown Township, bearing his name, was organized. Settlement advanced rapidly in all directions, covering the countryside with an expanding mosaic of fields, orchards, and woodlots around dispersed farmhouses. In 1790, 1,891 persons lived in Whitestown, in 1800, 4,212. Population passed 5,000 twenty years later. Within a half century of Hugh White's arrival, township farms annually yielded tens of thousands of bushels of corn, potatoes, and wheat; and dairying produced each year three million pounds apiece of cheese and butter. Pioneers occupied virtually all tillable land as early as 1820, ending the frontier epoch. During the ensuing twenty years young people emigrated away to seek land and opportunity elsewhere, much as their own forebears who had surged into Whitestown from New England.

While in its frontier phase, agricultural Whitestown saw the beginning of ancillary industries. Saw and flour mills, tanneries, distilleries, and carding factories scattered along creeks and roads running among farms served the needs of the countryside within a radius of five or six miles. Processing lumber, grains, hides, and wool, they furnished the community with a stream of products that were not processed in the home. Cash was very scarce in Whitestown's primitive frontier economy, so most exchange occurred through barter. Even the daughters and sons of local farmers who took jobs in the woolen mill of the Oneida Manufacturing Society received their wages in the form of room and board, goods from the company store, and yarn, for several years after the mill's establishment, around 1809. What little cash trade there was involved primarily a small selection of goods that could not be made locally.

Harbingers of economic change appeared early in Whitestown. The first merchant arrived in 1790. One of the largest speculative land development firms in western New York was on the scene soon after, as Holland Land Company agent Theophile Cazenove purchased a site for a market and export center that became Utica. By 1800, two bridges spanned the Mohawk, and John Post's store and Moses Bagg's hostelry were thriving. When three turnpikes converged in front of Bagg's establishment in 1805, a boom began in the newly incorporated village of Utica. A watercolor depicting the view from the hotel in 1807 shows some sixteen houses flanking the broad main street, most of them two stories tall, and four more houses nearby. The scene is one of calm; the two streets are virtually empty. No church or obviously commercial building is visible. The passage of a carriage, the tautly bent body of a woodchopper, and the presence of several onlookers, however, enliven the view in what appears to be a transplanted New England village.

Utica grew rapidly. Area farmers quickly shifted their trade from Albany, some ninety miles to the east. The passage of throngs of westward-bound migrants, whose groaning wagons sometimes numbered in the hundreds daily, brought added traffic. By 1811, travelers commented that around Utica "the houses were so thick, that it was for a considerable way like a continued village. Many of the buildings were elegant, with fine orchards attached to them, and the plots of ground adjoining were fertile and elegantly cultivated."[5]

The succeeding decades brought numerous challenges, as Uticans contended with the volatile business environment of the first half of the nineteenth century. When New Yorkers living farther west began to divert the shipment of their produce away from the route linking the Great Lakes to the Mohawk and Hudson, turning instead to the St. Lawrence River, Uticans and others in Oneida County looked to manufacturing to stimulate commerce. The organization of the Oneida Manufacturing Society attracted investment from many local merchants, a number of successful farmers, and at least one clergyman. By 1811, Oneida County boasted one cotton mill (which imported fiber through New York City), several woolen factories, many fulling mills, and ten carding machines. A year later, local entrepreneurs founded the Bank of Utica, setting the town on a course toward becoming a financial center as well. In 1817, when Utica legally separated from Whitestown, its inhabitants numbered nearly 3,000. It held at that time more than 40 percent of Oneida County's retail establishments and most of the financial and legal services that supported business. About a sixth of the entries in the first town directory, published that year, were for merchants of every character—wholesale, commission, retail. The town throbbed with energy and ambition.

Well it might, for in 1817 work began on the Erie Canal. The midsection, joining Utica to the Seneca River, was completed October 25, 1819, and the first packet boats began operating that year. By 1821, boats descended as far as Rockton, and by the end of 1822, 220 miles of canal were navigable. Open in 1825 the entire distance from Albany to Buffalo, connecting the Great Lakes to the Hudson River, the new waterway transformed Utica.[6] The arrival of a swarm of single male construction workers, with attendant boardinghouses, brothels, and grog shops, set off an explosion of population and business activity of every sort. Canal traffic stimulated continued growth afterward.

In 1832, as its population neared 9,000, Utica received its first charter as a city. At that time, it counted forty-four dry goods stores, sixty-three grocery and general foods stores, ten hardware concerns, nineteen milliners and dressmakers, five bookstores, twenty-nine smiths, seventy-nine cabinetmakers, more than seventy-five shoemakers, and four lottery offices. Nine stagecoach lines, forty-one canal packet boat departures weekly, and ninety-two mail deliveries a week linked it with the outside world. The small mercantile, banking, and professional elite that had formed in the early decades still dominated local affairs from their growing establishments along Genesee Street. Artisans and craftsmen, scattered among smithies, cabinetmaking and shoemaking shops, and myriad other trades, represented the largest occupational group, more than 40 percent of those gainfully employed. Enterprises were typically small. Nearly four-fifths of the local businesses were partnerships, half of them held within families. Here and there were a few firms that manufactured steam engines, wagons, mechanical instruments, rope, pottery, bricks, and boats.

Just outside of Utica, New York Mills, successor to the Oneida Manufacturing Society, was becoming an important cotton factory. The area's first genuine industrialist, Benjamin Walcott, had arrived and assumed control in 1825. He promptly introduced the Waltham plan of organization, providing separate, single-sex dormitories for farm youth recruited from the countryside to work as mill operatives. The growth of New York Mills forecast the time, not far off, when Utica would become a major manufacturing center.

The completion of the Erie Canal inspired more than the spurt of growth that made Utica, in effect, an "instant city." It also spurred efforts throughout the remainder of the antebellum era to extend the city's commercial importance, by improving its transportation and communication connections. These involved Utica centrally in the transportation revolution reshaping the country. Every technological advance that shared in the improvement of communication acted on the local stage. In some ways, the city's role was much larger than its size and situation predicted. The activities of Uticans ramified far beyond the immediate vicinity. Developments in transportation and communication placed the city, by 1860, squarely in an emerging national marketplace and economy. Changes in the local economy matched the dizzying pace of change on the national scene.

The brilliant success of the Erie Canal, which quickly drew the trade of the west to New York City and sped the development of western New York State, sparked fervent enthusiasm throughout the country for the construction of canals to provide inexpensive interior routes of trade. Uticans succumbed to the fever. After approval by the state legislature, the city in 1836 secured a water connection to the Susquehanna River at Binghamton. The Chenango Canal, four feet deep and ninety-seven miles long, introduced produce from Pennsylvania farms, as well as coal to heat local homes and fuel the fires of industry and trade.

A year later, as a major business depression settled on the nation, the completion of the Utica & Schenectady brought the first railroad connection. Although business languished until 1843, sweating gangs of construction workers continued to lay tracks as area cities vied with each other for competitive advantage. They drove the last spikes on the Syracuse & Auburn in 1839, and on the Utica & Syracuse soon after, bringing Syracuse to within nine hours of Albany and nineteen of New York City. In 1853, the many regional short lines united as the New York Central. Western New York by then possessed both a busy trunk line paralleling the Erie Canal, and numerous radiating local connections joining its cities and villages.

Meanwhile, a migrant from Berne, New York, with but meager schooling, had become a notable local figure. John Butterfield arrived in Utica as a stagecoach driver and quickly rose to dominate the stage routes of western New York. His interests proliferated rapidly, soon encompassing canal packet boats and steam boats on Lake Ontario. After 1847, they extended to plank roads throughout the region, as locals continued their ceaseless search for commercial advantage. One of the pioneers of the express business, he joined in 1850 with two others to form the American Express Company. Before the decade was over he led the way in establishing the first transcontinental mail and stagecoach services. By then he was also a pioneer in telecommunication. The wife of Samuel F. B. Morse, inventor of the telegraph, was a Utican. Butterfield in 1845 joined with one of Morse's local friends, Theodore Faxton, and others to organize the first telegraph company, connecting Albany with the city. Shortly after, Faxton founded the Associated Press in Utica, to take advantage of the new medium of communication. The telegraph company expanded swiftly, gaining control of all lines in the state. In 1846, it allied with its rivals to form Western Union, whose speedy extension of lines across the country joined with the advance of railroads as the key element in the creation of a nationwide market and economy. Butterfield continued to reside in Utica, developing real estate, directing the Utica National Bank, and serving as mayor before his death in 1869.[7]

The ambition that propelled Utica's efforts to improve transportation and communication linkages expressed itself in many other ways, as well. A piece of locally made china in 1824 proclaimed "Utica, a village in the State of New York, thirty years since a wilderness, now inferior to none in the Eastern Section of the State, in Population, Wealth, Commercial enterprise, active industry, and civil improvement." The burgeoning community entered the cash economy during the 1820s, uncounted local entrepreneurs adding to their business cards the words "Cash System." Others baldly sought farmers' produce with advertisements offering cash payment, or announcing in their quest for customers, "Money wanted." Fervent capitalists, Uticans used the word "capital" only slightly less often than the word "cash." Sermons preached of moral capital, the newspapers hawked offerings of capital stock, and the local credit agency busily investigated the "capital resources" of the populace. The city was a hotbed of aspiration.

Despite the onset of depression in 1837, Utica finished the 1830s with nearly 13,000 inhabitants, an increase of almost 50 percent in ten years. The Erie Canal, spanned by a series of "elevated and elegant bridges," ran through the city's heart. Eighteen churches ministered to its spiritual needs. Six weekly newspapers, a free public library, ten academies, and 188 shops provided numerous avenues of commerce. An 1838 lithograph picturing the view from the intersection of Washington and Genesee Streets showed rows of two-story houses and shops bordering the thoroughfares. Merchants Hall and First Presbyterian Church loomed larger than other structures, but (hinting at a parity of material and spiritual concerns) were themselves of equal prominence. Groups of people still engaged in neighborly conversation in the streets. The city retained many characteristics of a small town; at the time its built-up area was still but ten blocks square.

Over the next two decades, much changed.

Population fell during the depressed early 1840s. City leaders replied with a campaign to attract textile factories and diversify the economy after the example of an industrializing New England. Within two years, enterprisers launched the Globe Woolen Mills, the Utica Steam Cotton Mills, and the Utica Steam Woolen Mills. Three large garment mills, employing more than 1,200 workers, joined them in the following decade. By the eve of the Civil War, nearby New York Mills ranked among the nation's ten largest textile factories. As competition displaced less successful merchants and shopkeepers and industrial output grew, both the composition of the workforce and local class structure changed. Shopkeepers as a proportion of those employed fell by half, to 6.6 percent; craftsmen by a ninth, to 40.1 percent; while the ranks of industrial and factory laborers grew from 15.1 to 24.1 percent. As late as 1850, most firms remained small, employing ten or fewer operatives. The share of partnerships among city businesses plummeted, settling finally at about 10 percent between 1860 and 1865.

The arrival of large firms even on Genesee Street further evidenced the end of the era of exuberant small-scale capitalism. William Stacy's Dry Goods at number 104 expanded, pouring out a vast array of goods to consumers. Gaffney's Cheap Irish Shoes and the warehouses of G. W. Muir and of New York's Lord and Taylor added to the swelling supply of merchandise. A business recession in 1857, forcing failures of numerous smaller concerns, accelerated the general growth in scale. A mid-century engraving portrayed the new order, visually. The Utica & Syracuse Railroad and the Erie Canal cut across the foreground, setting off the city's commercial center, Bagg's Square. Large mercantile and industrial buildings loom five and six stories above hurried, tiny human figures and busy vehicular traffic that animate the streets. Heavy plumes of smoke trail from eleven industrial stacks that overshadow less prominent church spires standing out amid a mass of undifferentiated residential structures.

At the eve of the Civil War, the tiny frontier village with a rude barter economy had matured to a pulsing, medium-size commercial and industrial hub of more than 22,000. Foreign immigrants were conspicuous among the growing cohorts of factory workers. The founders of the old mercantile and professional elite were passing from the scene, leaving their descendants to share influence with more recent arrivals associated with the expanding industrial order.[8]

Profound social changes attended the swift maturation of Whitestown and Utica. Of these, two changes closely related and reflective of national tendencies stood out. The first was a transformation of the family. The second was the emergence of a new, urban middle class, with distinctive interests and values.

Hugh White and others of the first generation of settlers stood between two social worlds. Unlike many of their forebears, the first migrants from old to New England, these pioneers moved westward as individuals or as heads of individual families, rather than as members of migrating congregations with clerical leaders aiming to plant communities in the wilderness. Instead of acquiring lands in common through government grants, or as individuals in some form of leasehold subject to rents and feudal obligations, they did so for themselves through cash purchase, to become owners outright, in fee simple. They carved out and occupied dispersed farmlands, rather than closely settled villages.

But the earliest arrivals in Whitestown nonetheless replicated at first a seventeenth-century society in which family, community, and church were overlapping and mutually reinforcing entities. Religious faith, ancient habits, and laws assigned economic, educational, and religious roles to all three. The family was many things, but preeminently it was a miniature version of the covenanted society that God had ordained. As such, it reproduced society biologically, instructed the young in morality and the skills of living, and functioned as a locus of worship and prayer. The father held patriarchal authority as head of the family, with primary responsibilities for the maintenance of family order and the training of children. In an age in which the doctrine of infant depravity still held sway and eternal salvation beckoned as the goal, the preferred mode of child rearing was still that of old New England, will breaking. As soon as a child began to assert its own will, usually about the age of two, it was the object of stern discipline designed to produce consistent and unquestioning obedience to the will of the father and, in turn, to the governing purposes of God.

This mode of child rearing served a worldly purpose, too. Each household in frontier Whitestown was a little corporate economy or producing unit. Submission supported the productive needs of the family. It is no surprise, then, that children were often thought of as employees of the fathers, just as wives were dependents of the husbands. Whitestown's pioneer households added to the yield of fields, orchards, and barnyards such items as lye, potash, bark, and most of their domestic needs. As early as 1820, they averaged an annual output of forty yards of cotton, linen, or wool fabric each. Patriarchs sought to provide for continuity of the corporate household by arranging for descent of the farmstead to the eldest son; other sons, and daughters, inherited less. These same pioneer families also cared for less fortunate relatives, whether aged parents or otherwise, and as corporate units they often housed young laborers who were not relatives, but rather servants. In effect acting as social welfare agencies, sometimes with church assistance, they also in the early years were inti-

mately connected to government. Before the construction of public buildings and the elaboration of an array of civic offices and institutions,
neighbors met in homes to make decisions concerning the township. The
line between public and private spheres was blurred and indistinct in such
a society.

The corporate family economy persisted well into the nineteenth century. Early settlers introduced it into Utica and industrial operations of
the Oneida Manufacturing Society, as well as the countryside. The Society
initially employed entire families, housing them in a mill village designed
for family residence. By the second and third decades of the century,
though, a shift was evident. With the occupation of all tillable land, the
nuclear family was becoming predominant. Couples limited family size,
the average number of children falling from 5.1 for women born before
1805 to 3.6 for those born during the next ten years. New voluntary be-
nevolent associations began to care for infirm, indigent, and dependent
persons for whom families had often cared earlier. The Whitestown Charitable Society grew out of a sewing circle in 1806; the Female Charitable
Society formed soon after. These and similar bodies involved women in
new roles, outside of the home. The officers of the latter organization held
titles commonly assigned to men in corporate business. In 1827 Benjamin
Walcott's New York Mills counted but 25 percent of its employees in
family units, and wholly abandoned the family system a decade later.
Household manufacturing retreated, as a diversifying economy produced
growing quantities of staples commercially and drew exportable, expend-
able labor from farm and home to shops and factories.

The emerging business order held important social meaning. A swelling
corps of individuals found themselves cast as employees, and working outside of their residences. In some instances, formerly independent shopkeepers and artisans fell out of the middle class. In others, a growing cadre
of retail and professional workers termed "clerks" joined it to form the
core of a reconfiguring middling group. The departure of male workers
from the home displaced the corporate family economy, at the same time
undercutting the traditional authority of the now-absent father and husband and conferring an expanded role and potency to the mother and
wife. Patterns of inheritance altered, as urban ways and a cash economy
won ascendancy. More and more, fathers divided estates equally among
sons, with smaller shares for daughters, rather than attempting to preserve
a farmstead intact. Concurrently, beginning in the 1820s the coming of
scores of young single males and females seeking employment introduced
into Utica a novel and substantial population of boarders who were outside the traditional family structure.

The first conspicuous heralds of these changes were families that
emerged as Utica's mercantile and professional elite. Bearing names such
as the James and Jeremiah Van Rensselaers, Samuel Stockings, and Jesse

Doolittles, they amassed sufficient wealth to employ domestic servants. Wives and offspring gained freedom from household drudgery and the need to contribute to the family's earnings. By the 1830s wives of husbands working outside the home assumed an increasingly focal role in rearing their young. The children themselves were the first generation to benefit from the invention, practically speaking, of "childhood," a time of nurture and education rather than of employment. Formal schooling joined training in the home as a means of preparation for adult responsibilities. Delayed courtship prolonged further the time before the assumption of full adult and family responsibilities, girls learning great caution in the business of making a suitable match. Boys received instruction in the values and behaviors that would enable them, when mature, to pursue the ideal of the self-made man. In contrast, girls absorbed an emerging ethos defining the female sphere as the home, now increasingly viewed (given the separation of workplace from residence) as a private sphere and a haven for upper-and middle-class males engaged in the competitive struggle of business.[9]

The economic and social transformation of Utica reflected wider currents of change. The religious environment, however, as Mary Ryan showed in *Cradle of the Middle Class*, made the locale unique. Oneida County and Utica were the center of a region in western New York through which successive waves of religious revival swept with singular force for a quarter century. The revivals cut across all social classes and inflamed spiritual fervor to such a degree that the region came to be known as the "burned over district."

These upheavals were an extension of a movement that originated in Connecticut in the 1790s. Before they reached Oneida County, local settlers prepared a combustible mix of institutions. These constituted spiritual fuel, awaiting only a match to burst aflame. Local pioneers replicated the old New England ideal of a covenanted religious community, which embraced the corporate family economy and the patriarchal household. The Whitestown United Congregation embodied these elements at its founding. It introduced and sought to preserve deep-rooted customs of public and family worship, of moral training in the patriarchal home and in the church, and of conduct regulated by family, community, and church. Local laws and church discipline buttressed these efforts.

The rapid peopling and maturation of the region posed sharp challenges. A traveling clergyman inquired into the state of souls locally in the winter of 1813–1814, about when the revivals began. He found that most were Presbyterians followed by Methodists, Baptists, and Congregationalists and handsful of Quakers and Unitarians. More than half of the households contained no church members. Men, in particular, expressed disinterest in religion and disenchantment with preachers. But large numbers of women were deeply concerned for their salvation. Women led in church membership, and in response to the revivals. In 1814, they constituted 70 percent of the communicants of the First Presbyterian Society (later, Church), which had separated from the United Congregation the year before and which at once became the center of local religious influence and revivalism. Many of Utica's most prominent families were among the first converts in 1813 and 1814, including the Van Rensselaers, the Stockings, Ann Breese, the John Ostroms, and the Thomas Walkers. Within a year, Whitestown's Lydia Andrews converted. She later married Charles Grandison Finney, who in 1825 returned to Utica and introduced the evangelistic methods that have been employed in revivals ever since. Of the first sixty-four women to respond to the altar call, twelve, surprisingly, brought their husbands. Many were young, and pregnant, a quarter bringing infants to baptism within a year.

While the first revival was in progress, the Whitestown Female Charitable Society renamed itself the Oneida Female Missionary Society and redirected its efforts. The first of many such groups, it began immediately to sponsor missionary work in western New York and beyond. In the following years, proliferating women's societies provided an energetic network underpinning missionary and related activity. More than half of the 1814 converts at First Presbyterian joined the Oneida Female Missionary Society. Five teenage daughters in 1815 organized and taught the first Sunday school. Significantly, the husbands of 80 percent of these women were substantial merchants and professionals who worked outside their residences. Able to assign household tasks to hired servants, these elite wives employed their new freedom in religious, charitable, and related pursuits outside the home. By 1820, they were moving further into new roles, even conducting their own separate prayer meetings without male supervision. Their organizations raised and distributed money, published tracts and pamphlets, corresponded, and so on. Renewed revivals in 1819, 1825–1826 with Finney's return, 1830, and 1838 drew new converts, primarily from the middle ranks of society, and spawned further organizations. Spiritual and moral zeal excited in revivals inspired the formation of numerous associations bent on various reforms—aiming to stamp out prostitution and regulate the sexual conduct of Uticans, to prohibit the use of alcoholic beverages, to end slavery, and to combat myriad other ills, both real and perceived.

Meanwhile, the religious and theological understanding of the family underwent a fundamental change. By the end of the revival cycle, new conceptions of parental roles, and of the nature of children, had set aside the old patriarchal model. Fervent debate accompanied the process of change. The era began with a spirited defense of patriarchal authority. But as early as 1808 a Presbyterian sermon instructed that, instead of breaking the wills of children, parents ought to teach them Godly ways. By 1823, Utica's prolific religious writers were hinting that children might be innocent at birth, rather than depraved sinners bound for perdition unless redeemed by stern fatherly discipline that would break them to God's will. Finally, in the 1830s, the Reverend Beriah Green of Whitestown's First Congregational Church closed the argument. Because children were uniquely vulnerable and dependent, he wrote, they were uniquely susceptible to Christian teaching and the gift of divine grace. With infant depravity no longer a consideration, brief and decisive fatherly interventions to break wills were unnecessary. Instead, affectionate motherly guidance and monitoring would lead children to right ways. Religious sanction for a new approach to child rearing, with revised parental roles, served the circumstantial no less than the spiritual needs of the upper- and emerging middle-class households of Utica. The softened approach to rearing children accompanied a general tendency in preaching and practice to replace a faith of laws and predestination with one offering salvation to all who would accept a personal relationship with the Savior.[10]

James Dana, son of George and Elizabeth (Park) Dana, was born on May 19, 1780, in Ashburnham, Massachusetts, close to Fitchburg and the New Hampshire border about midway between the Connecticut River and the seacoast. When he was twelve, he moved with his family to Windsor, Vermont, about sixty miles to the north and west, on the Connecticut River. Shortly after coming of age, he forsook the well-settled lands and limited opportunities of the Connecticut Valley and joined the stream of immigrants drawn from crowded New England to the more expansive prospects of western New York. He paused for a year in Schenectady before moving on to his final destination in 1803. Unlike most earlier settlers, who had sought farmlands and who already promised to fill the countryside, Dana took up residence in the hamlet of Utica. He was poor in worldly goods, but he possessed some education. And he was wealthy in terms of ambition, probity, well developed habits of industry and disciplined work, business acumen, and a keen sense of opportunity.

Dana found employment as an assistant to Gurdon Burchard, a saddle and harness maker who had arrived from Connecticut with his wife a decade earlier. James learned quickly, soon becoming a partner and then, in 1806, setting up on his own. After a few years he abandoned the saddlery trade, concentrating on hardware. His firm prospered, adding new items of merchandise in cutlery, agricultural tools and implements, and seed as it grew. In a few years Dana emerged as one of Utica's foremost merchants and a member of the local mercantile elite. At mid-century his two-story building at 92 Genesee Street was one of the city's more imposing commercial structures. A director of the Bank of Utica for many years until his death in January 1860, he had built up a "handsome fortune" by the time he retired from the hardware business and passed the management of the store to his son George in 1850. His will devised his home and furnishings, and an annuity of $1,000 for the balance of her life, to his widow. It divided the residue of his estate, which may have approximated the then-considerable sum of $100,000, among his five surviving children.[11]

In successfully negotiating his enterprise through the economic cross-currents of the era, James Dana experienced directly many of the events then transforming the conduct and structure of business. Meanwhile his family lived through the contemporary metamorphosis of domestic life in western New York. In both instances, far-reaching changes forcefully impressed themselves on the Danas.

James Dana married Harriet Dwight in May 1812. Like her husband, who was twelve years her senior, she was originally from Massachusetts. A native of Williamsburgh in the far western part of the state, she had come to Utica with her parents in 1805. Her mother, Hannah, enjoyed a reputation for profound piety. Her merchant father, Seth, was far better known for his socializing habits than for his astuteness in business matters.[12] Nine months after James and Harriet wed, their first child, James Dwight Dana, was born. At two- or three-year intervals through 1835, nine other children followed. William Buck Dana, born August 26, 1829, was the eighth child. In all, seven survived to adulthood.

The clause of James Dana's will providing for Harriet illustrated his wealth, his generosity, his affection for her, and the adaptation of inheritance practices to a maturing cash and commercial economy. Historically, the right of dower entitled widows to claim life use of one-third of a deceased husband's real property. Dana stipulated that if she accepted the support proffered her, she did so in lieu of the right of dower. In either event, this prosperous hardware merchant conferred on his widow advantages of wealth.

Affluence and social position likewise afforded the Dana children significant advantages. Their circumstances freed them of the need to seek employment while still young. Able to enjoy prolonged dependency, they acquired education and married late, and well. Encouraged by their father's example and exhortations, by his willingness to make capital available to them for education and other expenses, and by his frequent reminiscences about his own route to wealth, the males absorbed his enterprising spirit, which reflected the optimistic capitalism of the age and of their community. All four who reached maturity made excellent careers. William became an attorney, John a medical doctor. George succeeded James in the hardware business, operated a lock factory, and was a prominent investor in a screw factory. James Dwight achieved fame as an entrepreneur in science. After stints as a student at Yale, in the navy, and as assistant to Yale's famed science professor, Benjamin Silliman, Jr., he returned to sea as the scientist for Lieutenant Charles Wilkes's South Sea Expedition (1837–1842). While exploring, in 1840, he became editor of

Silliman's prestigious *American Journal of Science*, accelerating a prodigious writing career that had begun with the *System of Mineralogy* (1837). He married Silliman's daughter, Henrietta, seven years after completing this seminal work, which organized mineralogical science. In 1849, at Silliman's retirement, Yale appointed Dana to his father-in-law's faculty position. He took up the post some years later, pouring out a stream of geological treatises, despite a series of serious illnesses, until his retirement in 1890. He died five years later.

The religious revivals that excited Utica swept through the Dana family as well, setting it on a course of spiritual fervor and piety that persisted for many years. Young Harriet was among the first converts at First Presbyterian Church during the 1813–1814 revivals. She had James Dwight baptized the next year, and John two years later. Parish records omit the remaining eight children, but it is clear that this redoubtable and kindly woman of faith exercised continuing spiritual influence in and beyond her home. In becoming an early member of the Oneida Female Missionary Society, she publicly accepted the moral and social responsibilities of her household. When her husband and her son John joined the church during the 1826 evangelistic crusade of Charles Grandison Finney, she must have felt great satisfaction. So, too, with the belated conversion of James Dwight, in 1838, an answer to years of prayer and hope. A later biographical sketch, reflecting the rise of the notion that a woman's sphere was in the home, mistakenly claimed that she rarely ventured beyond her family circle, while rightly describing her life as exemplary for its faithfulness and maternal devotion.

The influence of the conversions was as deep as it was durable. James Dana for thirty years was an officer of the Presbyterian church. For many years he taught Sunday school. He was known to delight in conversing about religious subjects, and to live a life founded wholly on his faith. Judging from the practices of his offspring, family prayer and worship were household fixtures. The ages of the elder Danas, the "firmly formed" habits of the father, and the conduct of the young Danas when grown all suggested that old-fashioned patriarchal authority reigned in the large Dana home at 24 Broad Street. This authority, with Harriet's support, reinforced traditional Protestant moral and religious values. It stressed submission to divine and all other duly constituted authority; careful regulation of ones conduct; diligence and industry at work; self-reliance; duty; and love of family that placed charitable works responding to the needs of the immediate and the extended family before all others. Business principles and calculation should govern charity no less than the other domains of action. Dana "systematically provided" for his charitable expenses. When he advanced money to family members—as he did $1,453 to George, $6,000 to James, $2,500 to Delia, $2,625.66 to William for his college and professional education and an additional $4,000 later for other purposes—he required each to execute an interest-bearing bond of indebtedness with strict repayment provisions. He could move forcefully to protect his interests, even when close relatives were involved. After Seth Dwight failed in business, Dana did not hesitate to foreclose on real estate belonging to his father-in-law as payment against a debt. A sense of fairness governed, too. The provisions of Dana's will canceling his children's debts to him stipulated that the value of the bonds yet outstanding be added to his estate and then "deducted from the respective shares" of the offspring whose debts had been forgiven.[13]

Utica's first common schools dated back to 1797, and from 1815 onward the community always had one or more academies, or high schools. However, Will Dana boarded in the village of Vernon, some eighteen miles from Utica, during his schooling. It is most likely that he received his instruction at the Vernon Academy for Young Men. Founded to "fit young men for the useful pursuits of life" and to "diffuse a literary taste in the community," the academy offered a classical course of study consciously designed to refine the manners, cultivate the virtue, invigorate the minds, and strengthen the bodies of its young scholars. Students traversed an academic year of four, eleven-week terms; completed exercises in composition and declamation on an average of once every twenty-eight days; and faced two semiannual examination days and one annual exhibition in declamation and composition. They studied astronomy, chemistry, French, Greek, geography, grammar, history, Latin (Ovid, Livy, Tacitus), mathematics, philosophy, reading, and rhetoric. Simple apparatus, including siphons, an air pump, a magic lantern and slides, a terrestrial globe, a hydrometer, and the like supported basic scientific demonstrations. The principal taught the fifty-odd boys in the classical department; two women taught in the English department and music. Tuition for classical scholars was $5 per term; room and board could be had in Vernon for from $1.50 to $1.75 per week.

Direct evidence of Will Dana's schoolwork is scarce. Two undated essays survive, of which one is revealing. Entitled "On a Story," it recounted how Will threw a tantrum after his mother forbade him to go (ice) "skaiting" with a friend. According to the tale he became grateful to her soon after, when he learned that the friend had broken through the ice and drowned. He closed with words indicating that he had already internalized some of the strict morality that governed his entire life: "Children, I warn you always obey your parents."[14]

Dana enrolled at Yale in 1847 and graduated four years later. His instruction at Vernon had apparently been thorough. He began college as a freshman in good standing, passing the "strict and comprehensive" August oral entrance examinations in selected works of Cicero, Vergil, Sallust, and Xenophon, and "Latin and Greek Grammar, Latin Prosody, and

Composition, Geography, and the theoretical parts of Arithmetic." The school was still small, to the point of intimacy, housed in only thirteen buildings. The "Annual charge for instruction" was $33, dormitory room rent $12, board for forty weeks $60 to $90, total annual cost per student an estimated $140 to $210. The faculty numbered thirty-five, half of them assigned to teach some 380 undergraduates and the rest to instruct 140 graduate students, most of them in medicine, divinity, and law. Before 1850–1851, regulations allowed undergraduates to reside off campus only when the four dormitories were full.[15]

Undergraduates lived under a strict regimen. The first of three academic terms constituting the school year ran fourteen weeks from around mid-September; the second from the third Wednesday in January; and the third, twelve weeks in length, from the last week in May. Commencement closed the year in August. Morning prayer, at 6:30 in winter and 5:30 in summer, began each day. A recitation period followed, then breakfast. A second recitation period occurred at 11:30, dinner at 1:00, evening prayer in the late afternoon, then a third recitation period at 5:00 and supper an hour later. Each Sunday students were required to attend two church services. The Reverend Eleazar Fitch provided most of the preaching in the College Chapel, combining a "simple evangelical gospel" that urged hearers to repent and escape the terrors of hell with a searching consideration of problems of "infinite difficulty—the duty and destiny of man." Not surprisingly, even on an inherently conservative campus stirred frequently by revivals, chapel services were often the scene of pranks and misconduct. Despite the strict schedule, students found time for recreation. They participated excitedly in three debating societies, in various social groups, and in scratch games of football, two old cat, and wicket. In summer they also enjoyed just sitting on the fence, savoring the scent of newly scythed grass in the yard.[16]

Yale aimed in Dana's day to offer students a thorough course of study, maintaining a proper balance among the disciplines and providing proper exercise "for all the important [mental] faculties." Students accordingly pursued a rigid, and conservative, prescribed and largely classical curriculum during the first three years of college. Freshmen read Livy, Homer's *Odyssey*, and parts of the Greek New Testament, working also through algebra and Euclid's hated geometry. Sophomores added Cicero's *De Oratione*, Seneca's *Heracles Furens*, Horace, and plane trigonometry, conic sections, and spherical geometry and trigonometry. Juniors concluded Cicero, read Tacitus, finished work begun the previous year with Aeschylus, studied Plato's *Gorgias*, and began natural philosophy with pneumatics, acoustics, optics, electricity and magnetism, and planetary astronomy. They added analytical geometry and fluxions (calculus), ancient history, and could at last elect one course from among Greek, Hebrew, and modern languages.

Only in the senior year did the curriculum turn substantially toward the study of modern works. The scholarly Theodore Dwight Woolsey, president from 1846 and professor of Greek for fifteen years before that, made sound scholarship the central theme of his administration. While adding academic scholarships for lower-class students, he emphasized strengthening the senior year. He made the final year more demanding, by adding a second required recitation period for seniors, and a more thorough system of examinations with orals at the end of every term. He personally directed seniors through a demanding course of study in modern history, philosophy, and political science. Completing astronomy and orations of Demosthenes, seniors turned to rhetoric, William Paley's natural theology, Victor Cousin's psychology, Thomas Reid's essays on human intelligence, Chancellor James Kent's legal commentaries, and Francis Wayland's political economy. Yale seniors gained through their program a comprehensive and consistent view of human affairs and of the world. Because his work as a senior completed the academic "furnishing" of his mind, the books that William Dana studied that year merit special attention.[17]

From the beginning to the end (the *alpha* to the *omega*) of its program, Yale directed the attention of its students to God. Religion permeated the college. Aspiring graduates met the deity finally and definitively during the second term of the senior year, when they grappled with William Paley's proofs from nature of God's existence. A graduate in mathematics from Cambridge and a Church of England divine, Paley published his *Natural Theology* in 1802. It quickly gained, and long held, wide acceptance as a text in England and in the United States. Paley introduced his argument immediately, with a story. He contrasted the reactions that one would feel after stumbling, respectively, over a stone and over a watch on the heath. If one wondered how the stone came to be in the way, one might conclude that it had always been there. Examination of the watch would lead to a very different conclusion. Composed, obviously, of many ingeniously devised and assembled parts for the purpose of telling time, a watch implied intention and an intelligent maker. Clearly a contrivance or mechanism, a watch implied a contriver or mechanic.

Paley followed with a train, drawn mainly from animate nature, of what he took to be examples of contrivance. Grant his premise, and a divine contriver was inescapable. Touching but little on physiology and biochemistry, he emphasized skeletal structures, the fit of joints, musculature, and various organs, in many species of living organisms. He dwelt at length on the organs of sight and hearing. The eye alone, adapted so perfectly (like all of his examples) for its purposes, was sufficient to confirm the existence of an intelligent creator–God. Intelligent, and also good, because, first, "in a vast plurality of instances in which the contrivance is perceived, the design . . . is beneficial," and, second, because "the Deity has superadded *pleasure* to animal sensation." Confident that a divine plan governed the world, human beings should, Paley concluded, "hope and prepare" for a "merciful disposal" at life's end.[18]

Victor Cousin lived from 1792 to 1867 and twice held posts in philosophy at the University of Paris. The author of multivolume histories of modern and of eighteenth-century philosophy, he incorporated into the latter ten chapters a critique of John Locke's theory that all knowledge derived from sensation. His critique, published separately as a collection of essays, won wide use in American colleges before the Civil War. He maintained that Locke's sensationalism was seriously flawed, because it necessarily implied materialism, fatalism, and atheism. Locke was also mistaken in regarding language as the result, rather than as a condition, of science. He erred further in grounding theories, of God, the soul, and liberty in the senses.

For Cousin (an indirect heir of the Scottish common sense philosophy of Thomas Reid) the human mind, or consciousness, contained three faculties: sense, will, and reason. Men perceived external reality through the senses. They acted and derived personality through will. Reason constituted intelligence. It was absolute and divine, not human, in origin and nature. It was the manifestation of God's eternal will in the nature of the universe, which was itself an imperfect reflection of the divine will. The rational principles that determined the creation of the universe also regulated the cosmos. And they governed the mind, the study of which Cousin defined as psychology. Consciousness, or mind, he taught, developed in two stages. Primitive consciousness was spontaneous, instinctive, universal. It was identical with the *logos* of St. John that made universal truths—God, time, space, the infinite, personal identity, good, evil—known to all men. Atheism, then, was actually a rejection of reason. Reflective consciousness, or intelligence, was the element of philosophy or thought that the will applied to the discoveries of primitive reason. Such a view of intelligence reinforced the religious precepts that mid-nineteenth-century American colleges taught and informed the understanding of many graduates long after they completed their studies.[19]

Introduced to this country at Princeton College, Thomas Reid's philosophy had gained great influence on American campuses by the middle decades of the nineteenth century. Of the writings of this famed Aberdeen and Glasgow professor, Dana and his classmates most likely studied portions of *Essays on the Intellectual Powers of Man* (1785) or *Essays on the Active Powers of the Human Mind* (1788). In either event, they learned that David Hume's skepticism was as wrong-headed as Cousin had shown Locke's sensationalism to be. Hume erred in maintaining that men could know only their own sensations, not even a hint of an external reality perceived through the senses. His corollary, that morality therefore rested on nothing more than subjective feelings, was also erroneous.

Reid opposed Hume through an appeal to the commonsense perceptions and understanding of all reasonable men, which he took to be valid. Indeed, he pointed out, even skeptics had to live *as if* the senses, and commonsense understanding, were reliable. "I never heard," he wrote, "that any skeptic ran his head against a post, or stept into a kennel, because he did not believe his eyes." For Reid, several faculties constituted the mind. Given to men as part of their nature "by the Author of our being," "God," these were sensory perception, memory, conception, analysis, judgment, reasoning, taste, moral perception, "and, last of all, consciousness." Each of these received extended consideration under the heading of powers of understanding, as opposed to powers of will or action. Reid's conception of the mind as a collection of faculties that, like muscles, could be developed through exercise found a congenial setting in American colleges whose instruction emphasized rote memorization, drill, written and oral exercises, recitation, and public disputations.

Reid treated human action similarly, reinforcing further the religious presuppositions of students. Action did not originate simply in subjective feelings. Instead, it sprang from appetites, desires, passions, and rational antecedents including the ability to calculate outcomes. Common sense attested that human beings were free. They possessed liberty, defined as the capacity to choose without being coerced externally to do so. Reid defended the existence of liberty on three grounds. First, the belief in liberty was so widespread as to make it likely true. Second, liberty was necessary if human beings were to be morally responsible for their conduct. Last, a complex train of actions leading to achievement of a particular goal was not possible unless a person was at least free enough to contrive and act on a plan. He added, finally, that all of moral science was deducible from first principles, made self-evident to mankind through a God-given "original power of the mind, which we call conscience, or the moral faculty."[20]

When Yale men turned to studying law and politics, they imbibed deeply of James Kent's *Commentaries on American Law* (1826–1830). A 1781 Yale graduate, Columbia law professor, judge, justice, chief justice, and finally chancellor of New York from 1814 to 1823, Kent was a towering legal influence. As chief justice, he introduced written opinions and much of French civil law into the New York legal system, and his opinions helped lay the foundation of equity jurisprudence in the nation. A lifelong Federalist, fearful of democracy, he opposed universal male suffrage at the 1821 New York constitutional convention. His *Commentaries*, modeled after those of the great English jurist William Blackstone, passed through many editions.

For Kent, law was a science. The laws of nations embodied both positive enactments and the principles of "natural jurisprudence . . . deriving . . . from the same principles of right reason . . . the nature and constitution of man . . . and Divine revelation, as those from which the science of morality is deduced." Law and ethics were intimately associated, and every state possessed the moral obligation to act with "justice, good faith, and benevolence."

The *Commentaries* advanced a blend of rationalism, wariness of democracy, and zeal to protect property rights that well served young men preparing for positions of leadership in an ebulliently capitalist America. Kent's readers discovered that the federal Constitution was a document of unrivaled wisdom. Its peaceful completion and adoption should stir pride in every patriotic breast. The great decisions of the John Marshall supreme court, asserting federal supremacy, drew lavish praise. Kent warmly approved Marshall's opinion, in *Gibbon v. Ogden* (1824), that within its sphere of authority to regulate international and interstate commerce, the power of Congress was "plenary and supreme."

Chancellor Kent applauded the division of Congress into two houses, to protect against "precipitate measures" resulting from "passion, caprice, prejudice, personal influence, and party intrigue" such as had tormented revolutionary Pennsylvania at home, and France abroad. He believed that American and English common law provided the best protections for civil and political liberty. For the all-important rights of property, the sanctity of contract, and freedom from capricious legislative interference in the conduct of business, he favored Roman law. Anticipating the role that courts would play in the late nineteenth century as guardians of vested rights, Kent determinedly defended the ideal of an independent judiciary. As a nationalist, he praised John Marshall's *McCulloch v. Maryland* (1819) ruling that the Constitution granted Congress implied authority to charter a national bank. As a defender of individual liberties, he also affirmed that the Constitution was "an instrument containing the grant of *specific* powers." The device of specific grants enabled the federal authority to act in designated domains and protected individual rights by withholding from it the capacity to exceed those grants. The difference between a limited and an unlimited government was absolute. The courts stood as a necessary independent guarantor of rights and held an obligation to "disregard" enactments that contravened the Constitution.[21]

Study of Francis Wayland's *Elements of Political Economy*, first published in 1837, completed the Yale senior year at mid-century. Quickly becoming the country's premier economics textbook, the volume passed through thirty-three editions by 1906. It collected "in substance" the lectures that Wayland, as president, delivered annually to seniors at Brown College. A clergyman like nearly all of his presidential peers, he incorporated economics into the ordered, coherent intellectual framework that Protestant religious tenets generally imposed on American campuses. Political economy for him addressed virtually the same questions as ethics, and it was a science. It was the science of wealth, science being defined as "a systematic arrangement of the laws which God has established, so far as they have been discovered [that is, deduced from self-evident first principles], of any department of knowledge."

Given the pervasive capitalist spirit of the time, it is no surprise that Wayland's text expounded principles that provided a rationalization for a capitalist order. Wayland made it clear that the American economic system was both natural and moral. Taking up production, exchange, distribution, and consumption in sequence, he founded his argument on the notion that reason and an appetite for pleasure were the twin wellsprings of human behavior. So animated, humankind quested for private gain and property, and at times for power. It followed that a free marketplace was the mechanism that best assured the satisfaction of individual and, in turn, social needs.

Wayland agreed with the classical economists that private property originated in the expenditure of labor on unowned raw resources. Stabilization of property rights propelled humanity from barbarism to civilization, then to culture, as it transferred the quest for pleasure and power from the physical to the economic realm. Capital accumulated, as a result, and a nation's standard of living rose as a by-product. The production and exchange of goods were self-regulating, if left to operate without interference. This was so because rational men, seeking to maximize their rewards and pleasure, would adjust their productive activities to demand, as measured by fluctuating prices. Left to themselves, naturally "adapted to labor," men would seek the "rich and abundant" rewards of industry and avoid the "several penalties"—ignorance, poverty, cold, hunger, nakedness—of indolence. Writing in an era of growth and the rise to triumph of a market economy, Wayland emphasized production and exchange, rather than distribution. He held speculation in contempt, as it added nothing to a nation's real wealth. He viewed consumption as the destruction of value, or of particular utilities. Although it was necessary to sustain life, consumption, because it annihilated value and thus the wealth of a nation, should always be as small as possible and should yield as large a result, or product, as possible. The maxim, "a penny saved is a penny earned," was true. Wayland optimistically believed that increasing a nation's capital more rapidly than population grew would maintain rising wages and an improving standard of living, even if population pressed heavily on the supply of land. The accumulation of capital was therefore all-important to a nation's economy.

Wayland's premises required that the economic role of government was to be strictly confined. He opposed a protective tariff and legislation advantaging particular enterprises as destructive of the operation of the marketplace. He believed that the convenience of using precious metals as a medium of exchange would have prompted their use as money without government action. He did not foresee the circulation of a national paper currency. Accordingly, the appropriate monetary function of the nation was to assure standardization and stability in value, of whatever circulating means of exchange a society chose. Government ought to encourage industry, but only through measures that allow natural market forces to operate. It could enact wise and judicious laws to protect individuals and property, refrain from interference in the operation of the market, protect international commerce, support education, and further the advancement of knowledge through support of such things as experimental farms and industries. "Internal improvements, such as roads, canals, and railroads may," Wayland wrote, "in general be safely left to individual enterprise." Ideally, care for paupers should be relegated to private charity.

While failing to anticipate urban business depressions that could cast multitudes into need, Wayland did recognize that there might be disasters so severe as to render private charity inadequate. In such instances minimal public relief expenditures, which did not sap recipients' will to work by rewarding idleness, were appropriate. All public expenditures, because they consumed value, should be strictly limited, as a matter of principle. Finally, Wayland believed that the "cheapest defense of nations" was "the exercise of justice and benevolence." If war did become necessary, it should be waged at the lowest cost consistent with victory.[22]

Will Dana lived off campus as a Yale student. He resided at a boardinghouse on Chapel Street as a freshman. For the following three years he rented a room in the home of Atwater Treat, a joiner, at 28 Elm Street. His academic record was undistinguished. His grade point average ranged between 2.32 and 2.70 per term, on a 4.0 scale, until the final term of his senior year, when it plummeted to 1.59. In view of his career in law and business journalism and his lifelong interest in theology, his poor performance in a last term containing courses in political economy, law, and theology was ironic.

Dana was unusually active in extracurricular life while at Yale. For all four of his student years, he was a member of Brothers in Unity, one of the college's literary and debating societies. He won increasing popularity among students as time passed. He belonged to the sophomore fraternity, Alpha Sigma Phi. The December 8, 1848, issue of its paper, *The Yale Tomahawk*, listing him as a staff member, is the earliest known record of his association with any publication. There is no evidence that he contributed to it, however. He joined a junior fraternity, Alpha Delta Phi. His even more extensive involvement as a senior may have contributed to his poor academic showing during his final term. As a senior he was librarian for the Brothers in Unity, and he accepted membership in Yale's oldest, most exclusive secret society, Skull and Bones. He was an enthusiastic Bonesman. On one occasion, he and three fellow members were disciplined for causing a "Difficulty at prayers [chapel service]," when they scuffled to prevent a rival from tearing down a Skull and Bones notice.

The friendly inscriptions in Dana's autograph book illustrate the regard that graduating classmates held for him. But his college record did not predict his later distinction. He checked out only three of the 11,338 books in the library of the Brothers in Unity as a student, although he did show excellent judgment in becoming their librarian. The office was one of but four that paid a stipend, $40 for the year. One classmate may have glimpsed Dana's promise. Possibly having in mind his meticulous management as librarian, one contributor to Will's graduation autograph book prefaced the customary references to friendship and kindness with a reference to his "financial ability."[23]

After graduation, young Dana returned to Utica. The city, with some 18,000 inhabitants scattered over about two-and-a-half square miles, was far too large to retain the intimacy of a village but not yet so large as to depersonalize life. One could still know directly a wide enough range of acquaintances to feel in touch with the community, especially if one occupied a prominent position. The business corporation, bank credit, written contracts, the use of legal advice in the conduct of trade and industry, and firms of increasing size were familiar features. Nevertheless, face-to-face agreements, sealed with a handshake and a bond of personal honor, remained possible. One's business affairs were confidential, often even within one's immediate family. A small circle of affluent old families still wielded great influence. Their members enjoyed support and encouragement from kin; and advantages that could accrue from intermarriage, friendship, and shared status; informal and formal business and professional relationships; and interests that frequently overlapped. As a member of a leading family, Dana could expect to find a suitable occupation and place without great difficulty.

Upon his return William boarded with his parents. He studied law, probably in the office of William Johnson Bacon. In practice since 1824, save for a two years' fling with newspaper publication, Bacon had taken a number of students over the course of time. A prominent citizen, he was among the first to invest in the Utica and Albany Telegraph Company. He served on numerous charitable boards and was a director of many corporations, including the Utica Steam Cotton Mills, the Second National Bank, the Utica Savings Bank, the water works, and the gas lighting company. A trustee of his alma mater, Hamilton College in nearby Clinton, he was a leading member of the Reformed Dutch Church. In 1853, elected to the first of two consecutive eight-year terms as a justice of the supreme court of New York's fifth judicial district, he became Judge Bacon. More to the point, for present purposes, his law office was next door to the Dana hardware store, and he was James Dana's attorney and coexecutor of the latter's will. He was also a close family associate, and after William Dana completed his training and began to practice law he was a frequent visitor to the latter's office. It was natural for Dana to take advantage of the web of connections and read law with Bacon.[24]

As a law student, Dana jumped into local affairs. Within a year of his return to Utica, he became an inspector of elections in the city's first ward, where the Dana residence stood. He was also paymaster of the Forty-fifth Regiment, Twenty-first Brigade of the New York militia. The post placed him on the staff of the regimental colonel. Both offices were useful for an ambitious law student and attorney. He subsequently served for a year as ward supervisor, continuing as paymaster until 1858.

Dana progressed quickly in his legal studies. In November 1852, the *Utica Daily Gazette* contained a notice for Jones & Dana, Attorneys and Counselors at Law. Again capitalizing on his connections, William occupied an office on the second story of his father's hardware building. His associate in practice was his brother-in-law, J. Wyman Jones, who played a fateful role in his life and who will be treated more fully later. Dana and his brother, George, were also at the time involved in operating an agricultural warehouse and seed store, under the firm name of Dana Brothers, at 91 Genesee Street. After Bacon abandoned his practice to serve as judge and Jones redirected his activities, William Dana joined with N. Curtis White in the firm of White & Dana. As before, the offices were situated upstairs at 92 Genesee Street. It comes as no surprise to learn that White had been Bacon's partner, and before that had preceded Dana as a scholar at the Vernon Academy and had read law in Bacon's office. The bonds joining profession to family tightened again in 1858, when White married Dana's sister, Delia.[25]

William Dana flourished as a lawyer. His name and family, and his partners and their associations, were immediate sources of clients. His ability, industry, and character brought more. His practice shortly involved travel throughout New York's fifth judicial district, which was made up of Oneida, Herkimer, Lewis, Onondaga, Oswego, and Jefferson Counties. Correspondence mentioned frequent trips to Rome, Syracuse, and Herkimer for the spring, summer, and fall sessions of circuit courts as well as for other scheduled proceedings. By late 1854, he was confident that the year's receipts of his firm would "not fall far short of from four to five thousand dollars." While he could not yet "say that I can depend on that amount every year . . . I expect it will be more the coming year." His share, after expenses, would be half. In contrast, factory workers averaged less than $290, and Yale professors earned but $1,300, annually. Dana appreciated at once that his professional practice was a business and must be managed methodically. He quickly learned the value of that most precious of commodities, his time, lamenting in one letter:

Here follows a long period of interruption. One man comes in and wants Something and another comes in but concludes he dont [*sic*] want anything, while a third and fourth amuse themselves by asking questions and obtaining advice for which of course they dont expect to pay—. . . .

As an attorney, Dana quickly gained experience in a broad array of business matters. He worked with transfers of personal and real property, mastering intricacies of contracts and contractual obligations. He became well versed in real estate affairs. He dealt with estate settlements. He learned firsthand of different forms of business organization, including the singly held firm, partnerships, and joint stock corporations. He gained substantial practical knowledge of financing and credit arrangements. He dealt with various tax problems, and liability issues, The growing centrality of legal advice and services in the formation and conduct of business assured that, as was common for contemporary attorneys, he was placed in frequent association with persons creating and operating enterprises. Like many of his professional peers, he was strategically positioned to hear quickly of new opportunities and ventures, and to absorb even more deeply the enterprising spirit of the age. William Dana developed a canny sense of opportunity and value, and he learned how to minimize risk.

Frequent trips to other cities, including New York, provided Dana with numerous occasions to use railroads and steamboats, and to observe changes in transportation, communications, and technology. Family ties contributed a chance to invest in stock in his brother George's screw company. An eminently eligible young bachelor and man of affairs, he was much in demand as a guest at parties, receptions, and other social functions. These included an open house celebrating the marriage of a fellow young Utica attorney who would later become United States Senator from New York, Roscoe Conkling. Family position, social and professional connections with individuals such as Judge Bacon, and an expanding law practice granted him growing stature in the community. By the late 1850s, he was clearly a man on the rise.[26]

William Dana's personal affairs took a decisive turn as he was embarking on his career in law. How, when, and where he met Katharine Floyd is unknown. A reasonable guess is that it might have been through her cousin and intimate friend, Cornelia Bacon, Judge Bacon's daughter. Cornelia often stopped by Dana's office after he entered practice, which indicates that she had become acquainted with him earlier, perhaps while visiting her father's office while Dana was reading law there. It would have been natural for her occasionally to bring Katharine along. The encounter, whenever it occurred, proved fateful. It set Dana on a course toward marriage that transformed his life and allied him with one of New York's eminent families.

Katharine Floyd was born on July 21, 1835, in Utica. Her great grandfather, signer of the Declaration of Independence and Revolutionary War general William Floyd, had in 1803 brought family and slaves from his estate at Mastic, Long Island, to occupy a large land purchase in Western Township some fifteen miles north and a bit west of Utica, on the Black River. Her father was John Gelston Floyd Sr. An 1824 graduate of Hamilton College, the younger Floyd had studied law with Utica's first mayor, Joseph Kirkland, with whom William Bacon had also read law. Floyd later married his mentor's daughter, Sarah Backus Kirkland, whose sister, Eliza, Bacon married.

John Floyd became well-known in politics as well as in law. He practiced singly and in several partnerships, the last with Charles Doolittle, 1840–1843. Elected twice to Congress, in 1838 and 1840, he founded the *Utica Democrat* in 1839. After completing his second congressional term in 1843, he returned to the 4,400-acre family estate on Long Island and quickly ascended to political leadership in Suffolk County. He served as state senator in 1848 and 1849, and again won election to Congress in 1850. Although a landed gentleman, he broke with the Democrats over the question of slavery to join the Republican Party upon its formation. His wife, a woman known for her intelligence, deep piety, and deeper hypochondria, lived in Utica until 1849, when she ceased traveling for conjugal visits and moved to reside with him in Mastic. The children completed their studies at boarding schools in Utica. Floyd died in 1881, an invalid, sometimes irascible and sometimes drunken, after a stroke shattered his health in 1857.[27]

As early as November 1853, Katharine Floyd and William Dana were exchanging correspondence and books, beginning with John Milton's *Paradise Lost*. Kate, or Kitty, was her father's treasure. Uncommonly bright, she was a graduate of the Utica Female Seminary, a classical high school for young women that leading men of the city had founded in 1837 as a counterpart to the academies available to their sons. She could be petulant, and lifelong she suffered a series of real and imagined physical afflictions. She was by nature inquisitive, talented and kind, with an electric personality. Fine-featured, a bit below medium height, delicate framed as a young woman, this blue-eyed light brunette with a commanding gaze captivated our young attorney. Well trained at drawing, she was an omnivorous reader who consumed poetry, stories, novels, George Bancroft's massive *History of the United States*, and works on oceanography, theology and devotional literature, and myriad other subjects. Throughout their courtship and marriage, she introduced Dana to social circles that outshone Utica. More important, she broadened his interests, reading, and range of knowledge. She became, and remained for as long as she lived, his adviser on writing and other matters, his intellectual companion, his confidante, his helpmate, and his one great love.

The courtship progressed fitfully, and against some formidable obstacles. Not the least of these was John Floyd's protectiveness. Kate's own temper

Katharine Floyd Dana (ca. 1857–1858) (top) and (ca. 1860–1863) (bottom). Photographs courtesy of William Floyd Estate/National Park Service, Fire Island National Seashore, Long Island, New York.

at times threw up barriers, too. But Dana persisted. By mid-1854, "My dear Mr. Dana" and "Miss Floyd" had become "My dear Willy" and "My Darling Katie," and he was asking Kate to correct his spelling and help him to improve his writing. He was also chafing at the elder Floyd's opposition and wishing that he and Kate could be seen openly together.[28]

Fortunately Kate, who was at Mastic for her annual summer visit, learned in July 1854 from her mother that her father was softening. "I *know*," her mother had said, "after next winter," when Dana's affairs would be "settled smooth . . . you will be allowed to do as you choose." She added, "Your Father's objections have not been against Mr. D., only against your marrying at all before you are 25."[29] Nevertheless, her father insisted on prolonging Kate's stay until November. Finally, in February 1855, she and her beloved announced their engagement with blessings all around.[30]

Later, Kate was back at Mastic preparing for the wedding, and William Dana was supervising construction of the house that would be ready for occupancy after they married. He bought a lot at 24 West Bridge (now Park) Street, where it intersected with Rebecca (now South) Street from his parents for $1,000, paying by taking out a bond of indebtedness to his father. Construction began just before the end of April, with the digging of the cellar. Framing was complete two months afterward. Roofing, enclosure, reconstruction of a collapsed chimney, installation of gas and water connections, finish work, and furnishing ran right up to the last minute. The finished house cost $5,000. Set on a fenced, landscaped lot, it held two parlors, a library, and a dining room on the first floor, a sewing room, bathroom, and sleeping quarters on the second floor.

Dana wrote Kate almost daily about the progress of construction, adding complaints about high costs and the slowness of the workingmen that will be familiar to readers who have built or remodeled homes.[31] His letters also indicated how deeply he had absorbed Utica's capitalist spirit. A year before, when it seemed that his income was too small to permit marriage, he had written to agree with Kate "as to the impossibility of our setting up in business with so small a capital." It was best to wait until he was sure of an income of $2,500 yearly. As the house rose, he observed that they should control costs, to permit a profit if the "possibility" should materialize for their selling it. When the builder offered to buy the dwelling back from them, William proudly wrote, "I told him he couldn't have it for less than ten thousand dollars." On the eve of the wedding, he penned, "I had a bona fide offer of $6,000$\frac{0}{00}$ for our home today," adding that even though he and Kate looked forward to occupying the house, "I like to have people think its [*sic*] worth more than it cost us."[32]

William Dana made his first, dreaded, often-delayed visit to Mastic at the end of May 1855, as construction on the house proceeded. Trunk in tow, he traveled by rail to Albany, steamboat to New York, and rail to the station at Yaphank, Long Island. A carriage met him at the depot for the six-mile drive to the Floyd home. There he met Kate and her family, and over the succeeding days friends and cousins. Visits followed again in July and August, as the wedding approached. Each trip strengthened a tie to Mastic, to which the Danas later returned each summer. Passions long subordinated to ingrained habits of self control and denied by months of separation erupted during the first visit. Exactly what occurred is not clear. But afterward William replied to a now-missing letter from Kate, proclaiming the purity of his motives and assuring her that "there is very little in what Baby refers to, except it makes me love . . . [her] far more than I ever did before, for it showed the confidence she placed in me, and made me feel that she was more entirely mine." They drew closer in every way during the ensuing hectic weeks, marrying at last at the Floyd home, surrounded by happy family members, on September 18. Dana had won his partner.[33]

The details of William Dana's course from law to journalism are obscure, but it is possible to reconstruct its main features. Brother-in-law J. Wyman Jones played a major role in his decision to change careers. There is evidence that a concern to relocate Kate to a less severe climate than that of upstate New York was a factor. A special *Commercial and Financial Chronicle* feature commemorating Dana's eightieth birthday recorded, "For reasons affecting the health of the dearest member of his family, it became important to change his residence to a more suitable climate." A desire to provide more generously for Katharine Dana may also have been involved, although by 1860 the Danas were sufficiently well off to employ two domestic servants.[34] The availability of *Hunt's Merchants' Magazine* for purchase, and a way for Dana to learn of it, were necessary conditions of the change. His share of his father's estate and earnings from his law practice provided him with the means to acquire the *Magazine*. That he grew up and worked in a community seething with ambition must have contributed to an openness to considering a new direction. An education steeped in capitalist values, an ability to gauge an opportunity, and a willingness to take an uncharacteristic risk while minimizing his exposure were also factors.

Born in 1822 to a prominent merchant family in Enfield, New Hampshire, J. Wyman Jones graduated from Dartmouth College and then studied law in Utica and New York City. After admission to the bar in Troy in 1843, he practiced for five years in New York City. He relocated to Utica after marrying Dana's sister Harriet. Enterprising and engaging, he soon made a place for himself in Utica society as well as in the Dana family. Throat problems forced him to abandon law in 1854 and seek more healthful pursuits in the country. Wyman Jones purchased 150 acres on Whitesborough Road near Utica and plunged into agriculture. He quickly emerged as a leader of Oneida County farmers. He and Dana, meanwhile, had become fast friends.[35]

In 1858, while visiting New York City, Jones heard from an engineer of the progress of construction of a railroad from Jersey City a half dozen miles into the pleasant valleys behind the Hudson River palisades in New Jersey. Intrigued, he inspected the area, returning sometime later for a second look. He liked what he saw, a lovely neighborhood of farms and woods only an hour and a half by train and ferry from New York. In 1854, several local farmers, seeking an inexpensive way to ship their produce to market, had won from the state legislature an act incorporating the Northern Rail Road of New Jersey. Financial problems had repeatedly interrupted construction, but completion was at last in sight. Jones quickly began to buy land, within months acquiring six farms containing 625 acres. He moved his family from Utica in the spring of 1859, turned to the speculative development of his holdings, and resumed legal practice in New York. After arranging for a survey, in August 1859, he filed in the Bergen County courthouse a plat of his townsite, christened Englewood. He was soon preparing promotional literature; arranging excursion trains for prospective buyers; involved in building of a hotel, a railway station, and a chapel; contributor of land for the First Presbyterian Church, of which he was for many years an officer and a Sunday school teacher; even organizer of a baseball club.

Although something of a plunger, Jones became hugely successful. He went on to develop the towns of Closter and Norwood and, later, lead mines in Missouri. Some time after Harriet died, in 1886, he married Mrs. Salome Hanna Chapin, widowed sister of Ohio's Republican United States Senator Marcus Alonzo Hana. Jones died October 27, 1904.[36]

Isaac Smith Homans, Jr. was one of several persons associated with Jones in developing Englewood. He moved there in 1859, when his father and his brother, Sheppard, also moved their families to the promising new townsite. He succeeded his father, an actuary for the Guardian Life Insurance Company of New York as Publisher of the *Bankers' Magazine* (the leading journal in its field). Like his father, he was a well-known writer on financial topics. He was also an actuary of the Mutual Life Insurance Company of New York and secretary of the state chamber of commerce. His brother, also an actuary for New York's Mutual Life Insurance Company, refrained from speculating in Englewood land but later, through his corporate connections, played a financial role in the town's development.

Although no direct evidence has come to light, there can be little doubt that the bullish Jones urged Dana to invest in Englewood. After a visit, the latter responded enthusiastically, when in May 1859 he bought the parcel of land on which he later built his imposing residence. With characteristic prudence, he paid but $300 with his own cash, financing the

balance of $20,550 with a five-year, 7-percent mortgage.[37] There still re-
mained the problem of earning a living in New York. Homans, Jr., whom
Dana must have met through Jones when he became interested in Englewood property, was probably the crucial link. Strategically situated as he
was in the New York business community, he was the one who would
have known that the *Merchants' Magazine* could be bought, and profitably
managed. After Freeman Hunt's death, George W. and John A. Woods
had become its publishers in April 1858. Thomas Prentice Kettell, a long-
time Hunt associate and well-known authority on the cotton trade, provided editorial direction. It appears, however, that when Dana bought
Hunt's its business was not good, for shortly after he acquired it he wrote
to Katharine Dana that he would "now endeavor to have the Mag. managed economically. It will pay if it is—it will *not* pay if it is not."[38]

How long it took to arrange the purchase cannot be determined. Dana,
with no publishing experience, surely hesitated. The risks were great, but
so was the possibility of gain. The Danas undoubtedly spent many hours
in searching conversation about a move to Englewood and a change in
vocation. Hesitancy most likely disappeared when Homans, Jr. and Dana
contrived a way to ease the latter into publishing. The plan was ingenious:
Homans would teach Dana to edit and publish. He would edit the *Magazine* while Dana learned. Risks now confined, on February 1, 1861,
William concluded two agreements. The first was to purchase *Hunt's*, for
$7,000. The second lodged editorial control with Homans. Dana would
manage business affairs, review all works of poetry and fiction sent to the
Magazine, and enjoy first claim to profits, up to 7 percent of his investment. Publication moved from the Woods' offices at 82 Nassau Street to
the Chamber of Commerce and Underwriters' Building at 61 and 63 William Street, where Homans published the *Banker's Magazine*.[39]

Always cautious, William Dana maintained his law office in Utica for
several years, until the results of his new venture should become clear.
But now an apprentice publisher and editor, he was ready to enter a new
world.[40]

NOTES

1. Agreement, February 1, 1861, in Dana Papers, copy in the author's posses-
sion. The originals of the Dana papers are in the archives of the William Floyd
Estate, a unit of the Fire Island National Seashore, Patchogue, Long Island, New
York. The writer holds photographic copies of this collection of materials.

2. Quotations here are from Anonymous [Freeman Hunt, Jr.], "Freeman
Hunt," in *Memorial Biographies of the New England Historic Genealogical Society*
(Boston: New England Genealogical Society, 1883), 3:203, 206; Frank Luther Mott,
A History of American Magazines (Cambridge: Harvard University Press, 1938),
1:697. Also *Hunt's Merchants' Magazine*, 1–41; (July, 1839; June, 1870); *New York*

Times, March 4 1858. Curiously, *Hunt's* is omitted in John Tebbel and Mary Ellen Zuckerman, *The Magazine in America, 1741–1990* (New York: Oxford University Press, 1991).

3. Robert Frederick Berkhofer, Jr., "The Industrial History of Oneida County, New York, to 1850" (master's thesis, Cornell University, 1955); Mary P. Ryan, *Cradle of the Middle Class: The Family in Oneida County, New York, 1790–1865* (Cambridge: Cambridge University Press, 1981).

4. Jack M. Sosin, *The Revolutionary Frontier, 1763–1783* (New York: Holt, Rinehart and Winston, 1967), 17–18, 32–33, 52–53, 152; Reginald Horseman, *The Frontier in the Formative Years, 1783–1815* (New York: Holt, Rinehart and Winston, 1970), 24–27, 67–69, 162.

5. Horseman, *Frontier in the Formative Years*, quoted 67, watercolor, 68, treats early settlement in western New York, 24–27, 67–69, 162. See also Ryan, *Cradle of the Middle Class*, 1–59; Codman Hislop, *The Mohawk* (New York: Rinehart and Company, 1948), 10, 223; and T. Wood Clark, *Utica: For a Century and a Half* (Utica, NY: The Widtman Press, 1952), 1–59.

6. Pomroy Jones, *Annals and Recollections of Oneida County* (Rome: Author, 1851), 545.

7. Clark, *Utica*, 38–59; George Rogers Taylor, *The Transportation Revolution, 1815–1860* (New York: Holt, Rinehart and Winston, 1962), 32–36, 78–80.

8. Discussion follows Ryan, *Cradle of the Middle Class*, quoted 8 and 9, lithograph and engraving 107, 151. Hislop, *The Mohawk*, 258ff, provided the 1840 description and discussion.

9. Ryan, *Cradle of the Middle Class*, especially 21–65, 98–104.

10. Ryan, *Cradle of the Middle Class*, 15–17, 60–61, 65–104, 108–127. Also, for formative influences in early America, see Bernard Bailyn, *Education in the Forming of American Society: Needs and Opportunities for Study* (Chapel Hill: University of North Carolina Press, 1960); John Demos, *A Little Commonwealth: Family Life in Plymouth Colony* (New York: Oxford University Press, 1970); H. Richard Niebuhr, *The Kingdom of God in America* (1937; reprint, New York: Harper and Brothers, 1959); (New York: Harper and Brothers, 1937; reprint Harper Torchbooks, 1959), 88–126, 164–198; Bernard A. Weisberger, *They Gathered at the River: The Story of the Great Revivalists and Their Impact upon Religion in America* (Chicago: Quadrangle Books, 1966), 63–126; and Whitney Cross, *The Burned Over District: The Social and Intellectual History of Enthusiastic Religion in Western New York* (Ithaca, NY: Cornell University Press, 1950).

Ironically, as Ryan points out, Utica's churches lost effective power to discipline members by means of church trials as revivalism progressed and, through the proliferation of competing congregations and denominations, gave members the opportunity voluntarily to change affiliation rather than submit to discipline.

11. For Gurdon Burchard, see Moses M. Bagg, *The Pioneers of Utica: Being Sketches of Its Inhabitants and Its Institutions, with the Civil History of the Place, from the Earliest Settlement to the Year 1825* (Utica, NY: Curtiss and Childs, 1877), 133 and for James Dana's life, 172–173, quoted 172 concerning his fortune. Also for Dana's life, in the collection of the Oneida County Historical Society, Utica, New York, see P. H. Fowler, *A Sermon Suggested by the Death of James Dana, Esq., and Delivered in the First Presbyterian Church Utica NY, January 15, 1860* (Utica, NY: Curtiss and White, 1860); for his bequests, will of March 1, 1852, and

codicils of May 29, 1855, and June 10, 1858, see Wills and Testaments, Oneida County, 15:453–460, in records of Oneida County Surrogate Court. James Dana reserved a capital sufficient to earn the annuity, probably some $15,000 at 7 percent, and bequeathed the residue of his estate by differing quantities of forty-fifths.

12. Bagg, *The Pioneers of Utica*, 222–223.

13. Quotation concerning James Dana's habits, William B. Dana to Katharine Floyd, September 1, 1855, see Dana papers; concerning charity, see Fowler, *A Sermon Suggested by the Death of James Dana, Esq.*, 22; children's debts, see James Dana Will; and conversions, see Ryan, *Cradle of the Middle Class*, 82, 84, 94–96.

14. Quotation from 1838–1839 report of trustees of Vernon Academy, in B. J. Peal, "A Glimpse into the History of Vernon, New York" (unpublished manuscript, collection of Oneida County Historical Society, Utica, NY, 1959), 32, which describes the academy. A set of trustees' records for the academy is in the possession of Mrs. A. J. Sforza (telephone interview with the author, March 17, 1992). For Dana's school work, "On a Story," and "On Fishes," undated manuscripts, Dana Papers, Box 4, Folder 24, William Floyd Estate; for Utica Schools, Clark, *Utica*, 173–177.

15. Yale College Matriculation Book, April 13, 1849 [1847?], referenced in Judith Ann Schiff, Yale University Archives (personal letter to the author, July 21, 1991). Also Yale College, *Catalog of the Officers and Students of Yale College* (New Haven, CT: Yale, 1847), quoted 29, annual costs 35.

16. James Hadley, *Diary of James Hadley 1843–1851*. Edited and with a foreword by Laura Hadley Mosely (New Haven, CT: Yale University Press, 1951), ix–xi; Brooks Mather Kelley, *Yale: A History* (New Haven, CT: Yale University Press, 1974), 171–202; Ralph Henry Gabriel, *Religion and Learning at Yale: The Church of Christ in College and University, 1757–1957* (New Haven, CT: Yale University Press, 1958), 133.

17. Noah Porter assumed responsibility for moral philosophy in 1849 (Yale College, *Catalog of the Officers and Students*, 1847–1850), all 31. Kelley, *Yale: A History*, 171–202; William Lathrop Kingsley, *Yale College: A Sketch of Its History* (New York: Henry Holt and Company, 1879), 1: 148.

18. William Paley, *Natural Theology; or, Evidences of the Existence and Attributes of the Deity. A New Edition* (1802; reprint, London: J. Christie, J. Richardson, R. Baynes, J. Walker, and W. Harrison, 1821), 391, 403.

19. Victor Cousin, *Elements of Psychology*, tran. with introduction, notes, and additions C. S. Henry (Hartford, CT: Cook and Company, 1834).

20. Quotations from Thomas Reid, *Essays on the Powers of the Human Mind*, (Edinburgh: Bell and Bradfute, 1819), 1:68–69, 424, 152; and Reid, *Essays on the Active Powers of the Mind*, introduction by Baruch A. Brody (Cambridge: MIT Press, 1969), 236.

21. James Kent, *Commentaries on American Law*, 12th ed., edited by Oliver Wendell Holmes, Jr. (Boston: Little, Brown, and Company, 1873), 1:2, 3, 222, 294, 437.

22. Francis Wayland, *Elements of Political Economy*, 4th ed. (Boston: Gould and Lincoln, 1860), iii, 1, 5, 106, 107, 370, 405. For Wayland's influence and the intellectual climate of antebellum colleges, see Stow Persons, *American Minds: A History of Ideas* (New York: Henry Holt and Company, 1958), 110–196.

23. Robert E. Daggy, Yale University Archives, personal letter to the author, January 15, 1965; Hadley, *Diary of James Hadley*, 176 regarding scuffle at prayers; Brothers in Unity, Yale College, "Library Circulation Records, 1850–1851" (unpublished manuscript, Yale University Archives); Brothers in Unity, Yale College, "Secretary's Records, 24 June 1840–20 May 1851," Book 6 (unpublished manuscript, Yale University Archives, 1851; for Skull and Bones, see "Henry F. Boyden, 1864," Russell Trust Association, *Catalog, 1864* in Yale University Archives; Dana's Autograph Book, in Dana Papers. Also J. H. Benham, *Benham's City Directory and Annual Advertiser, 1847–1848* through *1850–1851* (New Haven, CT: J. H. Benham, 1848–1850), respectively 24, 21, and 131; 18, and 14.

24. For more on Bacon, William L. Stone, *In Memoriam: William Johnson Bacon* (Utica, NY: n.d. [1889?]), pamphlet at Oneida County Historical Society, Utica, NY.

25. *Utica Daily Gazette*, November 27, 1852; *The Utica City Directory for 1852–1853* through *1860–1861* (Utica: publishers vary, 1852–1860), respectively 35, 21; and 93, 40, 59, 71 and 193, and passim. For more on White, see Daniel E. Wager, ed., "Family Sketches," in *Our County and Its People: A Descriptive Work on Oneida County, New York* (Boston: Boston History Company, 1896), 199–200.

26. Quotations from William Buck Dana (hereafter WBD) to Katharine Floyd Dana (hereafter KFD) September 27, 1854, and June 28, 1855; also WBD to KFD, August 22, and KFD to WBD, July 27, both 1856; in Dana papers. For industrial wages, see Stanley Lebergott, "Wage Trends, 1800–1920," in *Trends in the American Economy in the Nineteenth Century* (Princeton: Princeton University Press, 1960), 449–499; for Yale professors, see Kelley, *Yale: A History*, 171–202.

27. John G. Floyd, Jr. to KFD, March 14, 1879, Dana papers; *New York Times*, October 7, 1881; Anonymous, "Descendants of William Floyd of Mastic, Long Island" (unpublished manuscript, Genealogy Room, New York Public Library, 1896), 5; Moses M. Bagg, *Memorial History of Utica, N.Y.: From Its Settlement to the Present Time* (Syracuse, NY: D. Mason and Co., 1892), 178–179.

28. WBD to KFD, December 8, 1853; April 6 and 9, May 6 and 27, and June 10, all 1854; KFD to WBD, November 30 and December 13, 1853; February 21 and 24; June 10 and 20, August 6, September 1, October 8, and December 11, all 1854; all in Dana papers; Clark, *Utica*, 173–177.

29. KFD to WBD, July 9, 1854, Dana papers.

30. KFD to WBD, February 7; WBD to KFD, February 22 and April 6; all 1855, Dana papers.

31. WBD to KFD, February 26; April 15, 17, 19, and 25; May 4, 5, 8, 17, and 18; and June 3, 4, 9, 12, 16, 19, 23, and 26, all 1855; Dana papers.

32. *Book of Deeds, Oneida County, New York, 1855*, vol. 190, 19, recorded the sale dated May 1, 1855. Dana's parents later gave an added three-and-a-half feet of land to round out the lot. See WBD to KFD, April 17, 1855; for the marriage as a business, see September 27, 1854; for house costs and value, see August 28, May 8, July 26, and September 6, all 1855; all Dana papers. Kate's father encouraged building a house for $2,000 or $3,000, as being cheaper than buying an existing dwelling. KFD to WBD, February 7, 1855, Dana papers.

33. WBD to KFD, June 12, 1855; also April 6 and 15, May 20 and 23, June 3; July 26, August 25, and September 11; KFD to WBD, May 19 (visits), June 6;

WBD to KFD, June 9 and 28, August 7, and September 6 and 11 (marriage); all Dana papers. *Utica (New York) Morning Herald*, September 24, 1855.

34. *Commercial and Financial Chronicle*, August 28, 1909; WBD to KFD July 19, 1860, Dana papers.

35. WBD to KFD, April 6, June 12, and August 22, all 1855; May 10 and 13, 1861; all Dana papers. Also Anonymous, "J. Wyman Jones" (unpublished manuscript, Englewood Collection, Englewood, New Jersey, Public Library, n.d.).

36. *Englewood (New Jersey) Press*, October 29, 1904, and October 26, 1939. See also *Grantee, Index of Deeds, Bergen County, New Jersey, 1714–1962*, 41; *Index of Mortgages, Bergen County, New Jersey, 1766–1961*, 24; both passim and both in Bergen County Administration Building, Hackensack, New Jersey; and for Jones' reputation, see New Jersey, vol. 3, p. 19, R. G. Dun and Co. Collection, Baker Library, Harvard Business School.

37. James Greco, *The Story of Englewood Cliffs* (Englewood Cliffs, NJ: Tercentenary Committee, 1964); John K. Lattimer, *This Was Early Englewood: From the Big Bang to the George Washington Bridge* (Fairview, NJ: Englewood Historical Society, 1990), 120ff; Adaline W. Sterling, *The Book of Englewood* (Englewood, NJ: City of Englewood, 1922), 30–32, 37–38, 46–49, 52, 56, 61, 67–68, 95, 122, 226; Jeffrey A. Humphrey, *Englewood: Its Annals and Reminiscences* (New York: J. S. Ogilvie Company, 1899); and *Mortgage Index*, 13: passim.

38. WBD to KFD, May 10, 1861, Dana papers.

39. Agreements to purchase and with Homans, February 1, 1861, in Dana papers. For *Hunt's Merchants' Magazine* and *Bankers' Magazine* respectively, see Mott, *A History of Magazines*, respectively 1:696–698; 2:94–95. Inexplicably, Homans identified himself by full name and by both the initials "I" and what appeared to be a "J".

40. John G. Floyd, Jr. to KFD, September 11, 1861, in Dana papers.

2

Man of Enterprise

> I think exact methods and freedom from little wastes in handling money are an index to character.
> —William Buck Dana, December 24, 1896.

William Dana as an apprentice magazine owner faced numerous challenges. While skilled at management, he was ignorant of publishing and editing. The agreement with Isaac Homans, Jr. reserved to Dana the review of works of poetry and fiction, but even this task, and that of acquiring works to review, were unfamiliar. In May 1861 he wrote his wife Katharine that "very few" books were "published now," and "extremely few [are] recd by the Merchts' Magazine." Days later, he reported with surprise that Homans had told him, "I can get any books I want for *nothing* by simply writing the publishers for them & promising to notice [cite as new publications] them" in print.[1]

Meanwhile, the outbreak of civil war began a bloody, four-year test of the American union. Repercussions of the conflict resounded in nearly every corner of national life. The accelerating pace of events and change rendered a magazine that provided monthly accounts of business less and less useful. The requirements and effects of national mobilization diverted much of manufacturing and trade from accustomed channels. Before rising output for the war effort compensated, business contracted in the northern states. Dana found that his "presence was needed very much" at his office, to direct the affairs of *Hunt's Merchants' Magazine*. He ordinarily left Englewood by rail at "8 in the morning" returning at "half past five." Like other publishers, before the war's end he had to grapple with rising prices of ink and paper, and upward pressures on other costs of production. An 1861 letter illustrates the care that he applied to the enterprise. Remarking that he had sent two copies of *Hunt's* to Katharine's mother, Sarah Floyd, he commented that after she had read these through "she can have some more. If she wants it really & truly." He cautiously added, "I can send it to her without her subscribing." He mastered his new profession quickly, and well. In February 1862 he canceled his agreement with Homans and assumed full control of the *Magazine*, leaving his former associate free to direct the *Bankers' Magazine* and to pursue real estate speculation in Englewood and other interests.[2]

Under Homans' editorship *Hunt's* was unchanged in appearance and general makeup. Freeman Hunt's formulaic arrangement of the publication, which added to several articles numerous regular monthly topical and largely statistical "departments" devoted to various fields of commerce, continued. Nevertheless, war's dislocations of trade figured in a shrinkage of the average size of editions from 144 pages to 110 pages, from January to December, 1861. A year later, each number averaged ninety pages. By 1865, issues ran to only eighty pages, a length that remained the standard through the end of the *Magazine's* life. After Dana assumed direction, he began to experiment with the organization, appearance, and contents of the monthly. Throughout the war years, he struggled to control costs, adapt to evolving conditions, and generate operating margins that would allow the accumulation of reserves. Signed and unsigned articles gained greater prominence. The amount of space allocated to monthly statistical summaries declined, as events outran the tempo of publication and quickly rendered news stale. However, one monthly summary, the "Commercial Chronicle and Review" was expanded, incorporating many previously separate reports. More specialized accounts of such matters as nautical intelligence, commercial regulations, statistics of agriculture, postal intelligence, miscellaneous trade news, the book trade, and insurance appeared less frequently, and more irregularly. The reduction in the amount of statistical material gave the *Magazine* a more inviting aspect. Cotton remained an object of frequent discussion, Thomas Prentice Kettell continuing to write about this vital product. Kettell was probably the mentor from whom Dana gained expert knowledge of the world cotton industry.

The focus of *Hunt's* was always on business. By the end of 1862, though, measures associated with financing the Civil War commanded more extensive coverage than any other subject. Tariff enactments, the creation of a national banking system, and various monetary and tax proposals won ongoing discussion. The increasing importance of railroads, in turn, placed them in the forefront during the postwar years.

Whatever the subject at hand, the pages of the *Merchants' Magazine* revealed the lasting influence of Dana's formal education during the years of his editorship. They publicized the coherent, consistent view of economics, and by extension of the world, that he had absorbed as a boy and young man. Business was subject to laws ordained by a beneficent creator and discovered through the science of economics.[3] The protection of property rights, the establishment and preservation of a sound and stable monetary system, the maintenance of a free marketplace, honesty, and prudence were the principles that best served humanity and civilization.

Editorial policy at the *Merchants' Magazine* steadfastly opposed government interference with property rights and business. It greeted with skepticism proposals to nationalize telegraph lines and guarantee the bonds of a transoceanic steamship company. A subsidy for overseas mail service was conceivable, but "In the past whenever public or private matters have been mixed up, the public interest has often been the loser."[4] A gold standard of payments drew firm support. Of currency inflation, *Hunt's* observed: "If government, then, instead of doctoring banking systems, and printing bank notes, turned its attention to doctoring the laws, and printing the Statutes at large, it would find much more useful and profitable employment."[5]

As an editor and publisher, William Dana unswervingly echoed Francis Wayland, Brown University's president and author of the most popular college economics textbook, in favoring the most economic form of government: The war with the Confederacy should be waged at the least cost consistent with success. An advocate of low tariffs and minimum taxation, Dana on one occasion wrote, "There is room for criticism against every tax law . . . [taxation] is at best a necessary evil; but, perhaps the worst [tax] the country ever had, if it were once established and declared immutable, would be better than perpetual tinkering, lobbying, and suspense."[6] He admired initiative and genuine enterprise and was ever critical of speculation, chicanery and deceit, and imprudent risk taking, as these hindered progress and the growth of a country's wealth. When confronted with the problems of financial panics and business depression, he theorized that they were corrections that inevitably followed periods when misconduct and speculation stimulated an expansion of business that rested on false, inflated, rather than true, value.[7] He appreciated the primary roles of capital accumulation and the advancing use of labor-multiplying machinery in transforming the national economy. Nonpartisan and temperate in tone, he clung to the belief, popular in the America in which he had grown up, that labor and capital shared a mutuality of interests. Of a wave of strikes in 1866 he wrote that such contests between workers and management were "against reason and opposed to that community of interests which Providence has instituted between the workingman and the employer," contrary to natural law, and "consequently" injurious "to the most vital interests of society."[8]

Dana had regretted the coming of civil war. A conciliator by nature, even though a firm adherent to principles he took to be true, he favored a speedy and peaceful restoration of the Union.[9] By the end of the armed struggle, he had become an experienced and respected figure in publishing. He had developed his editorial "voice" and had begun to perfect the writing and editing habits that he would employ for the rest of his long career. He was ready for a bold new undertaking that would transform business journalism in the United States and make him its unrivaled leader.

William Dana's plans ripened quickly. They resulted, on June 23, 1865, in the appearance of the first edition of the *New York Daily Bulletin*. Its design, intent, and contents all evidenced the publisher's business acumen. Issued Monday through Saturday, the four-page *Bulletin* led off with detailed accounts of transactions in the New York financial markets, through a "Bond-holders and Stockholders Gazette" that covered securities trading and foreign exchange. It followed with "The New York Weekly Bank Returns," "The Commercial Times" reporting on activity in the produce and dry goods trades, and "The Almanac," which listed all steamship overseas mails scheduled for the coming week.

As forward-looking as the *Daily Bulletin* was in its intention to provide comprehensive reports for businessmen in the nation's commercial metropolis, it was not Dana's principal new venture. Its masthead shrewdly heralded: "The New York Daily Bulletin . . . Issued Gratis to Subscribers To The Weekly Commercial and Financial Chronicle." A half-column advertisement on the fourth page explained, "The Publishers of HUNT'S MERCHANTS' MAGAZINE beg to announce that they have resolved to issue, *in addition to the Magazine*, a weekly newspaper of THIRTY-TWO FOLIO PAGES, modeled after the celebrated LONDON ECONOMIST, to be called THE COMMERCIAL AND FINANCIAL CHRONICLE." To be published each Saturday morning, the *Chronicle* would contain "the latest Commercial and Financial news from all parts of the world by mail and telegraph up to midnight Friday." Already, the ad continued, a "large and efficient corps of reporters and editors have been engaged on each department, so that the most mature opinions, as well as the freshest intelligence, will be combined in the columns of this journal." Dana added to the promotional content of the first issue of the *Bulletin* by reserving a full column on the fourth page, which was blank save for the words, "This column is reserved for Advertisements, which will be taken at 10 cents per line daily: for longer periods a discount will be made." Within a day, commercial announcements filled the column. By Wednesday, June 28, they spilled back onto part of the third page. Dana immediately retreated in the next edition to a single page of promotions, so that he could provide intended news coverage. By August 1, he was able to convert from two to three columns of ads on the final page, devoting one column to publicizing the *Chronicle* and two to space sold to advertisers.[10]

The first edition of the *Chronicle* carried a publication date of July 1, 1865. A strong Gothic masthead preceded pages in which Dana proclaimed the principles that were at once his editorial position and a key element of his entrepreneurial strategy. He aimed to serve the nation's commercial interests as no other publisher. The *Chronicle* in calm, measured prose pledged to provide readers with "the best and most reliable sources of information needed in their daily pursuits." Although partisanship reigned in the contemporary press, it would exclude from "its columns" anything "having a partisan bias." At the same time, it would "endeavor carefully to elucidate the effects of political events and legislation upon commercial and financial affairs." Claiming that the end of the Civil War presaged "an era of peace and prosperity which only needs wise legislation to find encouragement," the introductory editorial made clear the urgency of remaining faithful to fixed principles of political economy. The *Chronicle* self-consciously purposed to publicize those principles, and to provide the commercial world with the information it needed to conduct its affairs wisely and profitably. Its aim, in fact, was to be a means by which businessmen could obtain timely and accurate information that would enable them to manage effectively and consistently with the laws that political economy had discovered. So employed, the information would promote the better operation of those laws.

Going on, our editor wrote that the late war had seen "one false [economic] theory after another" come to naught, as had a succession of schemes "for producing wealth faster than the measured action of industrial [economic] laws will permit." It was time to return "to the teachings of the great leaders in political economy for wisdom and guidance." The only proper basis for national policy was the needs of the country's "industrial and commercial interests." The *Chronicle* declared itself to be the first national paper wholly devoted to those interests. It would not confine itself solely to the

advocacy of correct principles, but will be in every essential sense a newspaper. All that the economist, the merchant, the banker, the manufacturer, the agriculturalist, the shipper, the insurer and the speculator [investor] may need to know in the course of his daily pursuits will be found duly chronicled in its columns.

With typical modesty, Dana ended the editorial with an invitation to the public to answer whether his paper successfully accomplished its announced purposes.

The *Chronicle* initially organized its thirty-two, 8 × 12¾-inch-page editions into two columns per page that conveyed the news under four main headings. The first was "The Chronicle," eleven pages of editorial features and statistics on leading events and issues of the week. "The Bankers' Gazette and Commercial Times" followed, consisting of thirteen pages with much statistical material on banking and on transactions in all lines of trade. Then came "The Railway Monitor and Insurance Journal," seven pages on investment activity and profit and loss statements of firms in these businesses, followed by a final page of advertisements. The price of subscriptions revealed the target audience: affluent and influential businessmen. Outside of New York City, subscribers paid $10 a year. City residents paid $12, for which, Dana assured them, they also received the *Daily Bulletin* at no added cost. The page of advertisements was set in three columns, allowing sale of more lineage than would have been possible if it had employed the two-column format of the rest of the paper. This arrangement allowed 435 lines of advertising on the page, for rates that ranged from twenty cents per line for a single placement to eight cents for weekly placements for a year. On a per-page basis, this translated into a maximum of $87 and a minimum of $34.80. The *Chronicle*'s address of publication, at the offices of the *Merchants' Magazine*, at 60 William Street, illustrated Dana's knack for holding down costs.[11]

A new firm published the *Chronicle*. On June 5, 1865, Dana had formed a partnership with Katharine Dana's younger brother John Gelston Floyd, Jr. "under the . . . name and style of William B. Dana Co." to edit and publish "in the city of New York a weekly financial and commercial newspaper to be known as the New York Chronicle . . . a daily newspaper to be known as the *Bulletin*." Their business would also include job printing. Floyd, born in Utica in 1841, was a graduate of Rutgers University and of New York's Albany Law School. In 1861, after finishing his studies, he briefly practiced law with Dana in Utica. Subsequently, he raised a company of soldiers at Mastic and enlisted as a second lieutenant in the 145th New York Volunteers. He saw action at Chancellorsville and Gettysburg and rose to the rank of captain before mustering out and moving to resume his career in law and to associate with Dana in New York City. Floyd contributed $5,000 of the partnership's $8,000 capital; Dana supplied the rest, apparently garnered from reserves accumulated through careful management of the *Merchants' Magazine* and his law practice. Floyd became business manager and Dana became editor of the papers. The latter retained liberty to edit the *Magazine* while working in the new enterprise. Profits were to be divided, with three-fifths going to Dana in recognition of his experience and editorial work and the balance to Floyd. Also on June 5, 1865, the company engaged Alexander Delmar, who was an experienced newspaperman and editor of the quarterly *New York Social Science Review*, to assist in editing and publishing the papers, for the consideration of 25 percent of the company's net profits. How long the association with Delmar lasted remains unclear.[12]

William Dana's entrepreneurial strategy in founding the firm that bore his name, and the *Daily Bulletin* and the *Chronicle*, was revealing. He continued to depend on the web of acquaintances and kin that had worked so well in Utica and in facilitating his move to Englewood/New York City. Turning to a brother-in-law for the larger share of the capital invested in his company, he minimized his own exposure to risk. He leveraged the firm's limited capital, and further reduced risk, by engaging the experienced Delmar to assist in entering the unfamiliar world of newspaper publishing. It is a reasonable conjecture, given Dana's generally cautious habits, that he and Delmar were acquainted through their common work as magazine editors in New York. Finally, and quite rightly, the organization of the new company, as reflected in its provisions for the distribution of profits, recognized that its principal asset was the knowledge that Dana had gained, of economics, of business, of editing, and of publishing.

There was more. William Dana had matured in and around Utica and could scarcely have failed to note the impact of rapid economic and technological change there. The transforming effects of railroads, of the growth of manufacturing, of telegraphic communication after the formation in Utica of both the first telegraph company—which soon grew to become Western Union—and of the Associated Press were prominent features of the local scene. As publisher of the *Merchants' Magazine* during the Civil War, he had repeatedly contended with the lag between the pace of events and the publication of a business monthly, as well as with the advancing development of a nationwide marketplace through the railroad and telegraph revolutions. He also observed that subscribers often returned for binding copies of the *Magazine* that were still in their original wrapping and unopened, and he concluded that the publication had been valued originally for its wealth of current statistics on business. A monthly no longer appeared frequently enough to convey very useful tabulations. With the suppression of the South and the restoration of the Union, he discerned an opportunity to establish the first comprehensive business weekly, taking advantage of the extension of railroads and telegraphic communication to serve the budding, reconstituted national marketplace and its financial center, New York City. He understood the critical importance of timeliness in reporting, of complete accuracy, of unparalleled comprehensiveness of coverage, of holding to a nonpartisan and authoritative stance, and of maintaining uncompromising independence of external interests in a weekly intended to serve the needs of financiers, investors, and businessmen in a reuniting nation. He buttressed his weekly with a daily for New York City, and with provision for ancillary job printing, as hedges. Meanwhile, continuation of the *Magazine* enabled him to spread his risks across four ventures in all. Moreover he saw a unique moment and opportunity. As business became national and global and as electric, steamship, and rail communication improved, an omnivorous demand for commercial information would follow. He intended to satisfy that demand.

The *Commercial and Financial Chronicle* established itself quickly. As early as December 1865, the *New York Times* began to refer to it, affirming its emergence as a respected source of news and opinion. Before its first year of publication was over, it announced that it had engaged an editor of none other than *The Economist* of London to provide a weekly report from Europe. At the end of June 1866, an editorial combining promotion of the paper with a tone of surprise at its quick success thanked subscribers for their support and remarked that "there is scarcely a city in the United States, or scarcely a country connected therewith in either hemisphere, which is not represented in our subscription list, yet that list is every day receiving large additions."

By mid-1866 the *Chronicle* had evolved far toward the format that characterized it until Dana's death in 1910. Each edition began with a half dozen or so editorial pieces occupying eight to ten pages. These were unsigned and typically contained at least one treating leading business events of the past week. There was often during the first year or two of publication a page or so of book reviews (mostly of works on business or economic subjects) current affairs, memoirs or biographies of public figures, or history, with occasional forays into imaginative literature. However, reviews soon gave way to space devoted to "hard" business subjects. The balance of the paper fell regularly into several weekly features. There were a page or two on miscellaneous business, two or three on the condition of the national banks with emphasis on those in New York and Philadelphia, one on the week's sales of corporate securities and of government bonds, four to six pages detailing trade in leading lines of merchandise, three pages minutely reporting current prices of all manner of goods, four pages on railroad securities and earnings, a report on world postage rates, and, finally, as many as three and sometimes four pages of advertisements. Brokerage houses, insurance companies, and banks in New York and other financial centers led among advertisers. Producers of railroad and mining equipment, firms marketing securities issues, and commission and luxury import merchants also commonly published notices.

In June 1867 Dana established a separate firm to publish the *Daily Bulletin* and doubled its size to eight pages "on account of its growing popularity and the desire of its publishers to furnish subscribers with a complete daily record of the commercial and financial markets" of New York City. For an additional six months it remained available to *Chronicle* subscribers "at the reduced price of $4 per annum." The following month a correspondent for R. G. Dun & Company's Mercantile Agency, forerunner of the modern Dun & Bradstreet, first took note of William B. Dana and the W. B. Dana Company. Attesting to the firm's growing stature he added a tantalizing remark that William had continued to practice law up to the birth of the *Chronicle*. Because the new publishing company purchased its paper from manufacturers "down east," its creditworthiness was not yet generally known in New York. One source had reported, though, that its owners were "highly honorable men, believed to be ... well possessed of abundant means for their bus." Dana, "the capitalist of the firm," already held property valued at nearly $200,000. His decision to end his relationship with the *Daily Bulletin* in January 1868 had no adverse effects on his progress. The *Bulletin* subsequently merged into the daily (New York) *Journal of Commerce*. Dana concentrated his energies on his weekly, whose growth consumed his attention. The *Chronicle*, uniquely accurate, impartial, and comprehensive, was achieving singular importance as a source of information for key decision makers in the business world.

Advertisers, especially banking houses, brokers, and firms offering securities issues, replied to the growing prominence of the *Commercial and Financial Chronicle* by purchasing more and more space for their notices. Within three years of the paper's establishment, promotional announcements filled six to eight of its pages each week. Four pages of commercial notices preceded the first page of editorial matter, two more concluded each edition, and up to two additional pages could be found inside the paper. At such a volume, advertisements could generate between $278.40 and $696 per week of receipts, depending on the amount of discount given for multiple placements.

The *Chronicle*'s (really, Dana's) editorial views commanded high regard. Its success was so great that in December 1870 the *Merchant's Magazine* announced that it was to be incorporated into the *Commercial and Financial Chronicle* for 1871. The monthly had become effectively obsolete. Ever alert to a chance to keep customers, Dana promised subscriptions of the *Chronicle* to the full value of any unexpired, prepaid subscriptions to *Hunt's*, and a month of the paper free to those whose subscriptions ran out at the end of 1870. Maintaining that absorption of *Hunt's* by the weekly and publication of a *Commercial and Financial Yearbook of Hunt's Merchants' Magazine* would fulfill the functions of the *Magazine*, Dana ended what was, in effect, its obituary with an expression of hope that friends and subscribers would stay through the transition. He also retained a titular vestige of the *Magazine* by changing the name of his weekly to *The Commercial and Financial Chronicle and Hunt's Merchants' Magazine*, although the paper continued to be known popularly by its former name.[13]

William Dana was entering the prime of life when he halted publication of the *Merchants' Magazine*. In his forty-second year, vigorous and ambitious, he was at the peak of his powers. Of medium height and build, he framed a strong face with a thick, wavy shock of brown hair that grayed but did not recede as he aged. Kindly, direct, ice-blue eyes peered out from beneath a broad, high forehead and strong brow, all characteristic of the men in his family. A strong, straight nose guarded a drooping mustache and determined mouth and chin. He dressed conservatively, customarily in a black frock coat, black trousers, shirt with stiff starched collar, bow tie, and congress boots. When out of doors, he added black gloves and a square-blocked derby hat. He was sober in manner without being somber, serious but not humorless, high-minded but not a prig, methodical but not pedestrian. His voice was light and musical, and he laughed readily and with a gentle humor. On one occasion he merrily described to his wife-to-be how, in his efforts to remove a spider from his sister Delia's bonnet during worship without alarming her, he found the situation so funny that he almost violated the prohibition against "speaking out in church." Physically active, he enjoyed walking, carriage rides, and riding horseback, finding the last quite "delicious" at the end of a hot summer day's work. He puffed an occasional cigar, favored claret with dinner, and from time to time succumbed, with dire digestive consequences, to a temptation to consume too many raspberries.[14] In substance, his appearance and actions were of a piece with the man. They were straightforward, decorous, dignified but not stilted, combining a certain simplicity of manner with the self-assurance of one who occupied—in no small part as a result of his own exertions—a prominent station in life.

The switch from law to publishing was only one of several major changes in Dana's life as the 1860s began. Relocation from Utica to Englewood was itself no less considerable. Wyman Jones had platted the town of Englewood, in New Jersey's northern valley, but lines on the map still outran reality. The Danas consequently built their new home in what was yet largely open countryside. They were apparently as new to country life as they were to journalism. In May 1861 construction had begun of a barn, outbuildings, and of a home a mile to the east of where Englewood was developing, at a point just north of Palisade Avenue where it strikes the top of the Hudson River Palisades in what is now Englewood Cliffs. The place was sufficiently remote that the couple obtained a yoke of oxen and a cow for milk from Katharine Dana's mother. Shortly after the cow's arrival, William Dana wrote his wife that they would need to find out from her mother when the cow "comes in"—adding, delicately but revealingly, "that means, 'has a calf,' I believe. We dont [sic] know abt milking her. She looks a little as if she might be milked, but the man says he has tried & its no go."[15]

Despite the challenge of getting a home built and preparing for life in the country while he was learning his new business, Dana wrote of Englewood with a note of excitement rarely displayed in his life. Eager to stir his wife to enthusiasm for the move, he praised the palisades for their sunshine, wonderful scenery, and healthful "good air." Once he even exclaimed, "I think I am becoming quite extravagantly fond of New York and Englewood life." The fervor subsided in time, but he formed and retained a genuine attachment to the new town. That attachment merged into an entrepreneurial vision for Englewood.[16]

Construction of the new residence was a daunting task. Many materials for the house—lumber, stained glass windows, oak wainscoting, and other items—arrived by schooner from Boston, for delivery at river's edge beneath the palisades. A narrow ravine provided a difficult but practicable route for a laborious haul to the top. Other materials arrived by rail and wagon, via the station at Englewood. At the site, the builder who had erected the Danas' Utica house, one of many Uticans who thronged to Englewood seeking fresh opportunities, oversaw work. An imposing L-shaped, two-story Victorian mansion of native "blue trap" stone, with lintels and exterior trim of pink New Jersey sandstone, gradually rose. A glass conservatory took shape at the south end, while a three-story square tower at the entrance afforded views all around. There were two gardens.

Initially, the plan was to complete the dwelling by fall, but the cost of the *Magazine* and the house evidently strained the Danas' resources. The Utica house had not sold, and when it did, in June 1861 for $4,500, the result was a loss of $500 excluding the cost of the land on which it stood.[17] In the late spring, Dana inquired whether they might be able to get along with one rather than two servants, so as to save money. He also reported that construction was progressing more slowly than anticipated. The house would be finished "in about a year. Even if we had the money," he continued, the house that fall would still be "too rough and unfinished to make it pleasant to live there before another year." In the interim he and Katharine would live in a suite of rooms at the home of Wyman Jones and Dana's sister Hattie (Harriet). He visited the construction site as often as affairs permitted. His wife had named the place "Greycliffs." It was finally ready for occupancy, mantels and grates installed, plastering completed, and "cheap furniture" bought at "auction houses," in the autumn of 1862. It was their home and principal residence for as long as Katharine Dana lived.[18]

William Dana's career as an entrepreneur and journalist cannot be understood apart from the rest of his life. There was a consistency that ran through all of his thoughts and actions. That consistency originated in his character, which depended, in turn, on deeply held convictions about the essential elements of life: conceptions of the nature of the world, of human nature, and of human destiny; convictions about morality and family; and understanding of the character and purposes of social, economic, and political institutions. His views about social, economic, and political institutions are treated later. It is useful to consider his fundamental thought about the remaining matters now.

Dana acquired the basic ingredients of his worldview from his family, church, and schooling. His worldview was at its core Protestant Christian and, in fact, Presbyterian. Church attendance was a regular and central part of his life. As a young attorney he often attended two services on Sundays, one at Utica's First Presbyterian Church and one at its Reformed Dutch Church. His zeal did have limits, though. He confided to Katharine

Greycliffs (ca. 1865–1868) and after its enlargement in 1901. Photographs courtesy of William Floyd Estate/National Park Service, Fire Island National Seashore, Long Island, New York.

in 1855: "Two sermons are about as much as I can comfortably listen to in one day." He taught Sunday school to a group of boys he found to be occasionally unruly, but in 1856 he modestly declined an invitation to become superintendent of Sunday school, pleading that he was unqualified for so demanding a post.[19]

Bible reading and study were regular activities throughout Dana's life. His personal correspondence referred often to a guiding providence. Ever mindful of the uncertainty of human life, he wrote of the death of an infant nephew as a release from the pain of this world. In prayer he found consolation and renewal. He shared with his wife a keen interest in collecting proofs of truths in the Bible, and especially of the fulfillment of Old Testament prophecies in the New, although he believed that the New Testament was its own best proof of its truth. At Greycliffs on Sundays, the Danas, unable to have children of their own, established a Sunday school for local children. Each first day, children who lived along the Hudson River beneath the palisades, in the area known as Undercliffs, scrambled up a steep path to the Dana residence. There, the "lady on the hill" and her husband instructed them with Bible stories, poems, and other tales.

Probably replicating the practice of his own parents, Dana made family prayer a regular fixture of life at Greycliffs. Every morning the household, dressed formally, gathered in the parlor, knelt, and each member read a verse of scripture and prayed aloud. William Dana's faith shaped in fundamental ways his sense of morality. Visiting Martha's Vineyard in 1882, he deplored "the free and easy way of living, and above all . . . the custom of the two sex [sic] going in bathing [swimming in the ocean] together." He keenly disliked avarice, dishonesty, and social pretension, as well. Writing a few days later from Bar Harbor, Maine, he drily described the place as "an attempt of people who could not get up much of a standing in Newport [Rhode Island] society to build up something similar where they would be first—on the principle that they would rather rule here than serve there."[20]

Although he was too moderate in outlook and temperament to slip into outright bigotry, William Dana was like many of his contemporaries who looked askance at churches other than their own. He viewed Methodists and Baptists with some condescension, and Roman Catholicism with genuine distaste. While touring Europe in 1881, he found a visit to the Roman Catholic cathedral in Brussels, Belgium, "rather oppressive, because so many that came in dropped into their devotions with such suddenness, crossings, genuflexions . . . that you could not help pitying their ignorance or hating their hypocrisy." He was later disappointed to discover that services at the American church in Paris were Episcopalian rather than Presbyterian, but he nevertheless took pleasure in the sermon that he heard there.

Throughout his life, Dana grappled with issues of faith in the face of changing social practices and advances in human learning. One major interest was the proper observance of the Sabbath. It resulted, after his death, in the publication of a book, *A Day for Rest and Worship*. The volume, which showed how far he had moved from the stern eighteenth-century faith of his father, was the fullest expression of his religious views. Consistent with his advocacy of an unregulated economy, he opposed the enactment of laws prohibiting the conduct of business or banning other activities on Sundays. He hoped, instead, to use persuasion to arrest the growing disregard of the Sabbath, demonstrating in his book the "indispensable office in man's career the day was designed by God to fill." He showed, through extensive analysis of scripture and learned quotations from writers such as Herbert Spencer, James Dwight Dana, John Milton, and John Dryden, that a loving God had created a world designed to meet the needs of humanity. Unthreatened, doubtless partly through the influence of his brother James, by the theory of evolution, he likened the days of creation in the biblical account to geological epochs. The story of divine dealings with humanity was one of a loving parent trying to nurture and persuade, rather than to coerce. If salvation was the greatest of God's gifts to mankind, the Sabbath even so was an important gift that served to promote health, enrich life, and permit worship. Dana's book exuded the spirit of moderation, simplicity, deliberation, and learning that had been so evident in his life and professional writing. It was a fit summation.[21]

William Dana's family life was as important toward an understanding of his character as were his religious convictions and practices. He enjoyed an uncommonly close relationship with his wife. Constancy, fidelity, devotion, ripening friendship and mutual respect, and deepening romantic feeling ran through their marriage. Attentive to each other whenever they were together, they corresponded regularly and frequently whenever they were apart. The years brought changes. He grayed and walked with less of a spring in his step, and she became a bit stout. But affection never diminished. "My Darling Kate" with the passage of the years came to be "My Dearest Kate," "My Precious Wife," and "My Beloved Wife." "My dearest Will" became "My dear husband" or even "My poor dear old Will." The same strong expression of love continued in their closing words, too, whether "Your own loving wife," "your loving husband," "From your [illegible] cross old husband" or "Your dear failure of a wife."[22]

There were disagreements, as one would expect from two such strong-willed people. The Danas held deep feelings for each other, and they were both capable of passionate outbursts despite gentle dispositions and well developed habits of self-control. She was fastidious and could be willful, impetuous, demanding, and could even desire to be babied. He could be stubborn. When anger flared, it was short-lived and ended in speedy reconciliation. Obliged one morning to leave home early for work, after a disagreement, he penned a note to her that he was "constantly grieved

Katharine Floyd Dana (ca. 1865–1868) and William Buck Dana (ca. 1868). Photographs courtesy of William Floyd Estate/National Park Service, Fire Island National Seashore, Long Island, New York.

and humiliated that my tongue can be such an unruly member. There seems to be in me so much of profession and so little of grace."[23]

The couple shared a special affinity of minds and spirits. Her active intelligence broadened his range of interests and learning into realms well beyond law, business affairs, and political economy. The Dana library collection reflected her influence. It sheltered, together with a complete set of the *Chronicle*, some 3,000 volumes. Among these were standard works of literature, such as the writings of Victor Hugo, Ralph Waldo Emerson, James Russell Lowell, Benjamin Franklin, Washington Irving, Charles Dickens, Emily Brontë, Sir Walter Scott, William Makepeace Thackeray, John Milton, William Shakespeare, Robert Browning, Samuel Johnson, and many others. There were numerous works of a religious nature, extending to commentaries on scripture, hymnals, devotional books, writings of Cotton Mather, and the like. There was an extensive list of scientific titles, including James Dwight Dana's classic treatise on mineralogy. An ample history section harbored titles by James Hildreth, William Hickling Prescott, John Lothrop Motley, George Bancroft, Edward Gibbon, as well as popular series of American biographies, the life and correspondence of Louis Agassiz, official United States documents concerning reconstruction after the Civil War, and more. Also present were official federal reports of output of precious metals and of agriculture, and activity in various lines of trade; bound series of such periodicals as *[Appleton's] Annual Cyclopedia*, the *London Quarterly*, and the *Edinburgh Review*; miscellaneous titles treating the Dwight family and Frederick the Great; and works of nineteenth-century poets. This extensive collection was not just for show—its many volumes were well-worn from use.

Dana's intellectual companion and confidante, Katharine, assisted him in improving his writing, and probably his editorial skills. Very likely she was a foil against which he could test many of his ideas and with whom he could share his thinking. Where he might speak and write in measured (and sometimes convoluted) tones, she tended to do so with spirit, although her views and those of her husband were for all practical purposes identical. A letter to the local administrator of the poor concerning the condition of the township poorhouse was illuminating. She bluntly described the facility, as a charitable institution, "as an utter failure and a miserable *sham*, for in my opinion it injures the body, mind and soul of every creature that it professes to benefit." Economically, the place was wasteful: the taxpayers supported a keeper and family numbering eleven, to care for only nine paupers. Educationally, it was worse. The illiterate keeper's wife spoke contemptuously of the physician's instructions for care of the sick, who nevertheless died "in a fortnight in spite of her superior practice. She probably would make a good undertaker," Katharine Dana jabbed, "but I could not possibly persuade myself to put any sick creature into her keeping." In terms of sanitation, the poorhouse was terrible. Morally, it was worst of all. Heatedly, she wrote that if the keeper did "not train . . . [the young inmates] to be devils incarnate, it was not because the township does not give him the chance." Besides providing no Sunday school and no Bible instruction, the keeper commingled inmates of diverse ages and both sexes.[24]

Her husband's encouragement, and his roles as an editor and publisher, afforded Katharine Dana an outlet for her ambition, intelligence, and talent. As early as March 1862, writing under the initials "O. A. W" (after all, what could a woman possibly have to say about serious commercial topics?) she contributed a lead article, "Commercial Phrensies," to the *Merchants' Magazine*. She followed, again as O. A. W., this historical account of speculative bubbles with a July piece, "Petroleum, Old and New," providing a history of the uses of petroleum. Later, unsigned book reviews, in both the *Magazine* and the *Chronicle*, bore the unmistakable impress of her vigorous prose. However, the focus of her literary efforts shifted.[25]

Katharine Dana's legacy as an author lies primarily in two domains: fiction for adults, and a wide range of children's literature encompassing works of religious instruction, poetry, word games, and fiction. As she gained confidence, the initials "O. A. W.," which at first signified for her "only a woman" became the pen name "Olive A. Wadsworth." William Dana was as much her partner, critic, and confidant as she was his. She wrote determinedly, in ink on ruled 8½ × 14-inch pages, making but few corrections as her work progressed. From her pen flowed a steady stream of pieces to leading literary and children's magazines. Her most important adult fiction appeared in *The Atlantic Monthly*. *St. Nicholas* and similar journals published the bulk of her writing for children.

"Our Phil," "Aunt Rosy's Chest," and "Marty's Various Mercies" were

Katharine Floyd Dana (from an oil portrait), 1871. Photograph courtesy of the
author.

Katharine Dana's best-known pieces of adult fiction. Set on a plantation
on antebellum Maryland's western shore and cast as recollections of a
narrator known when she was a young girl as "Miss Kate," all three tales
drew on characters and events on the Floyd estate on Long Island. Although they reflected the patronizing attitudes of racial superiority common among contemporary upper-class white Americans, the writer made
it clear that the plantation's owner had freed his slaves immediately upon
inheriting the property and that Blacks, however childlike they might appear, were equal to Whites in God's eyes. Gifted with an acute ear for
the nuances of speech, she wrote the stories in persuasive dialect.

"Our Phil" told how this "blackest darky that ever was born" descended, after his wife deserted him, into drunken dependency. He later
recovered, became a devout church member, and after enlisting in the
Union Army died on an unknown battlefield. The writer concluded her
account with words of assurance that a loving God had taken Phil to a
saintly rest. "Aunt Rosy's Chest" recalled how a beloved nanny had
snitched a valued family medal from the Order of the Cincinnati and con-
cealed it in the wooden chest where she kept her clothing and valuables.
Afterward, she took mysteriously ill. Almost miraculously, her appetite
and health returned as soon as she restored the emblem to its rightful
owners. "Marty's Various Mercies" recounted the humorous misadven-
tures of Marty, "a poor little yellow girl," in marrying Ed, "the most
chicken hearted darky that ever lolled against the south side of a barn."

Dated in many respects, these stories held sufficient interest, strength of characterization, effectiveness of dialect, and charm to warrant their republication in a volume, *Our Phil and Other Stories*, as recently as 1970.[26]

Heavenward Bound (1870) won a $250 prize from the Presbyterian Publications Committee in a contest to select "the best book of small size for the instruction of young converts." It offered youthful readers twelve topical lessons: on conversion, the growth of the soul, the Christian standard of attainment, Bible study, prayer, public worship, expressions of faith in the home and at work, and similar matters. Simply written and gentle and affectionate in tone, it reflected the nurturing and monitory ideal of child rearing that had come into vogue during the middle third of the nineteenth century. Katharine Dana repeatedly urged children to pursue lives of "affection, obedience and cheerfulness," productive activity, and reverence. However simple and direct its lessons, *Heavenward Bound* showed that Katharine's faith partook of the same mix of piety and rationalism that characterized William's beliefs. Of the relationship between faith and science she wrote, "We must not, however, be misunderstood as implying that the Bible should be used as a test of the truth of works of science, art, or history." In words that placed her far in advance of fundamentalists a century later, she continued, "[It] was given to teach us the plan of salvation, and not as a handbook of science."[27]

Among Katharine Dana's other books for children, *Over in the Meadow* has enjoyed the greatest success. A collection of twelve rhymes penned to help children learn to count, it was first published in 1906, with simple musical settings added to encourage singing as a way of aiding in memorization of the rhymes. The volume was republished in the United States and Canada in 1985 and appears frequently in library collections. It is, with *Our Phil*, a moving testimony to the durability of Dana's devotion to his wife, and of a literary collaboration that extended beyond her death. He arranged for Houghton Mifflin to publish *Our Phil* in 1888, two years after she passed away. It is likely that he also brought about the first publication of *Over in the Meadow*. Its preface, which told of its origin and publication with the addition of Katharine's rhymes of "twelve little sermons . . . all written by a man who hopes you will not dislike him for preaching," and which was signed, simply "MAN," is written in a tone and style that strongly suggests his authorship.[28]

It is ironic that the Danas, whose religious convictions emphasized family, who personally held family to be of utmost importance, and who showered love on children, could have no children of their own. Their impulse to nurture young persons nevertheless would not be denied. Over time, it found numerous outlets.

Among the children who scrambled up the path from Undercliffs to Greycliffs to attend Sunday school was William Allison. Born about 1849

to William Henry Allison and his wife, Billy was one of four children.
Some persons later recalled that he first climbed to Greycliffs to sell fish
and that Katharine took a liking to him and helped him to earn money
by letting him chop wood. He quickly found a place in the Danas' affection. They brought him to live with them, raising him as foster parents
when his own parents declined to release him for adoption. They gave
him a wide background in reading and culture and encouraged his education, paying for private schooling in Englewood. When Billy enlisted in
the Union Army as a drummer boy, William Dana, opposed to the Civil
War as unnecessary and eager to protect Billy, hired a substitute to take
his place. Dana sent Billy to work for a friend who owned the *Journal of
Commerce* in New York City.

Allison excelled at reporting on the oil, paint, and drug trades. His
weekly pay rose quickly from $7 to $40. In October 1871, after being
advised by a drug manufacturer to start his own paper, he launched the
Oil, Paint, and Drug Reporter in New York City. He worked long hours—
years later he told his children of toiling twelve hours a day almost single-
handedly to get his paper out—and lived frugally. Often, at the end of a
week's work, he trotted on foot to the ferry, in order to save cab fare, and
after reaching the Jersey shore walked the nine miles to Greycliffs to
spend the weekend with the Danas. After his paper began to flourish, he
added two more publications: the *Druggists' Circular* and the *Painters'
Magazine.* As early as 1876 he was investing in real estate at the top of
the palisades, beginning with a purchase from Dana's brother-in-law and
former law partner N. Curtis White. In time, he owned more than 800
acres of prime land above the cliffs. He died a millionaire many times
over, and left choice holdings to become a city park.

Allison remained close to the Danas as long as they lived. Never formally adopted, he was yet "family" in all but name. Katharine Dana, still
a young woman in her thirties when he reached manhood, touched him
profoundly. A son recalled many years afterward that he took "Outis" as
his middle name to satisfy a fancy of Mrs. Dana that his initials would be
the same as those she used as her pen name, although in reverse order.
Well into middle age he signed his letters to her, "Billy." A frequent
correspondent of the Danas and often a visitor to their home and William
Dana's office, he handled many sensitive personal matters for them. Dana
to the end of his life counted on Allison for help and associated with him
in various business ventures.[29]

Allison proved to be only the first of several young protégés of William
Dana. The Danas eventually adopted three children, all through the
American Female Guardian Society of New York. John Armstrong, born
in February 1862, became John (Jack) Kirkland Dana on May 17, 1865.
Fannie Oscarina Payfer, born in March 1866, became Ethel (Daisy) Floyd
Dana on May 15, 1868. George Knight joined the family soon after, as

Richard (Dick).[30] As parents the Danas pursued a family strategy consistent with their values and social position. That strategy, employed also with Allison, sought to perpetuate the advantaged status of the children through an upbringing that emphasized the virtues they held dear, a superior education, and in due course provision of capital to assure that they would enjoy a suitable income if they lived properly. This family strategy was akin to William Dana's business strategy in its reliance on ties of kinship and friendship.

John, Ethel, and Richard enjoyed the care and teaching of governesses, as well as parental attention, when they were small. All then attended boarding schools, repeating the experiences of their adoptive parents. Jack and Dick studied at St. Paul's School and the Peekskill Military Academy, both near New York City. Daisy, as Ethel was known in the family, received instruction in schools in New Berlin, Connecticut, and Minneapolis, Minnesota. Despite the care lavished on them, the children did not excel in school. Their letters to their adoptive parents are filled with excuses, promises to try harder, expressions of self-reproach and, in Daisy's case, pleas for more correspondence from "Mama." None went to college. Jack, after finishing his secondary schooling in 1884, took a job with Allison at the *Oil, Paint, and Drug Reporter*.[31]

While they were growing up, the children joined in a long-standing Floyd family ritual, making extended summer visits to the old family home in Mastic. William Dana gained a reputation for inventing games for the youngsters; his wife was memorable for her storytelling and kind nature. Among the numerous cousins who brought their families was "Fanny." Born Frances Louise Tracy, Fanny was the daughter of Louisa Kirkland Tracy, the sister of Katharine Dana's mother and the wife of Utica, then New York City, attorney Charles Tracy. Her father was one of the state's foremost lawyers, representing, among others, financier John Pierpont Morgan. Although there is no evidence that the association proved important in William Dana's success, Fanny widened his network of kinship ties when, in 1865, she became Morgan's second wife.[32]

Katharine Dana's attachment to Mastic never wavered. Her husband, in time, came to share it. Given their fondness for the place, it is not surprising that they built a second home there. Early in 1879 Dana created the opportunity. He resolved a thorny family problem, drawing on his lawyerly skills and good business sense to frame a plan to deal with the "aggravating" subject of stricken, old John G. Floyd Sr's. "affairs—both personal and property." The arrangement reserved all income from Floyd's property to pay for his care and defray the interest on his debts. Four of his five children, Katharine, John Jr., Augustus (Gus), and Sarah (Sadie) were to share equally in meeting any expenses that exceeded his income. The fifth, Nicoll (Nick) gained a release from his debts to the elder Floyd, and from any obligation to help support him. The estate was to be divided, equally. Katharine and Sarah were each to receive between 150 and 200 acres, along both banks of Poospatuck Creek and from its confluence with the Mastic River downstream to the boundary of Nicoll's land. Nicoll Floyd received a plot containing a summer house. Kate, Sadie, and Nicoll were to gain their parcels "free from any debt." The remainder, and the largest part, of the farm was to go jointly to Augustus and John Jr., "subject to all the mortgages amounting to $8336."[33]

In October 1880 Katharine Dana received a deed for twenty prime acres. Her land fronted about 600 feet of the south bank of Poospatuck Creek, then swung around the point where the creek entered the Mastic River and reached along some 1,500 feet of the river's western bank. A fringe of green rushes separated the dappled blue waters of the river and creek from the oak-shaded, white sandy soil. Within two years William Dana had arranged for a surveyor to map the shoreline, trees, and height of land, with the purpose of "fix[ing] upon a place for a house." By early 1883 a red brick and mortar foundation was under construction. Large quantities of bricks, laths and other materials were at the site, and there were three railcar loads of lumber at Forge Station, nearby. The house began as an oblong, three-story rectangle, its long wall facing the river and a round tower built on the inland side of the southern end.

The Danas both subscribed to the ideology of the "Big House" that enjoyed currency among affluent folk of the era. They believed that giving charity or alms without requiring work in return sapped the willingness of the poor to labor. Building large houses, rather than being mere ostentatious display or waste, was one way in which wealthy people believed that they could meet a moral responsibility to provide for the less fortunate, by furnishing employment rather than alms. The new Dana house expanded steadily inland, then turned north to form an L. Gables and a widow's walk joined the original tower, as a huge, rambling, pink shingle–clad structure, with forest green trim and a veranda running along the south and west fronts, took shape over several years. When the house was finally complete, the first floor contained a parlor, a library, an entry hall, a large formal dining room, and an ample kitchen and pantry. On the second floor were bedrooms and bathrooms, on the third a large study and a nursery. A back stairway connected the kitchen to servants' apartments—in clearly demarcated areas—on the two floors above. A bulkhead stabilized the riverfront, where there was also a dock. A gatehouse, replicating that at Greycliffs, guarded the entry. When it was fully staffed, the property employed some two dozen servants and groundskeepers. The study offered a stunning view of the creek to the north, the river to the east, and, to the south, Fire Island and the sea beyond. Katharine Dana named the place "Moss Lots." Occupied as a smaller dwelling in the spring of 1884, as other Floyd summerhouses rose on adjoining properties, it was the Danas' summer home, and Katharine's love, for the rest of her life.[34]

Moss Lots in 1965. Photograph courtesy of the author.

As it turned out, that was not to be long. Illness and pain had been Katharine Dana's companions since childhood. Whether or not encouraged by her mother's hypochondriac example, she endured recurring episodes of sickness throughout her life. Any exertion debilitated her and sent her to bed for one to three days, or as much as a week, even when she was a teenager. Severe headaches, high fever, "pain in every bone," toothaches, eye aches, respiratory problems, and a heart rate that reached 115, all troubled her. Whatever the causes, the pains were real, frequent, and intense, moving William Dana to a zealous protectiveness. As early as 1854, he described neuralgia as Katharine's "old friend." Correspondence to and about her referred to her "regular ill health," and often to "long sickness." We have already seen how a desire to remove her from the rigors of Upstate New York winters figured in Dana's decision to relocate to Englewood. In 1884 a broken rib joined her other torments. She sought escape from suffering through heavy (possibly in time, addictive) use of laudanum, an opium derivative in an alcohol solution that was taken orally. She died on April 6, 1886. Shortly before the end, she drafted a penciled will dividing her jewelry and silken shawls among family members and close friends. Her grieving husband and family laid her to rest in the family cemetery a few hundred feet from the old Floyd home in Mastic. Her passing ended a remarkable life and marriage.[35]

Perhaps it was fortunate that Katharine Dana died when she did. At least she was spared the distress and disappointment that William Dana endured in dealing with their adoptive children. All three, despite a family

Postcards picturing the verandas at Moss Lots (ca. 1910). Photographs courtesy of William Floyd Estate/National Park Service, Fire Island National Seashore, Long Island, New York.

strategy that offered them numerous advantages, fell short of their parents' hopes.

John Dana's stint with William Allison's firm was brief. Handsome, charming, even dashing, he gained notoriety for his wild ways and excessive drinking. When he fell in love with a well-to-do young woman, Tillie Feeks, whose brother Glendon was one of his prime drinking companions, William Dana at first opposed the relationship as one that John could not afford. He soon relented and acceded to a plan to separate his son from his riotous companions and drink, and to encourage a life of sobriety and self-sufficiency. In 1886 he spent several thousand dollars on a large farm, house and outbuildings, and livestock for the young couple, at Oakesdale, some forty miles from Spokane, in Washington Territory. Prudently, to prevent his son from frittering the farm away, he incorporated the property and placed it legally under Tillie's control. He provided the couple with an allowance of $20 a week and later, on condition that John and Glendon Feeks refrain from drinking, he furnished a 160-acre farm to the latter. His generosity was misplaced.

The carousing pair resumed—if, indeed, they had ever quit—their drinking, and John's marriage crumbled. Tillie separated from him. In March 1890 Dana unhappily cut his son's allowance to $10 a week, "one half your family being gone." Two years later, Tillie had relocated permanently to New York. John feigned reform, reporting that he was attending Bible class and singing in a church choir. He claimed that he was a new man: "I do not drink a drop now nor do I go into saloons anymore." He even professed to be reading law. His intentions became clear in September, when newspapers carried reports that he had eloped to Tacoma with the church organist, Catherine (Cassie) Helmer. Soon after, he fled to Vancouver, British Columbia, to escape Cassie's irate father and an angry Tacoma hotelier whose bill he had not paid. Piteously, he wrote his father for funds to keep him from going to jail for his debts. Before year's end he was in another scrape, accused of stealing $70,000 in securities from a drinking companion while they were drunk. He subsequently reunited with Cassie. There is scant evidence of any contact with his father thereafter. He died in 1906, without even reaching the age of forty-five.[36]

Richard fared little better. In 1890 he persuaded Dana to buy a twenty-acre ranch for him on Magnolia Avenue in Riverside, California, for $2,185. Over the following two decades Dana enlarged the property considerably, adding an orange grove and other lands to the original alfalfa field. He also furnished a monthly allowance that rose from $50 to $100 as the years passed. Richard Dana's enthusiasm for ranching subsided rapidly. By 1895 an acquaintance reported to the senior Dana that he was rarely on the property working. Two years later Richard's wife Hazel informed Dana that the ranch must be sold. Her husband was in poor health and treating her with unbearable unkindness. Wearily, Dana replied that he was sorry Richard could not make a go of it. "I am of the opinion," he continued, "that it will be better to dispose of the ranch and let future provision [for Richard and Hazel] depend upon circumstances.... I am too tired to write more."

Richard, meanwhile, always a bit unstable, had become, in Hazel's words, "nervous and morbid to an unusual degree." Bedridden with real and imaginary afflictions, on one occasion when troubled only by a cold he had insisted on a call from a physician and had received an injection of morphine. Early in 1898 he traveled to Los Angeles, where he enjoyed shopping, and disappeared. A tired Hazel returned to Pennsylvania to be with her relatives. Richard briefly sold shirts, on commission, was hospitalized in a sanatorium in the summer, and in September with his father's blessing took a recuperative cruise to Honolulu. Soon after, he was back at the ranch, on which Dana had by now spent $30,000. After returning to California, Hazel over the following years tried raising chickens. She and Richard added walnuts and mixed-grain farming, planting wheat, oats, and barley. Nothing seemed to work. Orange prices fell, frosts damaged fruit, grain harvests failed. Always, there was need for more money for electricity, a roof, paint, a mower, a hay rake, and so forth.

Allison visited the ranch in 1905 and was unimpressed. Two years later a homesick Richard tried to surprise his father with an unannounced visit to Greycliffs. The trip was a disaster. He had long expressed feelings of inadequacy, the result, he said, of his continued dependence on the senior Dana for support, and of the latter's high expectations. En route he lost his luggage, two suits, and his return train ticket. Crushed, because he had "tried to [sic] hard to have everything go smoothly and be independent," and failed, he fled to Hazel's family without seeing the elder Dana. Allison's son John many years afterward described him as a strange, dreamy, detached soul who arrived by boat at Mastic for William Dana's interment and stumbled drunkenly onto the dock. In his later years he became a recluse. The younger Allison claimed that he last surfaced in a magazine photograph, bearded and strumming a steel guitar.[37]

The principal differences in Ethel Dana's story were that she lived with her father during his later years, gave him a grandson, and cared for the aging editor. Married in 1891 to Frederick R. Shepherd of Minneapolis, she delivered William Dana Shepherd a year later. A daughter, Louise, was born in 1895 and died in infancy. William Dana sought to provide for Ethel as he had for her brothers. She and her family resided with him in his home, and both she and her husband received cash allowances. A banking position for Fred, whose father George B. was a banker, did not work out. Nor could Fred make a go of a position at the *Chronicle*. Young Shepherd, like his brothers-in-law, struggled with alcohol and dependence.

The marriage collapsed in 1903. Five years later, William Dana, still seeking an heir for the *Chronicle*, adopted his grandson on condition that the boy's name be changed to William Shepherd Dana.

Daisy's shortcomings were uncontrollable spending (including excessive charitable gifts inspired by her mother's own generosity in supporting worthy causes), self-indulgence, and an inability to exercise discipline in rearing her son. Dana tried heroically to improve her management of money. A December 1896 letter spoke volumes, indicating the consistency that ran through his business and personal affairs. As an experiment, he wrote that in 1897 Ethel Shepherd would assume full responsibility for her personal needs and those of the household. Her weekly allowance would rise by $40, to $130 (the average factory worker at the time made about $450 a *year*), and Fred was to continue to receive an added $20. Carefully reviewing household and other expenses she must bear, Dana observed that with "care and prudence you can easily pay all your bills, do more than you have ever done for . . . [charity] and save in a year twelve hundred ($1,200) out of your income." He had given her "a large sum of money and a correspondingly large responsibility." As an inducement for her to practice "economy and prudence" in managing her enlarged income, he added a promise: if she could save $1,000 or even $400, he would match her savings and invest the sum for her. Before closing with a generous new year's wish, he explained why he was "so urgent about this matter of carefulness in expenditures . . . I think exact methods and freedom from little wastes in handling money are an index to character."

Kind, and genuinely caring toward her father, Ethel nevertheless could not curb her extravagances. In 1902, Gorham Silversmiths sued to recover an overdue balance of $546.75. Allison helped negotiate a settlement through which Gorham agreed to sell Ethel no more merchandise on credit, and to charge no more sales to Dana without his written consent. Ethel's loose spending continued to surface from time to time. In 1909, she engaged Louis Tiffany, Jr. to redecorate Moss Lots. A spectacular new European chandelier cast brilliantly faceted patterns of light on parlor walls freshly covered with Flemish silk brocade. Among other purchases was an elegantly ornamented piano on which Ignace Paderewski had performed, imported to stand imperiously in the visual center of the room. Similar features transformed other parts of the house. Meanwhile, a succession of tutors for young William came and resigned, complaining that Ethel's constant interference made it impossible to teach and discipline him. He was a bright and affectionate lad, and badly spoiled. William Dana still lived unpretentiously himself, sleeping, while at Moss Lots, in a spare upstairs room containing a plain brass bed and simple wicker furniture. Apparently grateful for Ethel's care, he dealt with her problems as well as his advancing years allowed. She survived him by four years, living until 1914.[38]

William Buck Dana's bedroom and library at Moss Lots (1965). Photographs courtesy of the author.

William Buck Dana (ca. 1880–1881) and Katharine Floyd Dana (ca. 1880–1881). Photographs courtesy of William Floyd Estate/National Park Service, Fire Island National Seashore, Long Island, New York.

The scantiness of the evidence permits only conjecture about the reasons for which the adoptive children of two persons as loving, kind, and principled as Katharine and William were unsuccessful. Perhaps the Danas were caught between their own stern, patriarchal upbringings and the nurturing, maternal mode of child rearing that won favor with the upper middle classes in the middle third of the nineteenth century, and as a result were inconsistent in holding their children to a standard of conduct. Perhaps their inability to have children of their own encouraged a love that was too indulgent, and at times at odds with the standards that they believed were right but could not bring themselves firmly to uphold. Perhaps the explanation lay in Katharine Dana's repeated illnesses, or even in some degree to the numbing effects of a possible addiction to painkilling medication. Perhaps the problem was something else. Only investigation beyond the scope of this study, and possibly beyond the surviving evidence, can provide the answer.

William Dana held hopes for Englewood that were commensurate with his ambitions for the *Chronicle*. Much as his brother-in-law Wyman Jones had projected a genteel community in the valley west of the Hudson River palisades, he conceived of an exclusive settlement running along the clifftops. As early as 1860, he began to add to his first property, purchasing three parcels. Two of these he bought from Garret J. Lydecker, the storekeeper head of a prominent old neighborhood family and owner of a large farm dating back to a seventeenth-century Dutch colonial grant. By 1865 the Danas had acquired a dozen pieces of land, five of them from Lydecker. Buoyed by the success of the *Chronicle*, they bought another dozen through 1870. Their many-faceted partnerships extended to a number of these real estate transactions. They made two purchases jointly, and three in Katharine's name. Dana added thirteen more during the 1870s, and another twelve from then until 1905. He ordinarily financed his acquisitions with with mortgages, to leverage his purchasing power, and Katharine Dana was often a cosigner. On occasion, he borrowed from her: his records in 1884 contain a reference to a $2,000 debt to her. Further extending the web of personal association, he arranged many mortgages through Sheppard Homans, brother of his mentor at the *Merchants' Magazine*, with the Mutual Life Insurance Company of New York.

By the late 1870s, Dana properties in Englewood approximated 129 acres, extending along the river and palisades a quarter mile or more and westward along Palisade Avenue a quarter mile to Floyd and Dana Streets. Greycliffs, which William conceived of as the first of a line of substantial mansions that would one day command the view from the bluffs, included grounds of twenty-six acres with 520 feet of river frontage. At their maximum, in the 1880s, Dana properties in Englewood and other parts of Bergen County exceeded 220 acres.[39]

William and Katharine Dana paid for construction of the First Dutch Reformed Church near Greycliffs in Englewood. While this act could be construed as part of a strategy to create a community that would be attractive to prospective land purchasers, it is more consistent with the Danas' characters to view it as an act of faith and charity. The erection of a large resort hotel, however, was clearly an investment in the development of the heights atop the palisades. As William's only significant venture in real estate development, even this large undertaking did not deflect him from his primary interest in the success of the *Chronicle*. Here, as elsewhere, he displayed the familiar reliance on tightly-knit personal associations, and shrewd financial measures, that always characterized his entrepreneurial behavior.

Dana's associate in building the hotel (Palisades Mountain House) was Cornelius Lydecker, Garret's son. Born in 1827, Cornelius had left his father's store in 1849 to join the Gold Rush to California. He was back in New Jersey two years later, and married in 1852. Soon after, he embarked on a political career. Chosen Town (tax) Collector in 1862, then County Collector, he won election as a Democrat to the New Jersey state senate in 1872. He left the senate in 1875 to run for the office of state treasurer, remaining politically active in various capacities thereafter into the 1890s.[40]

Before commencing the hotel project, Dana expanded the Greycliffs estate in 1869, buying from William B. Leeds a parcel of land that gave him an additional 767 feet of frontage along the river to the north of his home, excluding a small inholding that Leeds retained. Typically, he paid but $1,000 of the $16,000 purchase price in cash. A second cash payment, also of $1,000, was due a year later. A four-year mortgage, with an interest rate of 4 percent annually on the unpaid balance, financed the remainder of the cost. Leeds later drew plans for the hotel.[41]

On September 4, 1871 Dana and Lydecker solicited bids for the construction of the hotel. Their request brought several responses, ranging from $24,750 for masonry work to $95,360 for the entire project, excepting stonework, outbuildings, furnishings, and grounds work. On September 18, they awarded the job to A[ndrew]. D[emarest]. Bogert & Bro., of Englewood, for $80,400, plus stonework at fifteen cents per cubic foot. The builder was to furnish all materials, including rough framing, wood siding, tin roof, iron columns, and so on. The agreement specified seventeen monthly payments. The first two, for foundation work, were respectively $2,000 and $3,000, followed by a third for stonework as mentioned, then $5,000 payments until the final installment of $10,400. Each payment was contingent on completion of a particular part of the project—foundation, beams, cornices, enclosure, floors, and so on.[42]

November 1 brought the first of a labyrinthine series of transactions toward financing the hotel that was to be built on the prominence known as Lydecker Point. Dana's and Lydecker's holdings to this point, obtained from Garret Lydecker, did not include the entire hotel site, and the two associates needed capital to pay for construction. They signed an agreement with William Walter Phelps and Jacob S. Wetmore, owners of land lying between Palisade Avenue and the hotel property to the south, and underlying part of the building site itself. Phelps and Wetmore were to provide a loan of $30,000, payable in installments of $5,000 a month over six months. Ownership of the land needed for the hotel was to pass to Dana and Lydecker when they obtained a loan of $50,000, to be secured by a first mortgage, for construction. Phelps and Wetmore's $30,000, five-year, 7 percent loan was to be secured by a second mortgage on both the property that they were conveying and "the land which . . . [Dana and Lydecker] are to receive adjoining, from Garret J. Lydecker." The deal enabled Dana and Lydecker to begin construction without committing cash of their own, and it provided leverage for obtaining the $50,000 loan that they needed, as well. It also substantially increased the value of Phelps and Wetmore's twenty-four lots ringing the hotel site to the north and west, and preceded a transaction through which Dana joined with the two in acquiring an additional seven acres. Meanwhile, Dana and Lydecker insulated themselves further from possible personal loss by incorporating the hotel. Each held 50 percent of the stock.[43]

Construction proceeded rapidly. By early 1872, workers were installing fifty-six Italian marble mantels, and a boiler and steam pump in a nearby eight-foot-square brick boiler house, to force hot water to a tank in the hotel attic for distribution. Close at hand, still other workers were completing a carriage house and a stable. Dana, with no intention to risk loss

through personal entry into an unfamiliar business, was concurrently negotiating to lease the hotel to experienced management. To one prospective lessee he wrote:

Perhaps we have built a better house [hotel] than was necessary. Be that as it may,
it cannot be changed now. Everything has been done with economy; and yet we
shall have spent about $150,000 (without counting the land, as worth one cent)
when it is completed the first day of May. We do *not* propose to furnish it but to
rent it unfurnished for $15000 a year say for about three years with the privilege
of renewing the lease at that time for 7 years more at an increase of rent to $20,000
so that we may secure a small interest in the land (about seven acres) which at a
low valuation is today worth $70000.

William added that the advanced state of negotiations with other prospects
prompted such candor, to avoid a waste of time if his present correspondent was unable to proceed along the lines he had laid out. He wrote
further that he and his associate had purchased a small boat to connect
the hotel with the train across the river, at Yonkers. Between their craft
and the three commercial steamboats already in service, "We shall have
arrangements for going to or coming from the City [New York] almost
every hour of the day."[44]
    The Palisades Mountain House opened in mid-1872 and operated for
about a dozen years. A separate Dana enterprise, the Englewood Dock
& Turnpike Company, linked it to a steamboat dock at river's edge, by
means of a "zig-zag macadamized road" hewn out of the cliffs "at great
expense." Users paid a toll of four cents per mounted rider, six cents per
horse and carriage, and six cents for each extra horse, making their way
to the hotel stable where forty horses could be accommodated. Dana and
Lydecker enlarged the Palisades Mountain House in 1875 and continued
to incorporate new, modern features throughout its years of operation.
Noted for its "splendid view of the surrounding country, New York City,
and the Bay," it boasted an unusual combination of luxury, natural beauty,
seclusion, and easy access to New York. When completed, it was a rambling, five-story, cupola-topped wooden structure that stretched 600 feet
along the clifftops, with a veranda along much of its length. It could accommodate 400 to 500 guests in 300 rooms, half with what was described
as cottage furniture and half with furniture of "black walnut of approved
patterns." The first floor held a spacious parlor with a piano and sump-
tuous furnishings and a large dining room. There were also private dining
apartments. A promotion for the 1881 season promised guests "gas, hot
and cold water, stationary basins, open grates, marble mantels, electric
bells, and steam heating" in both dining and sleeping rooms. Patrons could
enjoy the services of a newsstand, a billiard hall, a bowling alley, a barber
shop, a cigar store, reading rooms, and public and private parlors and

A photographic reproduction of an architect's rendering of the Palisades Mountain House, Englewood, New Jersey (ca. 1872). Courtesy of Palisades Interstate Park Commission (NJ Section) and Edwin Rizer.

reception rooms. Twice daily, morning and evening, an orchestra of "skilled musicians" performed, and there were weekly dancing classes in the ballroom. The establishment won favor with "large numbers of businessmen, lawyers, bankers, and others actively employed," who found it a pleasant alternative to the stifling heat and congestion of New York City during the summer.

Early in the morning of June 4, 1884, the sounds of crackling flames and falling cinders awakened the daughter of the hotel manager from her sleep, on the first floor, and another occupant, on the second floor. They found the dining room ablaze and quickly spread the alarm to some eighty-five employees, the manager, the lessee and his son, and the housekeeper, who were gathered to ready the Palisades Mountain House to open June 7 for the new season. Quick action averted a catastrophic loss of life but could not save the hotel. There was no fire hose, and a hastily organized bucket brigade could offer only futile resistance to the spreading inferno. In "a very short time the wooden structure had tumbled to the ground, a mass of flaming embers." There were no fatal injuries, but only a few trunks, and some chairs and sofas from the grand parlor, were saved. The hotel and contents, worth perhaps $200,000, were gone. Insurance coverage amounted to but $90,000.[45]

The hotel had never met Dana's expectations. Evidently he was unsuccessful in leasing it unfurnished. A notebook in which he recorded changes in his financial condition listed among his assets a $10,000 note, bearing 7 percent interest, for the purchase of furniture for the lessee. His papers also contain copies of $20,000 in insurance claims filed to recover the value of furniture consumed in the fire. Hotel rental income failed to meet projections. A major business depression during the period of 1873–1879 kept room occupancy down. In 1875 the lessee paid but $14,000 of the $20,000 due; the year after, only $10,000, of which $1,000 was in the form of a promissory note. Dana's personal income also shrank during the depression. In 1875 he expected $19,425 but received $13,837.50, with the hotel contributing a net of only $2,500. A year later, his income was $12,955, with the hotel providing "nothing" beyond the interest that the owners had to pay on outstanding mortgages. Affairs deteriorated before they improved. Although the Mercantile Agency's credit evaluation for August 1877 described the W. B. Dana Company as a "rich firm making $ quite steadily for their publishers & quite entirely safe for any contracts they will make," the evaluation for 1878 commented on Dana's personal reverses. His firm was still "safe & good," generating "a good income" to owners who also had "large outside means," but, the report stated, Dana had "lost money in Jersey Real Estate."

In "October, 1878," because of the latter's circumstances, Dana was "compelled to buy out Mr. Lydecker's interest in [the] Hotel." He paid an estimated $75,000, financing the transaction in part with a mortgage of

$60,000 with the Mutual Life Insurance Company, and another $5,000 with a private investor. Despite the return of prosperity in 1879, the Palisades Mountain House continued to earn less than Dana had hoped. In 1882 it rented for only $12,000. The next year Dana sold it, with grounds and outbuildings, to Allison for $10,000 in cash and "100 acres of back land at various points between Englewood and Alpine."[46] After the fire, Allison cleared the site and erected his own mansion where the Palisades Mountain House had stood. His was the only other grand house to be built atop the cliffs. Years later, in 1903, it also burned. Rather than rebuild it, Allison changed residences. Two years after the fire, he sold the land to the Sisters of St. Joseph, who built a novitiate, which is still in use, on it.

William Dana's vision for the palisades persisted lifelong. For about a decade after Katharine Dana's death, he resided during winters in a hotel in New York City, and during summers at Moss Lots. He never again attempted a development comparable to the Palisades Mountain House, limiting himself to occasional additions to his properties in and around Englewood and to building a few cottages for rental. In the mid-1890s he began again to winter at Greycliffs. With Allison, he was instrumental in winning approval for the separation of their neighborhood from Englewood and its incorporation as an independent borough in 1895, as a means toward realizing his dream for it. Allison became the first mayor of the new, one-and-one-eighth square mile jurisdiction, Englewood Cliffs, serving for eight years, until 1903. Dana became a trustee of the board of education and a member of the board of health. He succeeded Allison as mayor and remained in office until his death, when Allison resumed the position.[47]

In 1900 William Dana gave Englewood Cliffs the gatehouse at Greycliffs for use as a school. The building stood just northeast of the intersection of Palisade Avenue and Hudson Terrace, now overlain by the Palisades Interstate Parkway. Two years later, he sold the land and road of the Englewood Dock & Turnpike Company and five parcels along the river beneath the palisades to the commissioners of the expanding Palisades Interstate Parkway, respectively for $11,000 and $7,650.[48] In 1903 Englewood Cliffs sold the old Undercliffs School, which the Danas had built as an act of charity for the children who lived along the river beneath the cliffs. Dana, as presiding school trustee, contracted with the same A. D. Bogert who had built the Palisades Mountain House to erect a new public school for $6,583.[49]

During his years as mayor, Dana toyed occasionally with the possibility of disposing of part or all of his New Jersey land. Most of it remained as he had described it to a correspondent in the 1890s, "unproductive [undeveloped] real estate." An inquiry in 1906 from a representative of railroad magnate Henry J. Flagler about the availability of Greycliffs stirred him to write his realtor that "I will sell my house if you can get one hundred fifty thousand dollars for it." He inventoried his holdings in anticipation of a sale. Greycliffs, with the barn and surrounding thirteen-and-a-half acres, he valued at $140,000–145,000, an adjacent lot adding $20,000 more. The entire estate, of "about 85 to 87 acres all together," including the house, barn, lodge, and gardener's cottage, he set at $350,000–355,000. He assigned values respectively of $100,000, $35,000, and $30,000 for the 100 acres he had obtained from Allison and two more parcels, of ten and five-and-three-quarters acres.[50] Nothing came of Flagler's curiosity or Dana's inventory. Around 1909, the aging publisher–editor closed Greycliffs and took up winter residence in a suite of rooms, with Daisy and young William, at the Hotel Belmont in New York City. William Dana's activities in New Jersey real estate were at an end.[51]

The *Chronicle* was always William Dana's primary business interest. As it prospered, from time to time he relocated its place of publication to accommodate its expanding needs for space. A narrow, four-story brick structure at 60 William Street housed it from 1865 to 1868. For the following nineteen years, he published it at a larger, four-story building at 78–79 William Street. In 1887 he moved to 102 William Street, shifting again in 1896 to an address on Pine Street at the northwest corner of Pearl Street. Finally, in 1908, the *Chronicle* occupied a substantial, six-story masonry structure, with an imposing arched central entrance and three tiers of windows across the front, on Pine between Front and Depeyster Streets. It continued at this location for the balance of Dana's life.

Circulation figures are unavailable for the *Commercial and Financial Chronicle*. Fragmentary records of gross monthly receipts and disbursements, and profits, with published subscription and advertising rates, permit estimates accurate at least in suggesting probable ranges. Before the onset of the depression of 1873–1879, Dana's annual income from the *Chronicle*, representing three-fifths of its profits, reached $10,000 or more. Total profits would thus have been $16,500. For the first eleven months of 1911, profits slightly exceeded $90,000, suggesting a figure for the year of around $98,000, against total receipts of $265,000. Profits in 1911 fell just short of 37 percent of receipts. If the same ratio held for 1872—and Dana's management, we should emphasize, was notably consistent—receipts in that year would have neared $44,500. The upper limit for subscriptions would then, at $10 per year, have been 4,450 in 1872 and 26,500 in 1911. In 1911 advertising might have returned (figuring on 500 pages at published rates) as much as $150,835 or as little as $43,835, depending on the number of discounted repeat placements. Thus, the likely range of subscriptions was from 11,400 to 22,000—a median guess of around 16,000 to 17,000 seems reasonable—with the 1872 figure falling between 3,100 and 4,100.[52]

William Dana's management strategy was critically important in the suc-

The Palisades Mountain House (ca. 1880). Photograph courtesy of the Englewood Cliffs, New Jersey, Tercentenary Committee.

Pictures of various buildings housing offices of the *Chronicle*. Photographs from special volume published by the *Chronicle* commemorating Dana's eightieth birthday and his fiftieth year in journalism. Original missing; copy in author's collection.

cess of his paper. One key element in that strategy was a strict control of costs. The business of his company he "conducted practically on a cash basis." The company held virtually no assets, "other than the good will, except a few printing machines, office fixtures, library of reference, and cash [reserves]" Dana, in minimizing the capital expenditures of his company, held its obligations to a low level so that its profitability could be maximized. He added to his income stream from the firm by personally purchasing the buildings in which it published, and charging the paper rent.[53]

Dana devoted unceasing attention to his paper. He worked from sparsely furnished offices in his residences as well as at the *Chronicle*'s places of publication. Each contained a large desk, some straight-backed wooden chairs and a swivel desk chair, simply constructed wooden bookcases stocked with reference works and a complete file of the paper, and writing materials. Telephones appeared as soon as they were useful, complementing the company's access to telegraph lines. Letters forwarded inquiries about conditions in different lines of commerce worldwide; distant correspondents returned a steady stream of information by the fastest available means. When Dana was in his prime, his workday began as early as 4 A.M. at which time he devoted himself to thinking and pacing the floor, reading, writing, and editing for some hours before the family gathered for morning prayer. After breakfast, he commuted by train to the *Chronicle* building, arriving around 9 A.M. to resume work. He stayed until late afternoon, personally editing the weekly summaries of business and lead stories and writing most of the important articles himself. Later in life he slowed his pace, delegating more work, and in summer reducing the number of his trips to the company offices to two or three weekly. Even then, unless he was ill or traveling, he was present on days when copy was due and the paper went to press.

Handwritten drafts of editorials and articles reveal much about Dana's writing habits. Editor's marks for paragraph indentation, lines drawn through words and phrases and entire sentences, arrows indicating rearrangement, and interlinear additions all reflected ongoing revision, and a painstaking search for accuracy and precision, as a draft progressed. The passing years saw Dana's initially tiny, neat hand expand to a bold script and then deteriorate to an increasingly shaky scrawl. He wrote fluently but not hastily, usually in ink, making marginal corrections in both pencil and ink, thinking things through as he penned his words. Scrupulous attention to accuracy and care in reasoning shaped his prose. Usually, his writing was straightforward. He believed that commercial affairs deserved serious treatment. It is not surprising, then, that his prose was serious— one would not be tempted to describe it as sprightly. Occasionally it became entangled in awkward or ponderous constructions when he was dealing with subjects of unusual gravity or complexity. Secretaries converted

William Buck Dana's office at the *Chronicle*, 1909. Photograph from special volume published by the *Chronicle* commemorating Dana's eightieth birthday and his fiftieth year in journalism. Original missing; copy in author's collection.

his handwritten drafts to typed manuscripts. There were surely interruptions, conferences, and occasional lunch meetings, but none appears to have affected his writing.[54]

William Dana in founding the *Chronicle* targeted his audience carefully. His market was the select group that played a commanding role in the development of a corporate economy dominated by financial institutions. His readers were bankers, brokers, financiers, leaders of industry, and top government officials. That bank notices were the largest single source of the *Commercial and Financial Chronicle*'s advertising revenues identified

The *Chronicle*'s offices and library as seen from Dana's office, 1909. Photograph from special volume published by the *Chronicle* commemorating Dana's eightieth birthday and his fiftieth year in journalism. Original missing; copy in author's collection.

The mechanical (typesetting and press) room of the *Chronicle*, 1909. Photograph from special volume published by the *Chronicle* commemorating Dana's eightieth birthday and his fiftieth year in journalism. Original missing; copy in author's collection.

its core readership as members of the financial community. Virtually every important bank in the United States, from the 1880s onward, advertised in the paper. The volume of such notices ran to some 180 pages in the final year of Dana's life. The positions of the paper's readers encouraged stability, even growth, in circulation in good and bad times alike. They possessed the individual and corporate means to pay for subscriptions whatever the condition of business, and they needed the intelligence that the *Chronicle* offered in all seasons. In offering this key readership a common fund of information drawn from the entire nation, and the world, Dana forwarded the emergence of nationwide financial markets, of financiers as the nerve center of business, and of a truly national economy. He strove constantly to add to the value of his journal.

Cotton from Seed to Loom appeared in 1878. In writing and publishing it, William Dana evidenced clearly the disciplined industry and insight that typified him as an entrepreneur. Written when a severe depression had badly disrupted global cotton trade, *Cotton from Seed to Loom* demonstrated that he had learned well from Thomas Prentice Kettell at *Hunt's Merchants' Magazine*. Believing in a "divine law of progress," he showed how the emergence of India as a major exporter of the white fiber would meet the needs of a world no longer adequately served by the southern United States. Critical of sheer speculation, he minutely analyzed output, demand, changing markets, and prices to cotton to provide a sound basis for informed commerce in cotton futures. Dana's overriding conception was prescient: "in this day of steam and telegraphy, the world has a common centre of life, with a nervous system acutely sensitive in all its parts to every disturbing influence." Not coincidentally, the book's comprehensiveness established William Dana and his paper as the authoritative sources of information about all phases of the cotton industry worldwide.[55]

As time passed, our editor expanded the coverage and usefulness of the *Chronicle* through the addition of new features. Volume 24 (January–June 1877) began to provide separate indexes for "Editorial and Communicated Articles" and "Foreign Correspondence, Financial, Commercial, Railroads" (mainly weekly commercial news and current corporate reports) to make it easier for readers to locate items of interest. On December 4, 1880, Dana introduced a weekly column entitled "The Financial Situation." Although at first it wandered through the editorial pages, in time it became the weekly lead article and, as such, a distinguishing characteristic of the paper. With the passing years, Dana also added supplements. Each grew out of a regular department of the weekly. Because Dana was able to use the *Chronicle*'s network of correspondents and sources of information, its agents in London and Chicago as well as in New York, and printing machinery that was otherwise underused except for a weekly one-day press run, only a small marginal increase in the cost of production was incurred in publishing the supplements. They greatly expanded the space

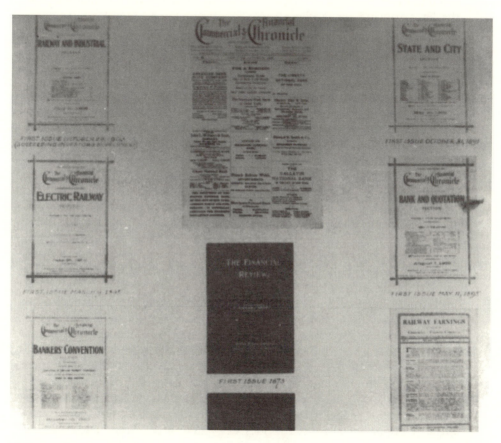

Pictures of cover pages of first editions of supplements to the *Chronicle*. Photograph from special volume published by the *Chronicle* commemorating Dana's eightieth birthday and his fiftieth year in journalism. Original missing; copy in author's collection.

available for advertising, which in turn generated enlarged cash receipts. They also capitalized on improvements in technology, without which it would have been impossible to introduce them. By the early twentieth century, the mechanical room of the paper boasted six Monotype machines, each capable of setting about one, seven-inch column per hour, or about a page of the *Chronicle* in six hours. Although records do not survive identifying the paper's presses, it is certain that they, too, represented the latest advance in machinery.

At first, *Chronicle* supplements were sold both to the general public and to subscribers at a reduced extra charge. Dana discovered that it was better for subscriptions to make them available only to subscribers, whose cost remained at $10 a year through his lifetime, at no added cost. He accordingly changed his practice, effectively adding to the value of a subscription. He promoted the additions as "supplements," but cleverly headed, formatted, and distributed them with weekly editions of the paper as "sections." The stratagem avoided the extra costs that a separate distribution would have involved, and it took advantage of postal rates that favored newspapers. The supplements extended the *Chronicle*'s commanding lead in its field, adding to its unrivaled comprehensiveness.

The first supplement, an annual reporting of the yearly convention of the American Bankers' Association, appeared as early as October 1868. Others followed, mirroring changes on the evolving national business scene. April 1875 brought the "Investor's Supplement," treating municipal, state, and federal bond issues and the financial condition and securities of all of the country's railroads bimonthly, later quarterly. The accumulation of a comprehensive record of trading in railroad securities generated a reference book, as a natural outgrowth. Dana's *Prices of Rail Road Stocks for 32 Years, 1854–1886* (1886) treated its subject in encyclopedic detail while requiring very little effort beyond assembling anew between two covers what the paper had already published. Government bonds gained separate attention in the "State and City Supplement," beginning in October 1891, and becoming monthly by the early twentieth century. The "Electric Railway Supplement" appeared in March 1895, testifying to the growing importance of this new industry and its stocks and bonds. In May 1895 came the "Bank and Quotations Section," which within a decade was a monthly, sixty-four-page publication detailing banking transactions and the market in bank securities. October 1903 brought the quarterly, 180-page "Railway and Industrial Supplement." It added to reports of trade in railroad securities accounts of transactions in the stock and bond issues of industrial corporations, heralding the advent of manufacturing corporations as a major new business force. "Railway Earnings," digesting monthly statements of railroad earnings sworn before the Interstate Commerce Commission, began in February 1910. All together these supplements, which accompanied a *Chronicle* that had swollen to sixty and more pages per week, numbered thirty-two per year by the time of Dana's death. In bulk they fully equaled the *Chronicle* itself, and they contained perhaps two-thirds to three-fourths of its advertising.[56]

The most important turn in the history of the *Commercial and Financial Chronicle* between its founding and William Dana's death occurred in 1894. That June, John G. Floyd, Jr. severed a partnership that spanned a generation. Floyd purchased and became publisher of the same *Bankers' Magazine* whose publisher and editor, Isaac Smith Homans, Jr., had taught Dana journalism at the *Merchants' Magazine* years before. Floyd abandoned publishing and retired about a year later. He devoted the balance of his life to a variety of religious, civic, and patriotic causes. Active in New York's East Side Young Men's Christian Association, his church, sundry historical and genealogical groups, and the American School of Patriotism, which sought to teach young men clean politics, he lived until November 1903.

When Floyd left, Dana incorporated his publishing enterprise as the William B. Dana Company. He paid Floyd off with $175,000 in bonds, to be retired over the following decade, and became sole owner of the company's 5,000 shares of common stock, which carried a par value of $100 each. The directors of the new corporation voted on June 19, 1904 to return its entire net income to Dana as payment for his services and for payment of the bonds. After the retirement of the bonds the board, on April 4, 1905, unanimously resolved "that the entire net income of this Company shall until the death of William B. Dana be paid to said William B. Dana as compensation for his services."[57]

Dana became president and chairman of the company and remained in control for as long as he lived. As he aged and his energies flagged, he was fortunate to enjoy the company of two associates who had first come to him as young protégés in ways not entirely unlike Allison. These two did much to maintain his paper in his last years, although he never relinquished final authority or active interest in directing its affairs. One of them was Jacob Seibert, Jr., who became vice president. The other was Dana's nephew, Arnold Guyot Dana who was named for his father, James Dwight Dana's, good friend the eminent Swiss geologist, Arnold Guyot. Arnold became treasurer. Both Seibert and Arnold Guyot Dana continued in their offices until William's death. Both also served as directors and gained significant stock holdings in the company.

Seibert joined the *Chronicle* in 1870 as a boy of thirteen. Already accepted to study at the City College of New York, he completed his education at Cooper Union. He began to contribute news and statistical matter to the paper long before his graduation in 1878. In 1880, after several years of managing coverage of railway earnings, he began to write editorial pieces. From then onward, he was the chief associate editor of the paper. He succeeded Dana in control of the weekly in 1910 and bought

William Buck Dana (from an oil portrait) (ca. 1890).
Photograph courtesy of the author.

it out in 1922. Seibert effectively absorbed all of his mentor's ideas and became an *alter ego*. A critic of high protective tariffs, of speculation, and of inflationary monetary policies, he championed the ideal of an unregulated economy and limited government. He imitated Dana in dress, manner of writing and speaking, and physical gestures. Even more private than his mentor, he shunned invitations to speak, club memberships, and public attention, although he corresponded widely and received numerous guests for interviews. As William aged, he depended more and more on Seibert. On March 10, 1905, Dana arranged for joint ownership, with him, of 620 Dana Company shares. A week later, he delivered to Seibert by trust deed an additional 655 shares. The deed directed the income from these shares, after Dana's death, to Ethel and to William Shepherd Dana.[58]

Arnold Guyot Dana came more circuitously to the *Chronicle*. Born in 1862, he studied at the Hopkins Grammar School in New Haven, Connecticut, graduated from Yale in 1883, and completed an additional three years at Yale's Sheffield Scientific School. His interests then shifted from natural science to economics. In 1887, at the age of twenty-five, he became a member of the *Chronicle*'s statistical and editorial staff. He rose to edit the investment news department, adding the role of managing editor of the railway and statistical supplement when it appeared in 1903.

Correspondence between Arnold and William Dana offers further evidence of the latter's management strategy and his continuing control of the paper. In 1893 Arnold skirted with leaving the weekly to become a partner in a Wall Street brokerage firm. He went so far as to ask William for access to or even a duplicate file of *Chronicle* supplements, and whether he might "be allowed the privilege of sending my circular to CHRONICLE subscribers." Our editor responded that some arrangement might be made for use of the supplements. The mailing list was another matter. Ever protective of his own trade secrets, he demurred, observing delicately that Arnold's request to use the list "might be open to the objection that it would not be kept private." Nothing came of Arnold's bid, and he remained with the company for another twenty-nine years. He collided with his uncle on at least one other occasion. In 1901, the aging publisher rejected an article that Arnold had written, urging him to rewrite it with a modified thesis. Ever a close analyst of the securities markets, the elder Dana acknowledged Arnold's correctness in noting a rising demand for stocks but thought that it could not be accounted for by a falling market for bonds. "So far as I know the facts," he astutely wrote, "I should judge that the inquiry [demand] for bonds has increased on a par with the demand for stocks." So it was, at a time when the formation of new manufacturing corporations was increasing issues of and interest in both stocks and bonds.

Arnold Guyot Dana left the *Chronicle* in 1922 when Seibert gained the controlling interest in the William B. Dana Company. He continued to write, adding to an already lustrous reputation with a 1928–1929 series of *Chronicle* articles that predicted the financial crash of 1929, and subsequently with a number of well regarded books on national and international business topics.[59]

William Dana prospered with the *Chronicle*. His personal income rose to nearly $20,000 per year before the business contraction of 1873, the paper contributing at least half of that amount. Although his income fell below $14,000, then to $12,955, over the next two years, and the weekly's contribution to $9,710, he had by 1875 accumulated impressive personal wealth quite apart from his interest in the Palisades Mountain House. In 1875 he valued the twenty-five acre Greycliffs property at $100,000, the adjoining fifty-nine acres at $160,000, and his interest in the *Chronicle* at $50,000. His mortgage indebtedness at the time was but $37,900. The paper's worth grew over the following years. In 1882 Dana reflected as much when he wrote of it only the words, "which I consider of large value." The Mercantile Agency's correspondent that year agreed. He characterized the firm as profitable, "worth 200 to $300,000," and "safe and good." The picture brightened during the ensuing years, as reports added reference to new Dana real estate holdings in Rutherford Park, New Jersey, and consistently granted his company the highest rating for credit and reputation. From its incorporation in 1894 until Dana's death the publication paid him yearly profits of $60,000 to $72,000, representing a return of 12 to 14 percent on the nominal value of capital. Meanwhile, by 1905 the publisher was sufficiently liquid to place, through Allison, sums of $25,000 to $65,000 on loan at call.[60]

The same alertness to change that kept the *Chronicle* current informed Dana's personal life for as long as he lived. The Electrical Exposition in Paris was the highlight of his summer 1881 trip to Europe, affording him an opportunity to study the potential for electrical power. An 1880 journey to Upstate New York to provide rest and recovery from a "horrid rash and swelling" and an 1882 excursion to New England for respite offered added opportunities to learn. When he traveled by rail to California and Washington in 1890 and again to California in 1892 to attend to the affairs of his adoptive sons, he took close note of irrigation and farming practices as well as of business and business prospects.[61] Several times he modernized Moss Lots. In 1896 he arranged to install "two beautifully appointed bathrooms, supplied with water from a windmill and tank and a laundry and large kitchen with every equipment to appease the tyrant of that department [the cook]," adding also major enhancements to the grounds. Two years later followed improvements to the gas lighting. In 1902 he provided for a modern septic system at Greycliffs, which he had enlarged in 1901. Six years after, he maintained close watch as Suffolk County property owners united to oppose efforts of Brooklyn to construct an aqueduct that would deplete the local water supply. At the age of eighty he purchased an automobile, a Stoddard "Runabout," in which to be chauffeured from place to place.[62]

William Dana remained a very private and modest man to the end. His paper rarely departed from the nonpartisan tone that was one of its hallmarks. Only family members, close friends, and Englewood neighbors had reason to know that throughout his adult years he was a loyal, conservative Democrat, or that he was for a time in the 1880s president of the local Democratic club.[63] He used complementary railroad passes on his 1890 western trip, as a matter of right for one in his position.[64] Still, he avoided ostentation. For many years he pedaled a large tricycle to the homes of neighbors in Mastic for Sunday visits, rather than ask employees at Moss Lots to violate the Sabbath by driving him in a carriage. Faith, family, and the *Chronicle* kept place at the center of his life. Besides citations of a few *Chronicle* pieces, a few personal maxims, and entries for selected relatives and for tradespeople who served his homes and business, his address book for the first decade of the twentieth century contained but a single entry, the name of a rising young financial writer, Alexander Dana Noyes. There were no entries for social contacts. He doted on his grandson and adoptive son, Bill, relishing days when he could stand at water's edge at

Mastic and watch the youth race in sailboats. On at least one occasion, wearing customary formal attire and overcome by excitement, he fell into the river.[65]

In charitable giving William Dana followed his father's example. He assisted relatives and acquaintances in need, gave to his church, and occasionally added other causes. He always treated his finances as a strictly private matter, and he viewed his comfortable position with modesty. An 1892 plea for help brought assistance. It also prompted the observations, "Now I do not know anything about your income . . . and do not want to know anything about it for it is none of my business," and, "My business income is good, but I have very little property except unproductive real estate." While averring that he did not possess vast wealth, Dana, with misgivings, provided a cottage in Englewood for his brother George's daughter, Mary (Minnie) Dana Knox. Later, he helped with the educational expenses of two young friends of the family, Elizabeth Simonton and her sister. He contributed toward construction of a new parsonage for the Presbyterian parish at Brookhaven, Long Island, New York. A participant in the reunion commemorating the fiftieth anniversary of his graduation from college, in 1901 he made two contributions totaling $1,250 during Yale's bicentennial campaign.[66]

William Dana completed his fiftieth year in journalism, and celebrated his eightieth birthday, in August 1909. His editorial and office staffs noticed the two occasions by preparing for him a special commemorative volume that pictured all of the buildings in which the *Commercial and Financial Chronicle* had been published, the first number of each of the supplements, different office scenes, and Dana himself. A lead story in the August 26, 1909 edition, entitled "A CHRONICLE ANNIVERSARY," mentioned that its editor–publisher had always been "extremely averse to personal mention of any kind" but added that the occasion was worthy of remark. Reflecting on his "skill and ability," the piece continued: "The history of the 'Chronicle' is the history of Mr. Dana's life." A bit more than a year later, on October 10, 1910, William Dana passed away quietly in his suite at the Belmont Hotel in New York City. He had suffered intermittently from pleurisy for many years, and since the 1890s from heart problems. He died of complications from a broken femur, the result of a recent fall. A funeral train carried the body to Mastic for interment after services at the Manhattan Congregational Church, Broadway and 76th Street, at noon on Wednesday, October 12. Mourners laid the remains to rest beside those of Katharine in the Floyd family cemetery, under plain five-inch by ten-inch stones reading, simply, KFD and WBD. After a quarter of a century apart, the devoted couple were reunited.[67]

Dana left an estate of nearly $2 million, a very large sum in 1910. His 3,009 shares of Dana Company stock were valued at $315,945. There were also holdings in the Fourth National Bank of New York City, the Southern Railway, the New York Central Railroad, the Pacific & Atlantic Telegraph Company, the Colorado & Southern Railway, and various companies devoted to the improvement of Englewood worth a bit less than $5,000, that sold for the sum of $91,566. Cash totaled $69,458. Greycliffs was appraised at $383,200; other New Jersey properties at $99,400. The *Chronicle* building carried a valuation of $160,000, other New York commercial properties an added $283,000, bringing the total to $1,402,569 without considering the eighty-seven acres at Moss Lots, or Richard and Hazel Dana's ranch in California, which was also in Dana's name.

William designated Ethel Dana Shepherd, Jacob Seibert, Jr., and his nephew George S. Dana of Utica as coexecutors of his will. Through a series of trust arrangements he assigned income from the Dana Company shares, the *Chronicle* building, his New York City properties, with Greycliffs and the New Jersey lands, to Ethel and to William Shepherd Dana. The trusts were to continue in effect "so long as William Shepherd Dana, my adopted son, or William Dana Seibert, son of Jacob Seibert Jr., shall live and twenty-one years shall not have expired since my death." When young Bill Dana attained the age of twenty-one he was to become cotrustee of the trust controlling Dana Company stock, and at the expiration of that trust he was heir to all of its stock except for 300 shares bequeathed to Jacob Seibert, Jr. Moss Lots and its grounds went to Ethel and Bill, the California ranch to Richard and Hazel, the Englewood cottage to Mary Dana Knox. Dana provided generously for various nieces and nephews. The children of his brother James—Arnold Guyot Dana, Edward Silliman Dana, and Maria Trumbull Dana—each received $10,000. Specified sums went to longtime family retainers and to those who cared for Dana during his final illness, while $12,000 was to be divided equally among a dozen long-term *Chronicle* workers. The residue of the estate was to be apportioned into five equal shares, one going to Maria Trumbull Dana and two each to Ethel and Bill.[68]

Material assets were the less important portion of William Dana's legacy. His major bequest was the *Commercial and Financial Chronicle* itself. The issues published during his lifetime remain an indispensable source of information about national economic development and the reigning business ideology of the era. Equally important, they constitute a window into the first, print, information age of modern business. A later publisher of the paper correctly observed: "The files of the 'Chronicle' are at once his biography and his monument." There was no greater measure of his influence and judgment than the fact that for a generation after his death his weekly still had no peer in American business journalism, even though its advance with the times diminished after he passed from the scene.

NOTES

1. William Buck Dana (hereafter WBD) to Katharine Floyd Dana (hereafter KFD) to, quoted May 10 and 15, 1861, in Dana papers.

2. WBD to KFD, quoted May 10 and 11, 1861, Dana papers. Publishing agreement with Homans, February 1, 1861, with Dana's handwritten notation: "canceled February 1, 1862," Dana papers. See also Frank Luther Mott, *A History of American Magazines* (Cambridge: Harvard University Press, 1938), 1: 696–698 and for Homans, idem. 2:94–95; and for general conditions confronting publishers, see John A. Tebbel and Mary Ellen Zuckerman, *The Magazine in America, 1741–1990* (New York: Oxford University Press, 1991), 47–53; and David P. Forsyth, *The Business Press in America, 1750–1865* (Philadelphia: Chilton Books, 1964), 86–87, 116–118.

3. "Commercial Chronicle and Review," *Hunt's Merchants' Magazine* 53 (October 1865): 305.

4. "Nationalization of the Telegraph," and "National Aid to Steamship Lines," *Hunt's Merchants' Magazine* 58 (June 1868): 441–43, and 46 (February 1867): 107.

5. "Journal of Banking, Currency, and Finance," *Hunt's Merchants' Magazine* 52 (June 1865): 449. Also, especially, "By a Western Banker," and "Commercial Chronicle and Review," respectively 53 (January 1863): 28–34, and 48 (February 1863): 128–136.

6. "Suspense," *Hunt's Merchants' Magazine* 62 (May 1870): 334.

7. See particularly, "Panics and Prevention," *Hunt's Merchants' Magazine* 58 (June 1868): 438–441.

8. "The Strikes," *Hunt's Merchants' Magazine* 55 (July 1866): 63; also "National Accumulation and National Income," *Hunt's Merchants' Magazine* 58 (May 1863): 353–360.

9. "The Crisis of Reconstruction," *Hunt's Merchants' Magazine* 58 (February 1868): 121–124.

10. *New York Daily Bulletin*, June 23, 1865; also June 24–August 1, 1865.

11. *Commercial and Financial Chronicle*, July 1, 1865; advertisement rates, November 26, 1870.

12. Partnership agreements June 5, 1865, July 1, 1866, and January 4, 1868; Delmar agreement June 5, 1865, all in Dana papers. For Floyd see John Gelston Floyd, (hereafter JGF, Jr.) to KFD, September 11, 1861, and April 20, 1861, both Dana papers; Cornelia Floyd Nichols, "As Told By the Attic Letters" Part 2, 44–45 (unpublished manuscript in collection of Suffolk County Historical Society, Riverhead, NY (1952); Anonymous, "Descendants of William Floyd of Mastic, Long Island" (unpublished manuscript at Genealogy Room of the New York Public Library, 1896), 5; *New York Times*, November 28, 1903. See also Forsyth, *The Business Press*, 86–87.

13. Quotation from *Commercial and Financial Chronicle*, June 30, 1866; also July 1, 1865–October 26, 1870; *New York Times*, December 17, 1865; April 17 and 22, May 13 and 20, and September 23, 1866; January 9 and December 3–6, 1867; and passim; "Hunt's Merchants' Magazine for 1871," *Hunt's Merchants' Magazine* 63 (December 1870): 401–403; and *Commercial and Financial Chronicle*, June 8 and December 28, 1867, and November 1, 1939. For the Mercantile Agency, re the *Chronicle* and Dana, see New York, vol. 434, p. 67, R. G. Dun & Co. Collection, Baker Library, Harvard Business School.

14. Quotations from WBD to KFD, June 9, 1855 and May 15, 1861; also see May 17 and July 28 and 31, 1855; all in Dana papers.

15. WBD to KFD, May 15, 1861, Dana papers.

16. Quotations from WBD to KFD, May 13 and 14, 1861; also see May 9, 1861; all in Dana papers.

17. The *Oneida County Deed Book*, 236: 246–247, recorded the sale to Mary Parker of Utica.

18. Quotations from WBD to KFD, May 13, 1861; information about servant, May 15, 1861; information about completion from KFD to JGF, Jr., September 17, 1862; all Dana papers. Author's interview with Frederick Foote, June 15, 1965.

19. Quotation from WBD to KFD, July 7, 1855; also August 7, 1855 and August 17 and 19, 1856; all in Dana papers.

20. WBD to KFD, August 10, May 13 and June 5 and 7, 1855; and May 24, 1856; quotations from August 6 and 12, 1882; all in Dana papers. See also John Allison, untitled history of the family of William Outis Allison (unpublished manuscript, collection of the author, undated), 4–5.

21. WBD to KFD, August 6, 1882, and August 16 and 18, 1881, all Dana Papers; William Buck Dana, *A Day for Rest and Worship: Its Origin, Development, and Present Day Meaning* (New York: Fleming H. Revell Company, 1911), quoted 7. See also WBD to KFD, July 26, 1855, Dana papers.

22. Quotations from WBD to KFD, June 12, 1854; October 20, 1880; and August 3, 10, and 12, 1882; KFD to WBD, June 14, 1860; February 9, 1873, and July 21, 1881; WBD to KFD, April 18, 1875, and October 17, 1880; KFD to WBD, July 10–12, 1860 and February 9, 1873; all Dana papers.

23. Quotation from WBD to KFD, undated, headed "Wednesday morning"; also August 17–19, 1856 and August 12, 1855, all in Dana papers.

24. KFD to John Van Hurt, Administrator of the Poor, April 6, 1870; Dana papers.

25. O. A. W., "Commercial Phrensies," "Petroleum Old and New," *Hunt's Merchants' Magazine* 46 (March 1862): 225–234; 47 (July 1862): 19–26; also 49 (July 1863): 85–86; 50 (January/February 1864) and 51 (October 1864); and for unsigned book reviews, *Commercial and Financial Chronicle*, October 7, 1865.

26. Olive A. Wadsworth, *Our Phil and Other Stories* (Boston: Houghton Mifflin and Co., 1888; reprint, Freeport, NY: Books for Library Press, 1970), 1, 100, 101. See also KFD to WBD, February 9 1873, in Dana papers.

27. Olive A. Wadsworth, *Heavenward Bound: Words of Help for Young Christians* (Philadelphia: Presbyterian Publication Committee, 1870), frontispiece, 118, 172–173. See also Olive A. Wadsworth, *Kit, Fan, Tot, and the Rest of Them* (Boston: American Tract Society, 1870).

28. Olive A. Wadsworth, *Over in the Meadow: A Counting-Out Rhyme* (San Francisco: Morgan Shepard Company, 1906; reprint, New York: Viking Penguin, 1985). See also Olive A. Wadsworth, *Bill Riggs, Jr: The Story of a City Boy* (Boston: Warren and Co., 1869); and "Three Rainy Days in Three Chapters" (unpublished manuscript, n.d., Box 7, Folder 2, Dana papers); and various undated poems including "Polly's Experience" (unpublished manuscript, Box 4, Folder 11, Dana papers); and "The M's and the N's" (unpublished manuscript, Box 4, Folders 9 and 10, Dana papers).

29. Allison, "Family," 4–5; author's interviews with John Allison, Frederick Foote, and Ella Lindley Dana, all June 15, 1965. Also William O. Allison to KFD, January 23, 1880; July 22 and August 20, 1884; and December 18 and 23, 1885; to WBD, February 16, 1901; December 8 and 12, 1905; January 2 and 19, 1906; all in Dana papers; *Grantee, Index of Deeds, Bergen County, New Jersey, 1714–1962*,

AAA–AMZ, 1:428–429ff; and James Greco, *The Story of Englewood Cliffs* (Englewood Cliffs, NJ: Tercentenary Committee, 1964), 36–44.

30. Information about the adoptions is contained in records of the Surrogate Court, Suffolk County, New York, concerning proceedings related to the estate of William B. Dana, whose will was admitted to probate there on November 28, 1910. A certified copy of this will was admitted in proceedings of the Special Term of the Court, October 19, 1918, relative to *William Shepherd Dana vs. Jacob Seibert, Jr., et al.*

31. See especially John Kirkland Dana (hereafter, JKD) to KFD, May 2, 1879; January 27 and 29, February 18, 22, and 27, March 7, 11, and 18, and May 16, all 1880; May 9 and July 29 and 31, 1884; WBD to KFD, September 19, 1883; Richard Dana (hereafter RD) to WBD, May 15 and 21, 1885; Ethel Floyd Dana (hereafter EFD) to KFD, May 24, 1874; December 26, 1877; October 1, 1878; February 16, 1881; and March 13, 1883; all in Dana papers.

32. Edith Dana Jones to WBD, December 15, 1904, in Dana papers. Also author's interview with Cornelia Floyd Nichols, September 2, 1965; Nichols, "As told by the Attic Letters," Part 2, 35, 43–45; and Sarah Floyd Turner, "Sunny Memories of Mastic" (unpublished manuscript in collection of William Floyd Estate with the Dana papers, Fire Island National Seashore, National Park Service, undated and with the notation, "Written in about 1889").

33. JGF, Jr. to KFD, March 14, 1879, and undated "Memorandum for Division," Box 7, Folder 5, both in Dana papers.

34. Nicoll Floyd to WBD, October 9, 1880; quotation about surveying, WBD to Nicoll Floyd, July 29, 1882; Marion D. B. Floyd to KFD, March 26, 1883; WBD to Nicoll Floyd, May 13, 1884; all in Dana papers. Also author's interview with Ella Lindley Dana, June 15, 1965; and, for the ideology of the "Big House," Edward Chase Kirkland, *Dream and Thought in the Business Community, 1860–1890* (Ithaca, NY: Cornell University Press, 1956), 101–107.

35. Katharine Dana is worthy of a study in her own right, and as a representative of a certain type of upper-class Victorian woman. Despite a remarkable intellectual partnership, lifelong bonds of deep affection, and even some involvement with William in business matters, she faced the usual contemporary obstacles to female achievement in the world of affairs. What role these obstacles played in encouraging her writing, artistic effort producing drawings that merited a special exhibit at the William Floyd Estate in 1991, her illness and resort to laudanum, and a desire to be babied, are all questions begging pursuit.

Quotations from KFD to WBD, August 6, WBD to KFD, June 21, both 1854; JGF, Jr. to KFD, July 24, 1861, all Dana papers. Also KFD to WBD, April 21, 1855; WBD to KFD, July 12 and 18, 1860; JGF, Jr. to KFD, August 17, 1879 and July 30, 1884; Anna L. Turner to KFD, February 11, 1886; "Bequests of Katharine Floyd Dana—Jewelry, shawls & other gifts," undated and with script notation "J[ohn]. Allison 1968"; all in Dana papers; and author's interview with John Allison, September 2, 1965.

36. WBD to JKD, March 7, 1890; JKD to Ethel Dana Shepherd (hereafter EDS), April 21, 1891, Dana papers. Also Tillie Feeks to KFD, December 25, 1885, and to WBD, September 24, 1887, and February 21, 1890; JKD to WBD, February 4 and October 19, 1892; WBD to JKD, February 26, 1890; all Dana papers. See, too, Glendon Feeks to WBD, "General Release," dated March 8, 1892; Feeks to WBD, May 26, 1892; WBD to Feeks, June 4, 1892; and *New York Times* and

Tacoma (Washington) Ledger, September 27: *New York Times*, September 30 and December 3; *New York Morning Advertiser*, December 2; all 1892.

37. Quotations from WBD to Hazel B. Dana, August 21, 1897; Hazel B. Dana to WBD, August 11, 1897 and September 2, 1907. See also WBD, undated memorandum to himself, 1890; Hazel B. Dana to WBD, undated and July 3, 1898, and March 26, 1905; Arthur C. McCann to WBD, June 10 and 17, 1898; RD to WBD, June 15 and August 14, 1898 and March 21, 1903; WBD to RD, September 17, 1898; H. Frank Sherman to EDS, October 4, 1904; all in Dana papers. Author's interview with John Allison, September 2, 1965, in which he recalled—probably erroneously—that the magazine photograph appeared in *Life*. It seems, however, that the subject of the photograph in question, in *Life*, was not Richard.

38. Quotations from WBD to EDS, December 24, 1896. See also George B. Shepherd to WBD, December 8, 1890 and January 16, 1891; WBD to George Shepherd, December 29, 1890, and January 24, 1891; Frederick R. Shepherd (FRS) to WBD, January 28, 1891, and January (n.d.) and October 25, 1899; WBD to FRS, January 17, 1899; JKD to EDS, April 21, 1891; William O. Allison to WBD, February 16, 1901; Ernest R. Tooker to Mrs. Frederick R. [Daisy] Shepherd, August 17, and George B. Shepherd to EDS, both 1903; bills of sale, The Gorham Company, to EDS, December 4, 1902; Lyman A. Spaulding to WBD, July 12, 22, and 24 and November 11, all 1903; WBD to Lyman A. Spaulding, July 21 and 24, 1903 and June 16, 1904; sheaves of receipts, April–August 1909 (copies in author's collection; most of originals now missing); Kathleen R. Glass to WBD, March 16 and 27, 1901; Ida M. Gardner to WBD, March 4, 1902; all in Dana papers.

39. *Grantee, Index of Deeds, Bergen County, New Jersey, 1714–1962*, DAA–DMZ, 19:107; William Buck Dana, Notebook, February 1, 1871–February 1, 1884 (catalog number I.S. 3242, Dana papers), 1ff; *Index of Mortgages, Bergen County, New Jersey, 1766–1961*, DAA–DELI, 12:91.

40. Robert C. Lydecker, comp. *Lydecker Descendants: Ryck Lydecker, 1650* (Short Hills, NJ: Lydecker, 1987), in collection of Bergen County Historical Society, Johnson Free Library, Hackensack, NJ.

41. Articles of Agreement, William B. Dana and Lewis B. Leeds, November 1, 1869, Box 7, Folder 23, "Palisades Mountain House," in Dana papers.

42. Agreement, A[ndrew]. D[emarest]. Bogert & Bro. And William B. Dana and Cornelius Lydecker . . . September 18, 1871, Box 7, Folder 23, "Palisades Mountain House," in Dana papers.

43. Agreement, William Walter Phelps and Jacob S. Wetmore . . . and William B. Dana and Cornelius Lydecker . . . September 18, 1871, Box 7, Folder 23, "Palisades Mountain House," in Dana papers. Inasmuch as Dana soon afterward noted that he shared ownership of an additional seven acres with Phelps and Wetmore, there is reason to believe that he and Lydecker may for a time have belonged to a syndicate with these two and Lydecker's father. See Adaline W. Sterling. *The Book of Englewood* (Englewood, NJ: City of Englewood), 116; and Dana, "Notebook," 1. The details remain obscure.

44. Quotation from William to S. C. Cozzens, February 17, 1872, Box 7, Folder 23, "Palisades Mountain House," Dana papers.

45. Quotations from *New York Times*, July 18, 1872, May 8 1881, and June 5, 1884. See also Greco, *The Story of Englewood Cliffs*, 27–28. Contracts for construction of the road, still the route from the end of Palisade Avenue down to the park on the riverfront, are dated January 25 and July 12, 1870; in Dana papers.

Also Sterling, *The Book of Englewood*, 116. In 1883, Dana appears to have projected a railroad from the dock to the hotel. WBD to KFD, September 4, 1883, in Dana papers.

46. Dana, "Notebook," 1, 22–24, 28; deed dated March 10, recorded March 14 1883, *Grantee, Index of Deeds, Bergen County, New Jersey, 1714–1962*, DAA–DMZ, 19:108. See also, for W. B. Dana Company, New York, vol. 434, p. 067, R. G. Dun & Co. Collection, Baker Library, Harvard Business School; for Palisades Mountain House, New Jersey, vol. 3, p. 213; and for Allison's interests in the Palisades Mountain House and in the Palisades Stone Co. New Jersey, vol. 4, pp. 428, 555, all in R. G. Dun & Co. Collection, Baker Library, Harvard Business School.

47. Greco, *The Story of Englewood Cliffs*, 23, 41–42, 181, 235–238.

48. Receipt from Commissioners of Palisades Interstate Parkway January (n.d.), 1902; Dana papers.

49. A[ndrew]. D[emarest]. Bogert to William, May 9, 1903, Dana papers; Greco, *The Story of Englewood Cliffs*, 178–184.

50. Box 4, Folder 13, Dana papers, contains envelopes postmarked October 26, 1906, with *Chronicle* letterhead and a notation in Dana's hand, "Burdict and Patterson about purchase of land & house. Nov. 1906." Inside are several letters, one dated October 26, 1903, from O. C. Weathersby to William, and an unaddressed, undated draft reply, quoted, together with several 1 ¼ × 4-inch sheets of paper containing estimates of the value of his property.

51. Author's interview with Frederick Foote, September 1, 1965.

52. Addresses of publication, with drawings of the *Chronicle*'s various buildings, undated 1909 private publication for Dana commemorating his eightieth birthday (author's photographic copy survives; original missing); advertising and subscription rates, *Commercial and Financial Chronicle*, July 1, 1865–January 1, 1910; also handwritten records of monthly receipts and disbursements, January–December 1911; in Dana papers.

53. Deposition of Wood Drake Loudon, October 23, 1911, in proceedings relative to William Dana's estate, records of the Suffolk County Surrogate Court, Riverhead, New York.

54. For Dana's information-gathering methods, James P. Kimball to WBD, January 17, 1888, is revealing. See also "Explanation of an Apparent Financial Absurdity" (undated manuscript), both in Dana papers; "80th Commemorative," and author's interviews with John Allison, Frederick Foote, and Ella Lindley Dana, June 15, 1965.

55. William Buck Dana, *Cotton from Seed to Loom: A Handbook of Facts for the Daily use of Producer, Merchant, and Consumer* (New York: William B. Dana and Co., 1878), 29, 244.

56. *Commercial and Financial Chronicle*, October 10, 1868, January 15, 1873; April 13, 1875; October 31, 1891; March 9, 1895; May 11, 1895; October 24, 1903; and January 1, 1910. Dana also introduced a year-end wrap-up for 1869, *The Commercial & Financial Register* (New York: William B. Dana and Co., n.d. [1870?]), and "The Railway Monitor," reporting the financial conditions of the railroads, January 15, 1873, a precursor to "The Investor's Supplement." See also William Buck Dana, *Prices of Rail Road Stocks for 32 Years, 1854–1886* (New York: Printed at the office of the *Commercial and Financial Chronicle*, 1886).

57. Quotation from Deposition of Jacob Seibert, Jr., April 27, 1912, in proceed-

ings relative to William Dana estate, Surrogate Court, Suffolk County, New York; see also Loudon, "Deposition."

58. *Commercial and Financial Chronicle*, November 4, 1939. Seibert died in 1934. His two sons, Herbert D. and William Dana Seibert succeeded him in control of the *Chronicle*.

59. Quotations from Arnold Guyot Dana to WBD, May 29, 1893, and WBD to Arnold Dana, May 31, 1893, and June 4, 1901, all in Dana papers.

60. Dana, "Notebook," 21; Mercantile Agency quotations, New York, vol. 434, p. 191, R. G. Dun & Co. Collection, Baker Library, Harvard Business School. See also pp. 1, 7, 12–13; Loudon, "Deposition," and Allison to WBD, December 8 and 12, 1905, January 2, 1906; all in Dana papers save Loudon in records of proceedings re Dana will in Surrogate Court of Suffolk County, New York.

61. Quotation from WBD to KFD, October 16, 1880; also WBD to KFD, August 3, 6, 10, and 12, 1882, and July 21, August 14, 19, 25, and 28, 1881; JKD to WBD, August 5, 1890; "Journal of 1890 Railroad Trip" (unpublished manuscript, 1890) in Box 4, Folder 16; all in Dana papers.

62. Quotation from Nicoll Floyd III to JGF, Jr., March 24, 1896. See also E. S. Morrison to WBD, June 29, 1898; "Sewage Disposal System," October 1902; map, "Proposed System for Supplying City of Brooklyn With Water From Suffolk County," August 5, 1908; and W. Bayard Cutting et al., Executive Committee to . . . WBD, August 6, 1908; all Box 7, Folder 4, Miscellaneous Dana papers; and Columbia Insurance Company Policy No. 7938, E. C. Midgely to E. A. Perry, April 6, 1909, and document dated April 8, 1909, posting bail for chauffeur's traffic violation; also in Dana papers.

63. Sterling, *The Book of Englewood*, 122.

64. J. N. Reichert to WBD, July 15, 1890; J. H. Morrison to WBD, October 25, 1890; November 5, 1890 entry in "Journal of 1890 Railroad Trip," Box 4, Folder 16, all in Dana papers.

65. Address Book, probably for 1904, Box 4, Folder 22, Dana papers.

66. Quotations from WBD to Alice W. Knox, June 27 and May 30, 1892; also E. Elizabeth Dana to WBD, April 27, 1906; Elizabeth Simonton to WBD, May 20, 1906; WBD to Elizabeth Simonton, September 8, 1906; Edith Dana Jones to WBD, December 15, 1904; all Dana papers. Also notation in *Directory of the Living Graduates of Yale University* (New Haven, CT: The Tuttle, Morehouse and Taylor Press, 1899), and confidential report of pledges "For the Use of the Committee Only Yale Bicentennial Subscriptions November 1900" and ledger sheets for July 1900, 12, and September 23, 1901, 44; both in Yale Archives, Treasurer's Records: Benefactors, YRG 5–13, Series 4, Box 373, Folder 23; and "Building Specifications, Presbyterian Parsonage, Brookhaven, NY, Box 7, Folder 19, Miscellaneous Dana papers.

67. "80th Commemorative," *New York Times*, October 11, 1910, mistakenly set the death at Mastic while placing the funeral at the Manhattan Congregational Church. The *Utica Daily Press*, October 11, 1910, placed the funeral in a Presbyterian church. See also *Commercial and Financial Chronicle*, October 15, 1910.

68. Will, dated April 12, 1909, 1; codicil, September 13, 1910; both in Dana papers. Also deposition of Jacob Seibert, Jr., April 17, 1912, in records of Surrogate Court, Suffolk County, New York, of proceedings relative to Dana estate; and Gwin & Pell to William Shepherd Dana, November 18, 1918, in Dana papers.

3

The Natural Order
of Things

[a]lmost all the ills from which humanity from time to time suffers
would cure themselves if natural laws were left free to work their own
cure.

—William Buck Dana, August 4, 1906

If any single belief underpinned William Dana's view of the world, it was
his unwavering conviction that natural laws reigned. Had he been a philosopher, economist, or political theorist, one could fairly expect of him
rigorous consistency in his thoughts and the reasoning that he employed
to express them. One could also fairly insist on a logically constructed
system of ideas that proceeded in orderly steps from his conception of
human nature through his understanding of natural principles and how
they could be discovered to a tightly argued notion of how these operated
in the affairs of humankind. But philosopher, economist, or political theorist he was not. He left no systematic and comprehensive exposition of
his thought. He was a journalist and entrepreneur. And not a journalist
who aimed to reach a mass, undifferentiated readership. His paper addressed particular needs of a particular audience during a particular epoch,
that of America's second industrial revolution. To recover and systematically reconstruct his conception of the natural order of things requires a
careful reading of a few scattered fragments of personal correspondence
but, to a vastly greater extent, the much larger body of hundreds of unsigned editorial features that he wrote or personally reviewed, edited, and
approved for publication in the *Commercial and Financial Chronicle*. It is
chiefly from these pieces in the *Chronicle* that it is possible to cull his core
ideas.

There was a general consistency to Dana's ideas. This held true throughout his life. There was relatively slight change over time, with a few conspicuous exceptions that will be treated in due course. As a result, it is a relatively straightforward task to unravel his thought; and chronology rarely limits the selection of illustrations. Of course there were instances of inconsistency and incongruence or noncongruence, as well as of faulty logic. Dana was human. He strove constantly for accuracy, clarity, and dependability in his paper. He also found it impossible to avoid being drawn, from time to time, into the major controversies of his day. To a large degree, whenever his views wavered they tended to do so in response to the pressures of current events. Time for reflection usually brought a restoration of perspective.

When the *Commercial and Financial Chronicle* was born, newspaper publishing in the United States, like the nation itself, was undergoing great change. Photography, mechanical typesetting, and the rotary press revolutionized newspaper production in the generation following the Civil War. They made mass circulation inexpensive dailies feasible at the historical moment when the emergence of metropolises provided potential mass readerships. These readerships, in turn, could be targets for advertisers just as increasing use of instruments of mass production made possible the rise of a consumer economy.

This was not all. The American newspaper business in the last third of the nineteenth century was intensely personal. Editors and publishers weaned on the country's booster spirit openly gibed their rivals in print, derided competing communities, and introduced new features as ways of advantaging their own papers. Joseph Pulitzer's 1883 acquisition of the *New York World* was a major turn. He immediately proclaimed that the *World* would take the journalistic lead in defending democracy. It would fearlessly expose sham, fraud, and public evils. For good measure and in a shameless bid for market dominance, Pulitzer added sensationalism: stories employing sexual allusions to titillate his readers and features on human and other genetic monstrosities. Rival Charles Adams Dana's *New York Sun* replied with a new genre, the human interest story. Whatever else they might have done, these democratic papers—addressed to the masses—besides disseminating news satisfied a psychic need of fresh migrants to cities that was itself as novel as the emerging metropolises. That need, conscious or not, was for the sort of information that helped them feel less isolated and anonymous, and more connected to their communities.

This type of news was the print equivalent of backyard gossip in small-town America. Interestingly, in hundreds of rural and small communities across the land there were comparable pressures working to encourage personal journalism. The most important was the fact that in such places people often heard the "news" in which they were most interested, that from their hometowns, orally before it ever got into print. Editors had to give stories some personal twist in order to maintain reader attention. Often, in small places, they had to meet competing publications head-on, as did their counterparts in the cities. And like their urban peers, they needed advertising revenue.

Finally, partisanship dominated the press, nearly everywhere. Ideals and ideology drove a good bit of this partisanship. Self-interest also played a large role. In small communities, contracts to print public documents and notices might mean the difference between survival and failure. In larger cities, they could be a significant source of added revenue. In both settings, advantages attached to association with the political party that held the reins of power.

Whatever the setting in which these general readership papers flourished or struggled, they had to operate on the basis of some guiding conception of the nature of the world, and of their readers. This conception might or might not be explicit, but it was axiomatic that an editor with no audience in mind, no conception of the needs of that audience, or no comprehension of the nature of his audience's world would soon be out of business.[1]

The very qualities that might have made for success among the mass urban dailies or the rural and small-town dailies and weeklies would have disadvantaged the *Commercial and Financial Chronicle* from the outset. It was aimed at the nation's business leadership. It sought to inform and advocate for what Dana conceived to be the country's great commercial, financial, and manufacturing interests. This constituency was not united in political affiliation. A partisan tone, and sensationalism, would have repelled many potential readers. Biased coverage that too obviously favored one principal industrial interest over others would also have done so. Editorial idiosyncrasy would have likewise been a distinct negative.

It did not follow that the *Chronicle* was not an instance of personal journalism. Its editor's personal propensities and writing tone were simply less obtrusive than was often the case in the more popular press. In its roles as nonpartisan provider of essential information and advocate for our leading business interests it was, as we have seen, an extension of Dana's personality and convictions. The latter to a remarkable degree probably converged with those of his readership. The *Chronicle*'s editor and audience did tend to share certain characteristics. These included at least a degree of affluence, educational advantage, some acquaintance with the world's affairs, and an inclination toward conservative views. They naturally incorporated a desire to protect business interests, with all that that implied. If readers were of William Dana's generation and were college- or university-educated, they were likely to have studied the same texts that he had. While the introduction of the university on the German model in 1876, and of the elective curriculum, brought changes later on, significant resemblances of class and outlook remained.[2]

William Dana's understanding of the natural laws that governed the world drew directly and heavily on his formal education, his experience, and a temperament that favored order and stability. He filled his writing with references to natural law. These references repeatedly reflected the influence of those who had taught him at home, in Sunday school and church, and especially at Yale. They also drew on his lengthening career, with its sustained analysis of business. Francis Wayland's influence was evident even before the Civil War ended and the *Chronicle* began publication in Dana's editorials in *Hunt's* advocating sound money. The sway of Victor Cousin's, Thomas Reid's, and William Paley's convictions about the rational character of the universe and the human race that a beneficent Providence had created were no less evident. When discussion turns, later on, to legal matters, the impact of Chancellor James Kent's views will be similarly clear.

In 1873, as opposing forces fired the first shots in what was to be a quarter-century battle over monetary policy between proponents and opponents of expansion of the supply of money, the *Chronicle*'s editor set out his views clearly in an article entitled "THE DEMAND FOR MORE NATIONAL BANK NOTE ISSUES." He stoutly challenged inflationists, basing his argument on "the elementary teachings of economic science" These assured us that "the three chief instruments which combine for the growth of national wealth are industry, capital, and currency." Of these the first two created wealth and the third distributed it. Continuing, he framed an analogy between the economy and a living organism in nature. Industry was analogous to the vital force or energy "with which nature has endowed all living organisms, capital is the material substance of each structure, and *currency* is the circulating blood which distributes vital force and activity of function in every organ." Like blood, if currency was too plethoric in supply it could disturb the equilibrium between the normal demand of industry (the body) for the circulating medium and the supply of that medium needed to sustain it. The error of inflationists was to repeat the theory of the notorious eighteenth-century speculator John Law. Acceptance of Law's ruinous confusion of the quantity of currency with the amount of real capital had plunged France into its first national bankruptcy, in that century. If it followed Law's perilous course, the United States risked the same fate. Dana had absorbed his economics well at Yale.[3]

Thirty years later, the aging editor explicitly acknowledged the importance of his collegiate studies in shaping his fortunes and, implicitly, his thinking. He conceded in an editorial that a business college or a university commercial course might more readily pave the way to prominence and success. Nevertheless, he continued, "If one has the time the old academic course is, we still think, the best." Such a course enlarged the mind, cultivated a thirst for knowledge that was, after graduation, an "unfailing source of pleasure," and helped one to make the most of one's life. "We get an idea of a college education's value," he went on to say, "from the fact that no graduate of a college would at any price part with what he has thereby gained." Should a career in business be one's goal, the study and then practice for a few years of law were important additions. They tended "more than anything else to take the hysteria out of a man and give him an orderly mind."[4]

During the intervening years the *Chronicle* fairly bristled with references to "natural law," the "immutable and natural law of business management," "certain moral and economic verities," "necessities of the case," "self-interest," the inexorable "law of supply and demand," "Providence," and more as unvarying constants on the scene.[5] Dana did not often address directly what he thought to be the source of these laws, but on occasion he did. Writing in 1873 about proposals to repeal usury laws, he went directly to the Bible. True enough, he wrote that the Old Testament contained a prohibition against usury. But the New Testament, with its story of reward for the faithful steward who had multiplied his master's money, must also be considered. The Old Testament had been written, he opined in his most lawyerly fashion, only as "a temporary municipal code for the Jews alone" during that brief period when they had controlled the Holy Land. In contrast, the New Testament "was intended for all nations and will be in force until the end of time."[6]

A quarter century later the explosion of the battleship *Maine* in Havana harbor and the ensuing diplomatic crisis with Spain prompted a less oblique hint at the source of natural law. Faced with growing public furor, and the growth of warlike sentiment toward Spain, our writer counseled caution. War with Spain and the associated sacrifice of lives and goods should be entered into only "in obedience to the requirements of a high moral obligation." Readers ought to ask whether "as followers of Him who said the blessed are the peacemakers," it did "not become this great Christian nation" to act only upon the best evidence. And "to compel peace whenever it is compatible with justice."[7]

Clearly, Dana was no deist, nor was his God a remote watchmaker. Instead, the deity was personal and active. In ordaining natural laws that human reason could discern, He had made economic science possible. This science took as its province the operation of economic ordinances in the lives of individuals, families, firms, and nations. It could and did generalize, but its generalizations derived from the application of reason to the study of observed behavior. It was thus far more humanistic and, one might add, less pretentious in its claim than what economics has now become. Dana would not have known what to make of the sigmas, deltas, streams of numbers generated through multiple regression analysis, and other arcana that now camouflage the fact that the further the study of economics strays from a regard for actual human behavior in time, the more barren its results become. For him, economic knowledge and science were practical matters. They bore on the destines of real live people, firms, and nations. They had nothing to do with advancement to a university position with academic tenure.

As editor of a publication aimed at leading manufacturers, traders, and financiers, Dana maintained that the laws of economic science held unrivaled place among natural laws. They were inseparable from morality itself. In believing thus, he positioned himself lifelong with his teachers. Together they all stood in the long shadow of Adam Smith, the University of Glasgow professor who had founded classical economics with the publication of *The Wealth of Nations* (1776). Dana acknowledged this debt in an 1874 article on the origin of classical economics. Aroused by the claims of a French scholar that eighteenth-century French court physician François Quesnay had anticipated Smith's ideas with his *Tableau économique* (1758), he showed that Smith had actually incorporated them into his lectures as early as 1748. Smith was not only the founder of classical economics; he gave us as his crucial idea the notion that the material needs and happiness of a society were best served when "administrative [governmental] interference with commercial movements and industrial growth" was restricted to the "narrowest possible limits."[8]

The rest followed inevitably from these first premises. Close to the end of his life Dana summarized his mature views. For him, mankind was not intrinsically evil. The modern world—and here we can discern a theory of social evolution or progress as one of the principles that he saw at work—had advanced beyond the old view that imperfect human nature required close regulation of behavior by church and state. He had abandoned the oppressive doctrines of original sin and stifling predestination of former generations of Presbyterians for a gentler (and perhaps less demanding) faith. Liberty in trade did not, he believed, necessarily spell the triumph of avarice. Liberty in politics need not foretell social violence. Liberty in morals could lead elsewhere than to blasphemous "wickedness." Rather, "[h]uman nature was better than had been thought" in earlier ages. "Man was not in a state of war with his Creator and all his fellow men." One could, of course, be too optimistic, given the present imperfect state of human development. Dana did not subscribe without qualification to the idea of Progress that had taken such deep root in nineteenth-century America. But if government could be restrained from meddling, he was hopeful for the future. "Humanity," he claimed, "left to itself," "gives hope of becoming more and more harmonious until rational egoism and rational altruism tend to coincide." In case any reader missed the point, he illustrated it by showing to his own satisfaction how the progress of the railroads, and their earnings, had been greatest when they were free to operate with the fewest restraints. The introduction of effective federal regulation in 1906 and 1907 brought a marked deterioration of affairs for them.[9]

Human beings occupied the pinnacle of creation within the natural law-governed world that William Dana inhabited. Their commercial and financial activities were the epicenters around which his paper orbited. To a great extent, he explained changing business conditions and advocated for the interests of business on the basis of his understanding of human nature. Yet, as a practical man of affairs he wrote relatively little about human nature as such. He aimed primarily to report and analyze commercial developments. What he wrote, however, left enough raw material to guide one to discover that he held to a few general and consistent conceptions about human nature. His views also contained some troubling contradictions.

As anyone of his era conversant with the reigning principles of economics, Dana accepted that rational self-interest was one of the innate characteristics of human beings. That quality was essential as the basis of the impulse for survival. It led individuals to calculate how they might exchange goods and services to best advantage. Delivering goods and services most in demand met social need and promised the greatest return to individuals. As they thus prospered, so would society. But possessed in excess, self-interest could be destructive. Unrestrained, if it led to "command of the market," it could result in the "great practical danger" of attempts to "restrict production rather than extend it; to cling to old methods rather than to new ones." Were that to happen, "any gain in stability" arising from market domination would be "offset by a sacrifice in efficiency." Even worse, exploitation, social violence, and international conflict might ensue. Fortunately, humankind also possessed reason and the capacity for altruistic behavior. It was these that moderated recurrent social conflict and completed the triad of qualities that made progress possible. Just as self-interest stimulated competition, reason and altruism could direct and limit it. The more closely they converged, we can infer, the greater the degree of progress and human happiness. It was in the unregulated, competitive marketplace that these forces best operated. Because there was nothing to indicate that "human nature" was changing or was likely to, Dana was "certain" that political action could not refashion it. Hence, governmental interference with free competition negated the benefits that would otherwise arise.

Dana might not recognize as conservatives many Americans who today claim to be such. His regard for the social good, for the happiness of the community, preserved a moral end that is all too often missing today in conservative rhetoric. For him a *laissez-faire* market economy was a means, not an end. Humankind was much more than *homo economicus*, however fundamental the impulse to rational self-interest might be. He was also *homo spiritualis*, *pater familias*, *homo moralis*, *homo civitas*, and *homo ludens*. Much of what our editor wrote could be, and was, used to defend the *status quo*. But clearly he did not see in change a threat to stability. Conservatism did not mean stasis. In all of this he stood closer to the English tradition of philosophical conservatism than what passes for conservatism as America enters the twenty-first century. Even though he used the term "class," he did not do so in a rigorous and consistent fashion. For him the word did not connote a group defined, as Karl Marx proposed, in terms of its relationship to ownership of the means of production and distribution. Class was more generic in its meaning. It denoted groups— say, the educated as opposed to the uneducated, entrepreneurs as opposed to wage earners, exclusionists as against those favoring unrestricted foreign immigration.[10]

Naked self-interest and pure altruism were, of course, contradictory qualities. They were not the greatest of the contradictions in Dana's view of human nature. The major industrial advances of the day, even the ordinary business success stories of the day, called for special qualities. These included "personal and official rectitude," "strength" and a "peculiar genius" for creating and "building up enterprises." They required a capacity to carry designs "through to success." They included the ability to stand "firm and resolute" in times of crisis. And, surely, hard work.

Success . . . requires on the part of the employer [a] full day's work and in most cases a good part of the night, too, to be reached. But the employees have no responsibility beyond the hours employed, and those they can regulate; yet in this case, too, the resolution to be successful must be kept within the possibilities of the capital in use. . . . Labor ought to be able to see that it cannot permanently secure more than the business will bear.[11]

Remarks such as those quoted above tempt one to believe that Dana subscribed to the "Gospel of Wealth." Propagated by a number of prominent industrialists, preachers, and writers subsequent to the 1889 publication of Andrew Carnegie's famous essay "Wealth," this loose collection of ideas quickly won currency within certain social groups. It glorified the accomplishments of the entreprisers who were leading in the creation of an industrial, urban nation. It was especially congenial to people for whom the new order was prospering most greatly. For many among the newly- or super-rich, it was an irresistibly seductive means of self-justification.

The reasons for the appeal of the new ideology were painfully obvious. The biblical Gospel of St. Matthew records a dialogue between Jesus and a wealthy young man who faithfully met all the formal requirements of Judaism and asked what he must do in addition in order to be assured entry into the kingdom of God. The response was sobering: the young man must also sell his possessions, give all to the poor, and follow the Nazarene carpenter. After his visitor went away "with a heavy heart, for he was a man of great wealth," Jesus shared a further remark with His disciples. It was "easier for a camel to pass through the eye of a needle than for a rich man to enter the kingdom of God." The "Gospel of Wealth" offered a stunning inversion of this message. Wealth had formerly stood as an obstacle to entry into the heavenly kingdom. Its acquisition had been associated with false, material values that diverted one from higher spiritual and moral concerns. Now, twisting the old and familiar notion of stewardship, wealth was celebrated as a means with which to multiply good works. Its acquisition was now in itself a virtue and the result of virtuous conduct: industry, thrift, prudence, sobriety, and so on. The larger the fortune, the greater the potential for good works. The more likely, too, eternal reward for the benefactor.

For those who aspired to great fortunes, the new view appeared to hold out hope, a recipe for success. Both lay in virtuous conduct, especially in the practice of the business virtues. Conversely, it explained poverty as the result of defects of character. It was the inescapable reward of vice—sloth, profligacy, improvidence, promiscuity, drunkenness, or worse. This was comforting news to those who wished to assume no responsibility for the less fortunate. Wealth was something actively to be sought after as a means of enlarging one's capacity for doing good. These notions lost their luster, at least for a time, when the Great Depression of the 1930s provoked widespread popular hostility toward big business and persons of great wealth. A profound abyss seemed to separate those who had amassed great fortunes from the multitudes for whom the business crisis of the 1930s was a disaster. Revelations of speculation and chicanery among captains of industry deepened social divisions. The disparity of circumstances was too great to evade notice, accept easily, or escape becoming politically charged. With the passing of the generation that experienced the economic calamity of the 1930s, our social memory is now fading. Colossi of enterprise are again emerging as cultural heroes, icons to be regarded with awe and reverence. If there is a difference from the ideas prevailing a century ago, the greater part of it is that a sense of philanthropy seems to occupy a much smaller place now than it did then. Wealth is more openly and unapologetically pursued for itself.

It would be too simple a conclusion to characterize William as an adherent of as transparent a collection of ideas as those constituting the "Gospel of Wealth." True, he subscribed to the ideal of the "Big House" as we have already discovered. He also took recourse to the biblical parable of the faithful steward to justify lending money at interest. That same parable lent support to the larger notion of stewardship that figured so prominently in the new view of wealth as a token of virtue. He was well aware of the great benefactions of his era that the "Gospel of Wealth" had helped to inspire. But he also knew of too many rich people who had won their fortunes by wrecking companies, speculating, misleading investors, and even commiting crimes to embrace uncritically the economic ideology that Carnegie and a battalion of others were promoting in the 1890s and the early twentieth century. There is no evidence that he regarded it in its entirety as anything other than what it far too often was: self-serving claptrap and theological and moral snake oil. Virtue neither assured wealth nor necessarily resulted from it. Wealth was, nevertheless, a trust. It imposed on a person enlarged moral responsibilities to society, as a steward of what Providence granted.

While the tendencies of self-interest and altruism stood in opposition, they were not beyond reconciliation. William had shown the way through reference to the operation of the third fundamental aspect of human nature—reason—as a mediating agent. But his notion of human nature contained another, much more difficult contradiction, one so difficult as to be paradoxical. It was this. The same brilliant, imaginative, bold, hardworking capitalists responsible for the development of the United States were also timid. They were easily frightened. When they became fearful, they withdrew their resources and energies from active investment. They battened down their financial hatches, avoiding new enterprises and scaling back existing ventures. Often they sent financial resources overseas, usually to Europe, to employ profitably in a safer environment. While this timidity was evident in many ways, it exercised its greatest influence in connection with the business cycle. The code words covering the prevalence or absence of timidity were "confidence" and its opposites, "uncertainty" and "lack of confidence."[12]

The most important clue toward understanding how vision, ambition, and ability could founder in a sea of uncertainty resided in another maxim of the economic science to which Dana subscribed. This was the notion, central to classical economics, that a national, market-based business system unburdened by government interference tended toward a certain characteristic set of conditions. Both sellers and buyers competed to dispose of or to obtain goods on the most favorable terms that they could. As a result, production and demand, defined as ability and willingness to purchase, inclined toward meeting. Employment and wages similarly converged with the demand of employers for labor, whose efforts transformed raw material into goods. Labor's wages never reached the full (natural) value of its product, as measured by the effort expended. The difference lay in profits. These were necessary incentives to induce people to enter business. They were needed to cover nonlabor operating expenses. They were essential, too, as a source of capital for investment in machines and other assets required to increase managerial effectiveness, operating efficiency, and the productivity of labor through expanded mechanization and specialization. When the economy was operating with a balance among output and demand, costs and prices/receipts, employment, wages, and profits, Dana and his business peers judged it to be functioning "normally" or "naturally." Production, demand, prices, costs, employment, wages, and profits were all at "natural" levels. The economy was in a normal state, defined as "equilibrium." It followed that anything threatening the maintenance of equilibrium signaled danger.[13]

And signals there were. One cannot read the *Chronicle* during William's editorship without being struck by the frequency and severity of contemporary business downturns. In 1899, a generation after he had begun publication, he directed a major portion of the week's "Financial Situation" to "a quite serious question, why is it that the cycles of buoyance in this country must be so extreme and so short?" He rejected the claim of some that the nation's youth was a factor, because youth typically exhibited exuberance. But he granted as an undeniable fact "that we quickly overdo every combination of favorable conditions and then have to suffer a retribution," because "the many reverses of recent years" showed that America's "temerity" could "not be denied." No other nation had "such a financial history. The course of the malady seems to be a short, feverish excitement, then quickly following this is a corresponding reaction." Given that underlying business conditions were often sound, he wrote that much of the problem was to be found in public sentiment against business and the resulting fear among businessmen.[14]

The record since 1873 was sobering enough. By early September of that year news of short harvests in Europe stirred massive grain shipments in the Midwest. A huge flow of funds to the interior to move the crops ensued, testing "the stability of our financial machinery." Pressure eased midmonth. Then the suspension of a major New York financial house caught short of cash because it had committed excessive resources to assist construction of a railroad portended trouble. On September 18 the suspension of Jay Cooke and Company, likewise overextended in connection with the building of the Northern Pacific Railroad, struck as a thunderclap. Panic flared. Stock prices tumbled. Depositors rushed to convert balances to cash. Restrictions and outright suspensions of cash payments, some of them involving leading banks and investment houses, continued to the month's end.

In the following weeks the *Chronicle* hoped that confidence would quickly return, bringing renewed prosperity. Rapid improvement was natural in a young organism. Lacking as yet the mature perspective of his 1899 editorial, Dana was optimistic, because this was a youthful country. Prosperity, he predicted, would come, if slowly, "after confidence has been restored." Past failures would be a pedestal for future achievement. Nevertheless, the situation was risky. There was insistent popular and political agitation for government action to inflate the money supply, which struck fear into conservative owners of capital. The "destruction of capital" resulting from failures had surely crippled firms. The outlook could have been more promising "if we had not the daily reports from various quarters of diminishing employment for labor," light contracting for trade, and indications of "prudence in buyers . . . in taking on new liabilities."[15]

Depression ground on for six long years, until a coincidence of short crops in Europe and large ones here stimulated recovery. During this time William Dana repeatedly mused on the sources and nature of commercial downturns. At the beginning of 1874 he somberly intoned that there would be "many less failures in the world" if more people would "allow themselves to remember long" the lessons that experience could teach. Immediately after a panic everyone appeared resolved to start on a new basis, depending less than before on borrowing to finance their ventures. "Overtrading, as it is called," had always existed, and there were already signs that it was resuming. Adventurers were disregarding the fact that "pretty much the same epitaph can be written above each business prostration— here lies the result of an attempt to do too much with too little capital." History would probably repeat itself. There seemed always to be available "a new crop of victims . . . for the Wall Street whales to swallow," and a large group of investors who appeared "to like the sensation consequent upon going to sea in a bowl. Rudder, compass, and anchor are words suggesting constraint, and therefore too confining for such spirits."[16]

A year into the slump Dana published an editorial on the causes and character of business crises. Praising a recent speaker before the New York Chamber of Commerce who had reiterated his own largely correct ideas, he expanded on some earlier writing. The debacle of 1873 had resulted from investing too much too quickly, with too great a reliance on credit, to build railroads to open the West for development. Economic science taught that there were three kinds of business panics. They had to be distinguished if they were to be considered intelligently. While qualitatively different, each could affect other aspects of business. The first was a currency panic. One of these struck in 1857. It left parts of the country without a currency system and paralyzed what was left. The second was a credit panic, such as occurred in England in 1866 after a leading financial institution failed. Capital and currency were abundant, but credit, which moved them, vanished. Without it the banking system, which operated like a machine to move capital around, lacked the essential motive power. The third sort of panic was a capital panic, which was what had struck the United States in 1873. It was simpler than the other two and easier than they were to remedy. Likening the financial system to a living organism, the article contended that a "malady whose centre is in one vital organ seldom fails by sympathy to reach other centres; without, however, losing its distinctive character or its specific systems." This fact was particularly notable in capital panics. The cure for this sort of downturn was easier than for the others because the excessive expenditure of capital that prompted it contained its own antidote. The public works upon which that capital had been spent would "with few exceptions" in time "produce all that they cost and more." They would give market value to worthless land and open it to production.

The only remaining question, then, was how to keep banks strong enough to meet demands of incipient panics when these appeared. The sole way to keep banks strong was to follow "the good old rule of rejecting bad business and keeping large reserves. If our banks last year had refused to lend on unbankable securities there would have been no panic." If they had complied with the warnings of the *Chronicle* and many other publications during the months when kindling and fuel for the conflagration were being piled up, it might have been averted. So, too, future financial fireworks.[17]

Dana's reflections extended into the succeeding months and years. On October 10, 1874, while the usual harvest shipping season's tight credit ruled, he explained current business failures in part in terms of debts left over from the panic. He also observed that as many as a third of the failures involved "speculations outside of the legitimate business of the insolvents." Had these adhered to the maxim that one's capital was nowhere so valuable as in one's own business, they might have averted insolvency. Tellingly, he rejected what he termed as cynical the view that contemporary commercial troubles were "a normal 'struggle for existence' ending in the 'survival of the fittest.' " Unwilling, yet, to embrace Social Darwinism, he continued. "Leaving this fashionable philosophy . . . to spin its shining web and to apply its specious theories where it can, we agree with it so far as this," that the depression was not without the promise of adequate recompense to the country. Experience taught sternly, but well.

This last point received elaboration in an editorial describing prosperity as the pleasantest companion and adversity as the best teacher. Persisting commercial prostration carried important lessons in political economy. One was that Americans when they were prosperous had been prodigal. They erected insubstantial buildings, then pulled them down. They wasted vast quantities of food. They lacked the thrift of the Germans and the capacity of the French for clever manipulation. The country had been, "as the saying goes, smothering in its own grease." Given as much, hard times were a blessing, forcing everyone toward greater economy and efficiency. The lesson of prudence and economy came at just the right time, for the country had probably reached the close of the era of development by geometrical progression. Henceforth, growth would be slower. It would therefore call for more steady, substantial building. Then, if we must continue at intervals to "stumble industrially," the intervals would lengthen and the falls would become gentler. In the opening era, wealth generated by steadiness and thrift would serve much better than wealth that could be had for the stooping.[18]

As late as 1878, our editor was still drawing lessons from the downturn. He had, in particular, resumed emphasis on the role of a lack of confidence in prompting and prolonging it. The decade's growing clamor against banks and capitalists, and for monetary inflation and ideas that many deemed socialistic, had led investors to withdraw their capital to "hiding places" until they could foresee an outcome.[19]

Commercial instability in the 1880s, with a moderate recession during the period 1882–1886, drove Dana repeatedly to take up his editorial pen and attempt to explain what had gone wrong. In doing so he left evidence that affords us a better grasp of his conception of business cycles.

As formerly, uncertainty and lack of confidence played key roles. The *Chronicle* pointed to several sources of apprehension during the early 1880s. One was the country's monetary policy. The Bland-Allison Act of 1878 required the Treasury to buy and coin between $2 million and $4 million in silver each month. It always purchased the minimum, but the result (with silver selling at a discount) was to coin yearly more than $24 million of silver dollars whose value by weight was less than their face value. When a trade recession lessened the demand for money, banks held on to their gold and paid the Treasury in currency or silver. The onset of gold exports on February 16, 1884 and the Treasury's announcement a week later that declining gold receipts might force the government to pay in silver were major blows to confidence, wrote Dana.

The National Banking Acts of 1863 and 1864 added further complications. Certain features, treated more fully in Chapter 6, of the banking system that the laws created, allowed smaller federally chartered banks to deposit a portion of their required reserves in banks in designated central reserve cities. Demand naturally drew a great proportion of these reserves to institutions in the country's financial center, New York City, where they drew interest. If these deposits exceeded the normal needs of commerce, reserve banks sometimes invested them speculatively. As long as confidence ruled, the system worked reasonably well. If confidence weakened and country banks suddenly recalled their reserves, reserve city banks that had invested them could be caught short, and fail, provoking a spread of distrust, runs, failures, and depression. In May 1884 all of these ingredients were present. And there was an additional problem in the banking system, with revelations of dishonesty among bankers. The Second National Bank of New York fell on May 8 because its president had stolen $3 million. The run that followed on May 9 began a general panic, precipitating a wave of failures. As Dana reviewed the wreckage some months later, he commented that the "May panic was virtually a moral panic, not strictly a financial one, and breaches of trust have become almost a daily development since that occurrence." Already suspicious, the public when confronted with "revelations of bank defalcations, deficiencies and rascality" lost "the last vestige of confidence" and succumbed to "unreasoning fear."[20]

Dana identified the remaining major deterrent to prosperity during the mid-1880s as the tariff that Congress had enacted on March 3, 1883. Although it had reduced rates, it retained too much of the protectionist principle. Excessive protection, he believed, fostered artificially high prices. These induced domestic manufacturers to rush into business. Manufacturing output soared. High prices brought high profits and increases in wages and other costs of operation. Industry reached a stage at which production overtook or even outran consumption, while high domestic prices to a degree allowed foreign goods to compete. As markets became congested with goods, producers struggled vainly to maintain prices, output, and profits. A downturn inevitably followed until the normal state (equilibrium) was restored. The weakest firms were forced temporarily or permanently from the field. Such a "never-ending but quickly revolving circle" prevailed in every commercial country. But too protective a tariff made the cycles brief, more sudden, because of its perturbing effects.[21]

The following decade contained mild recessions during the periods 1887–1888 and 1890–1891, and a catastrophic depression, during the period 1893–1898. How Dana explained them further extends our understanding of his conception of business cycles. To a growing degree he found the fiscal circumstances and practices of the federal government to be the most important source of uncertainty and distrust among business interests. His editorial comments reflected a shift in focus, but fidelity to the economic precepts that were central to this thinking.

Among disturbing influences were recurring federal surpluses during the years 1867–1893. These accumulated in the Treasury removing money from circulation. When Congress failed to reduce taxes sufficiently, the Treasury turned to premature retirement of bonds in order to expand currency available for commercial use. To some degree this effort was negated by a legal requirement of the national banking system. Banknote issues had to be secured by deposit in the Treasury as a reserve against note issues of U.S. bonds equal in value to 90 percent of the face value of notes issued. Retirement of bonds forced retirement of notes. Ingenious congressmen found other ways—not all of them reassuring—to get the accumulating surplus back into circulation. In 1887 and 1890 they passed two successive Dependent Pension Acts for Civil War veterans. For the first time these based pensions on service alone, rather than service-related disabilities. The latter extended the benefit to certain widows and dependent children and parents. Yearly pension expenditures shot up from $56 million in 1888 to $135 million in 1895. The McKinley Tariff of 1890 assaulted the surplus by placing sugar, a major revenue source, on the free list, while raising duties on most goods to 57 percent. Such high rates discouraged imports, further reducing customs receipts.

Chapter 6 will treat monetary issues at length, but some discussion will be helpful here. The year 1890 also brought the Sherman Silver Purchase Act. The new law required the Treasury to purchase 4.5 million ounces of silver monthly, the nation's current output. It was to coin the silver as standard silver dollars and issue against these certificates redeemable at its option in gold or silver. The net effect of the act was less than proponents of silver inflation hoped. The money supply grew about 3.5 percent from 1889 to 1890, enough to meet commercial needs. As noted, Treasury repurchase of bonds prevented a greater increase.

One further feature of the monetary system needs mention. An 1875 law required that beginning on January 1, 1879 the Treasury redeem in specie the $356 million of Civil War legal tender notes (greenbacks) whenever holders presented them for redemption, and that they be maintained at par with gold. The Sherman law placed a new burden on the Treasury reserve, as it was required to maintain the 1890 notes at par with gold. This obligation reinforced the preference of note holders to be paid in specie. An earlier, 1882, law completed the scene. It authorized the circulation of up to $100 million in a new currency: gold certificates. Whatever amount was actually issued had to be backed 100 percent by a gold reserve. Given these circumstances, the business community by the end of the 1880s came to regard $100 million as the minimum needed to ensure the government's ability to pay in gold. Potential for a financial hurricane lurked in the unstable, partly contradictory mixture just described. If enough people came to fear that the Treasury might be forced to abandon gold payments, or that there was an increased danger of this eventuality, a small tropical breeze might quickly build into a storm of devastating violence.[22]

Dana's paper recorded these events, and the course of commerce, warily. It noted that even during the more prosperous period of 1889 and 1891–1892 trade fell below expectations. A deep depression in Europe, with resulting foreign sell-offs of American securities, did not go unnoted. Neither did declining European trust in the ability of the U.S. government to continue payments in gold. The suspension of the great London banking house, Baring and Brothers, in November 1890 prompted only a momentary panic on this side of the Atlantic. But as late as January 1893, Dana observed of the year just closed that the country had "been in the midst of prosperous conditions . . . without achieving prosperity." While many avenues of commerce, including falling railroad investment and earnings, reduced exports of produce and a substantial outflow of gold to Europe were discouraging, he still hopefully claimed that business displayed many "decidedly encouraging" signs for 1893.[23]

By February, the *Chronicle*'s editor was less confident. Citing annual meetings of several of the so-called "industrial companies," he offered some stern warnings. Each year the reports of these entities were becoming "more meagre and more entirely useless." Insiders were making immense profits by working the stocks of many of these firms. Worse, some were rashly financed, and others were endangering themselves through unsuccessful attempts to corner markets. Caught with large inventories of coal and a weak market after the collapse of an anthracite combination, the Philadelphia & Reading Railroad failed on February 20. A brief financial disturbance followed. On May 4 the gathering storm finally struck, with the announcement that one of the strongest industrial firms, the National Cordage Company, had entered receivership for want of credit. A selling wave inundated the stock market. Credit disappeared. Banks washed away like sand castles in a rising tide as depositors rushed to obtain cash during the months of May and June. When banks restricted cash withdrawals, currency went to a premium. The eye of the storm brought two weeks of deceptive calm as July opened. Mid-month, the backside of the tempest struck, bringing another fall in values and rush of failures. Responsibility for the calamitous loss of confidence, upon which the *Chronicle* placed responsibility for the crash, lay specifically and solely with the operation of the silver purchase act and uncertainty about the continuing safety of the country's monetary system.

In a representative editorial written after the House of Representatives in late August voted to repeal the Sherman Act, Dana exclaimed, "if the cause of the lack of confidence . . . be removed . . . if the Senate passes an unconditional repeal measure within two weeks and Congress adjourns for one or two months," the resilience of the American people would restore normal conditions in short order. He returned to this theme time after time over the next three years, until William Jennings Bryan failed in his 1896 bid for the presidency on a silver free-coinage platform. On one occasion he sympathetically reported an interview with a leading manufacturer who said that foreign and domestic capital had become equally alarmed. Capital had "run into a hole and will not come forth to embark on enterprises which create prosperity until it is established that the American people borrowing in gold" would repay a dollar of equal value.[24] In the meantime, the mass of industrial ruin wrought in 1893 had apparently erased Dana's earlier reservations about Social Darwinism. In the midst of the turbulent events of that May, he editorialized that the argument of the president of the American Iron and Steel Association for a protective tariff was "more ingenious than convincing." But he agreed that "the law of the survival of the fittest is inexorable and merciless."[25]

It was the expanded interventionist and regulatory tendencies of the federal government during the presidency of Theodore Roosevelt that impelled Dana to craft his fullest exposition of the crucial role of confidence.

Commenting on the financial panic of October 1907 and the near failure of the Tennessee Coal & Iron Company, he placed the blame squarely on the government. The panic of the season was at its core an instance of "capital on the run—at its wit's end to find a place where it could be out of the reach of the confiscatory action of the Administration." Would it be safe in stockings? That was apparently the only choice. "Little and big deposits—those in savings banks where the widow's mite" found lodging, as well as those in "our largest financial institutions" all sought some place of "concealment."[26]

Fittingly, a lengthy piece on currency reform written in 1908 brings discussion in this chapter full circle, uniting all of its themes. Banks and business, wrote the *Chronicle*'s editor, were so interwoven that legislation directed at one must also look out for the other. Legislation that crippled one would cripple both. The role that banks played was so focal that these institutions must be made to serve business, and "paper representatives" of business, whether currency, checks, or securities, must be good for their declared values.

It is all right to demand on the part of man-made law that the corporation shall do this and that, but unless the demand is in accord with the life of the institution according to the natural law of service, there will be no good effect follow the law. To do this is a vast undertaking. It means that the natural laws of business are coming to be known as stronger than any laws that Congress can make. These natural laws cannot be evaded. The others can. The natural law acts instantly though it may not be observed for years. The other law often serves as a shield to hide behind.

We are beginning to understand these principles. You may hammer a business to death by your inconsiderate talk, but when you cure one evil this way you make another far more harmful. Men are now talking of confidence. . . . Confidence in the ability and honor of men, confidence that business is for service as well as profit, confidence in the continued tireless activity of those who plan and toil, confidence in the right of man to own that which he can honestly acquire in the vast marts of the world, that which fate sends him in the mine, that which his own unaided genius brings into existence in the discovery and control of natural laws. . . . It is all right to punish those who disobey the laws of the land. But they will meet their doom sooner or later under the operation of the natural law, which is as fixed as the laws of planetary motion, and business must wait on this. If there is watered stock, if there is the buyer who is willing to take his chances as a non-participating stockholder in something he does not understand and cannot control, then there will be personal loss to the end of time. But it is better that these few suffer in the natural way than that all others suffer by reason thereof. Business makes its own laws, founded on right and justice, as it is interwoven with the powers and destiny of man. And there is no other salvation. This is the end. The banker and the businessman are woven together by the coils of a fate that lies in the constitution of things—helping and harming each other, as the case may be.[27]

From the perspective of a century, it is easy to view Dana's ideas about human nature, natural law, and business cycles and their causes as quaint, old-fashioned, and obsolete. This is true, with few exceptions, for persons at either end of the spectrum of mainstream American political and economic opinion. Yet, inspection suggests that we may not have come quite so far after all. The new monetarists, of whom Milton Friedman has been most prominent, have rediscovered that there is a connection between the volume and velocity of money in circulation, interest rates, and the pace of business growth and activity. The institutional economists, preoccupied with tracking measures of business activity and classifying them as leading, synchronous, or lagging indicators, likewise continue to pursue the Holy Grail of predicting the future course of business. Both monetarists and institutionalists incorporate into their ideas deterministic elements that are not entirely unlike the determinism inherent in the equilibrating mechanism of competition in classical theory. Both have replaced references to human nature with discussion of individual and aggregate behavior. Both aspire to moderate, if not eliminate, business cycles. Our self-styled political conservatives, meanwhile, lavish praise on free markets (which, of course, include tax and other advantages for wealthy interests). Even the few remaining vocal advocates of liberalism too often substitute ideology for thought.

Our national conversation about economic history and policy, such as it is, tends then to traffic in "thought-bites." For example, since 1941, Thomas Cochran and William Miller's famous remarks in *The Age of Enterprise: A Social History of Industrial America* have acted largely as received wisdom.

In the nineteenth century, depressions were viewed simply as the results of errors of judgment that would not be repeated. They were regarded merely as periods of penance for economic sins, and recovery was expected as soon as rituals of liquidation and reorganization could be performed. Thus, instead of destroying hope, depressions paid dividends for faith. They presented opportunities.[28]

In fact, for Dana they were morality plays and more. They should have been, since Political Economy originated as a branch of Moral Philosophy. Given the unlikelihood of change in human nature, he doubted that we would escape business cycles in the future. He was also aware of the range of extrinsic and intrinsic influences on business conditions. Meanwhile, leading economists of our time, whether monetarists or institutionalists, still include in their theories deterministic elements such as the role from the 1870s through the 1890s of contemporary ideas about money. These inescapably involved some plan to repay debts with an honest currency. Such talk centered on morality. Modern scholars likewise write, as did Dana and his peers, of "the job of cleaning out firms which needed to be reorganized or liquidated," and of the pursuit of Treasury policies whose effect was to "enforce the monetary contraction that was necessary to produce a balance of payments permitting the export of capital."[29] Turning to the depression of 1893, and granting the possibility of wishful blaming, they concede that fear was a potent determinant of behavior. Milton Friedman and Anna Jacobson Schwartz wrote that the entire silver episode was a "fascinating example of how important what people think about money can sometimes be. The fear that silver would force an inflation sufficient to force the United States off the gold standard made it necessary to have a severe deflation in order to stay on the gold standard." Institutionalist Rendigs Fels in his superb study, *American Business Cycles, 1865–1897* (1959), after weighing all the endogenous factors, concluded that "the real villain" was the "silver problem, without which the contraction of 1896 would have been mild and that of 1893–94 little worse than 1882–1885."[30]

It is even more interesting to relate Dana's ideas to those elaborated in John Maynard Keynes's *The General Theory of Employment, Interest, and Money*, published in the middle of the Great Depression of the 1930s. Classical economics allowed for persistent, widespread unemployment only when labor refused to accept low wages offered to it as a response to reduced demand. Keynes looked at the real world and concluded that it did not comply with the laws of supply and demand in all cases. There could be an equilibrium between supply and demand that would tend to leave a large reservoir of able and willing persons who were *involuntarily* without work. Where large involuntary unemployment existed, cuts in both interest rates and wages could stir increases in investment. But not increases sufficiently large to eliminate redundancy in the labor supply.

If too high a wage level, or the wrongheadedness of labor in refusing lower wages, were not causes of persistent unemployment, what was? The fact, not fully explored in classical theory, that every transaction involved two elements pointed Keynes toward the answer. The recipient received the sum the payer expended. Income flowed in a circle through the economic system. Any shrinkage in general demand must therefore result in a shrinkage in the flow of income. One must then discover who was holding money out of the flow, and why. Obviously, it was not those who were spending. Keynes knew that savers and investors were not always the same people. Some savings flowed into insurance, savings banks, or the like, to remain quiescent until someone activated them for investment or consumption. Downward or upward swings in the stream of aggregate income resulted from withholding more or less money from consumption than was being invested. Turning earlier writers on their heads, Keynes argued that interest rates did not determine investment. Instead, the reverse was true. Further, the "expectations" or "anticipations" (which might not always be rational) of enterprisers chiefly governed their investment decisions. Finally, at all levels of activity an economy was in equilibrium if *intended* savings equaled *intended* investment.

Knowledge of classical theory led Dana to appreciate the roles of consumption, savings, and investment. Practical experience and direct observation taught him, too, that contrary to classical economics, investment did not always equal savings. The reason was found in the expectations of businessmen, for which he employed terms such as "confidence," "lack of confidence," or "uncertainty." He did not press these ideas to their full implications. These awaited discovery by Keynes, as we shall see later. Nevertheless, it is reasonable to suggest that at least in his case a revision of the stereotypical interpretation of late-nineteenth-century business thought is in order. There were in his ideas elements that pointed toward the future, just as there are elements alive now that connect us to the past. We presently maintain a "consumer confidence index." Stock market analysts daily examine entrails in attempts to read the minds of investors and fathom the future. And we still contend with the havoc wrought by financial misconduct of plutocrats. We yet confront shameless theft such as that which shared responsibility for the savings and loan crisis of the 1980s. We learn of insider trading in junk bonds. We witness the looting-by-dismemberment of corporations seized through leveraged buyouts during the following years. The difference is that with a weakened moral sense and an emasculated capacity for indignation we reward such conduct with praise for the culprits for their cleverness or, at worst, with light slaps on the wrist. There is just enough remediation to reassure the unwashed masses that all is well.

William Dana was a transitional figure, grappling with emerging economic realities. In doing so he expressed considerably more subtle and sophisticated views about human beings, and the workings of the economy and business, than we often associate with business spokesmen of his era. Retaining a deeply ingrained ethical sense as a journalist and advocate, he emerges also as a social thinker of consequence.

NOTES

1. The standard reference for newspapers is still Frank Luther Mott, *A History of Newspapers in the United States through 260 Years, 1690–1950*, rev. ed. (New York: Macmillan, 1950). Also useful for context are Bernard A. Weisberger, *The American Newspaperman* (Chicago: University of Chicago Press, 1961); Daniel J. Boorstin, *The Americans: The Democratic Experience* (New York: Vintage Books, 1974), 371ff, 402–404, 659–660; Father Walter J. Ong, *Orality and Literacy: The Technologizing of the Word* (New York: Methuen, 1982); Robert A. White, "Mass Communication and Culture: Transition to a New Paradigm," *Journal of Communication* 33 (Summer 1983), 279–301; Janet E. Steele, "The 19th Century *World* versus the *Sun*: Promoting Consumption (Rather than the Working Man)," *Jour-*

nalism Quarterly 67 (Autumn, 1990): 592–600; Janet Steele, *The Sun Shines for All* (Syracuse, NY: Syracuse University Press, 1993); and the subtle and sophisticated argument that appears in Sally Griffith Foreman, *Home Town News: William Allen White and the Emporia Gazette* (New York: Oxford University Press, 1989), 1–3 and passim.

2. Frederick Rudolph, *The American College and University: A History* (New York: Vintage Books, 1965), and *Curriculum: A History of the American Undergraduate Course of Study Since 1636* (Chicago: University of Chicago Press, 1978). See also Francis W. Gregory and Irene D. Neu, "The American Industrial Elite in the 1870s: *Their Social Origins*"; William Miller, "American Historians and the Business Elite"; and William Miller, "The Recruitment of the American Business Elite"; *Men in Business: Essays on the Historical Role of the Entrepreneur*, ed. William Miller (New York: Harper & Row, 1962), respectively 193–211, 309–328, 329–338.

3. *Commercial and Financial Chronicle*, June 14, 1873. For Wayland, unsigned article, "The Strikes . . . ," *Hunt's Merchants' Magazine* 55 (July 1866): 63–65.

4. *Commercial and Financial Chronicle*, January 17, 1903.

5. *Commercial and Financial Chronicle*, July 5, 1902 and August 4, 1906; December 4, 1909; July 5, 1902; January 10, 1903; October 26, 1889; and October 9, 1886; "The Strikes . . . ," *Hunt's Merchants' Magazine* 55 (July, 1866): 63–65.

6. *Commercial and Financial Chronicle*, March 15, 1873.

7. *Commercial and Financial Chronicle*, April 2, 1898.

8. *Commercial and Financial Chronicle*, April 18, 1874. Adam Smith, *An Inquiry into the Causes and Nature of the Wealth of Nations*. With a new Preface by George J. Stigler (Chicago: University of Chicago Press, 1976). Dana knew Smith through direct study, as well as through Francis Wayland, *Elements of Political Economy* (Boston: Gould and Lincoln, 1860). He was also aware of Smith's 1759 *Theory of Moral Sentiments*; and from Wayland he may have learned that no later than 1759 Smith had crafted a series of lectures on jurisprudence that formed the heart of the *Wealth of Nations*.

9. *Commercial and Financial Chronicle*, September 5, 1908. See Chapters 1 and 2 for more on religious views. Key references for the nineteenth-century idea of Progress include Arthur Alphonse Ekirch, Jr., *The Idea of Progress in America, 1815–1860* (New York: Columbia University Press, 1944); Stow Persons, *American Minds: A History of Ideas* (New York: Henry Holt and Company, 1958), esp. 153–162, 163–250; Sydney E. Ahlstrom's massive, *A Religious History of the American People* (New Haven, CT: Yale University Press, 1972), esp. 429–895; and Martin E. Marty, *Pilgrims in Their Own Land: 500 Years of Religion in America* (Boston: Little, Brown and Company, 1984), esp. 271ff.

10. *Commercial and Financial Chronicle*, April 11, 1908, July 28, 1888. Conservatism: Clinton Rossiter, *Conservatism in America: The Thankless Persuasion*, 2d ed., rev. (New York: Random House, 1962), esp. 128–163; and James MacGregor Burns, *Roosevelt: The Lion and the Fox* (New York: Harvest Books, 1962), 234–241. Burns's characterization of conservative opposition to Franklin Delano Roosevelt as little more than a rationalization for greed seems as apt now as it was when he wrote it. For Dana's use of the term "class," see *Commercial and Financial Chronicle*, May 5, 1888 and January 17, 1903. Perspective: Josep Pieper, *Leisure: The Basis of Culture*, trans. Alexander Dru (New York: A Mentor Book,

1963); and Dana Gioia, *Can Poetry Matter? Essays on Poetry and American Culture* (St. Paul, MN: Graywolf Press, 1992).

11. *Commercial and Financial Chronicle*, May 8, 1886.

12. *Commercial and Financial Chronicle*, September 16, 1899; August 18, 1900; September 11, 1909; October 17, 1900; and May 8, 1886. Limitations of space permit only a brief introduction to the vast literature bearing on the "Gospel of Wealth." Clinton Rossiter in *Conservatism in America* offers a still-useful introduction to the "Gospel of Wealth," which took its name from Andrew Carnegie, "Wealth," *North American Review* 168 (June 1889): 654ff. Also useful, Moses Rischin, ed., *The American Gospel of Success: Individualism and Beyond* (Chicago: Quadrangle Books, 1965); Edward Chase Kirkland, *Dream and Thought in the Business Community*, 1880–1890, (Ithaca, NY: Cornell University Press, 1956), 27; H. Wayne Morgan, "An Age in Need of Reassessment," and John Tipple, "The Robber Baron in the Gilded Age: *Entrepreneur or Iconoclast?*" both in *The Gilded Age: A Reappraisal*, ed. H. Wayne Morgan (Syracuse, NY: Syracuse University Press, 1963), respectively 1–13 and 14–37. See also Lewis Atherton, *Main Street on the Middle Border* (Bloomington: Indiana University Press, 1954); Irvin G. Wyllie, *The Self-Made Man in America* (New Brunswick, NJ: Rutgers University Press, 1954); and for the biblical quotations, see Matthew 19:21, 19:24, *Revised English Bible* (Oxford: Oxford University Press, 1989). For recent works that bear on the influence of the "Gospel of Wealth" and stand out among more relevant biographies, see Ron Chernow, *Titan: The Life of John D. Rockefeller Sr.* (New York: Random House, 1998), 561ff and Bibliography; and Joseph Frazier Wall, *Andrew Carnegie* (New York: Oxford University Press, 1974).

13. *Commercial and Financial Chronicle*, October 11, 1873; January 2, 1882; December 8, 1888; January 2, 1892; December 20, 1902; and February 25, 1905. It is interesting to note that Dana in his view of equilibrium and the importance of demand, hence consumption, was far closer to Adam Smith than he was to his teacher Francis Wayland. See Smith, *The Wealth of Nations*, I:17–14; and Wayland, *Elements of Political Economy*, 154–187. For Smith, the social benefits of the free market were *unintended* results of an *intentional* pursuit of individual gain, but that fact in no way diminished their importance. For equilibrium, implied in the operation of supply and demand, see *Wealth of Nations*, I: 271.

14. *Commercial and Financial Chronicle*, June 3, 1899.

15. *Commercial and Financial Chronicle*, September 13–October 15, 1873, quoted September 13 and October 4, 25.

16. *Commercial and Financial Chronicle*, January 24, 1874. Useful studies of the depression of the 1870s include Rendigs Fels, *American Business Cycles, 1865–1897* (Chapel Hill: University of North Carolina Press, 1959), 83–112; Samuel S. Rezneck, "Distress, Relief, and Discontent in the United States during the Depression of 1873–1878," *Journal of Political Economy* 38 (December 1950): 494–512; Edward Chase Kirkland, *Industry Comes of Age: Business, Labor, and Public Policy, 1860–1897* (New York: Holt, Rinehart and Winston, 1961); Milton Friedman and Anna Jacobson Schwartz, *A Monetary History of the United States, 1867–1960* (Princeton, NJ: Princeton University Press, 1963), 15–88. There are also scattered, but still-useful, passages in Thomas Cochran and William Miller, *The Age of Enterprise: A Social History of Industrial America*, rev. ed. (New York: Harper and Brothers, 1961), 142, 143, and passim.

17. *Commercial and Financial Chronicle*, October 3, 1874.

18. *Commercial and Financial Chronicle*, July 22, 1876.

19. *Commercial and Financial Chronicle*, August 31, 1878.

20. *Commercial and Financial Chronicle*, May 31, quoted August 16, 1884. Brief but incisive treatments of the contractions of the 1880s are in Fels, *American Business Cycles*, 128–178; Friedman and Schwartz, *A Monetary History*, 99–102; Oliver Mitchell Wentworth Sprague, *History of Crises under the National Banking System*, (Washington, DC: Government Printing Office, 1910), 109; Samuel S. Rezneck, "Patterns of Thought and Action in an American Depression, 1882–1886," *The American Historical Review* 61 (January 1956): 284–307.

21. *Commercial and Financial Chronicle*, February 13, 1883.

22. For summaries of these events see Fels, *American Business Cycles*, 159–219; Friedman and Schwartz, *A Monetary History*, 101–151; Davis Rich Dewey, *Financial History of the United States* (New York: Longmans, Green, 1903), 443ff; and Douglas Steeples and David O. Whitten, *Democracy in Desperation: The Depression of 1893* (Westport, CT: Greenwood, 1998). For more on the Sherman law see Friedman and Schwartz, *A Monetary History*, 106–33; Fels, *American Business Cycles*, 165–204. The Resumption Act passed on January 14, 1875.

23. *Commercial and Financial Chronicle*, January 7, 1893; Steeples and Whitten, *Democracy in Desperation*, 1–21; Fels, *American Business Cycles*, 155–192.

24. *Commercial and Financial Chronicle*, May 23, 1896.

25. *Commercial and Financial Chronicle*, May 13, 1893.

26. *Commercial and Financial Chronicle*, October 19 and 26 and November 7, 1907; January 4, 11, 18; and November 2, 1908. Election of 1908: July 25–October 24, 1908. Crisis of 1907: Friedman and Schwartz, *A Monetary History*, 156–168; William H. Harbaugh, *The Life and Times of Theodore Roosevelt*, new rev. ed. (New York: Oxford University Press, 1975), 295–300; Robert H. Wiebe, "House of Morgan and the Executive, 1905–1913," *American Historical Review* 65 (October 1959): 49–60; Robert H. Wiebe, "Business Disunity and the Progressive Movement, 1901–1914," *Mississippi Valley Historical Review* 44 (March 1958): 664–685; George W. Stocking, *Base Point Pricing and Regional Development: A Case Study of the Iron and Steel Industry* (Chapel Hill: University of North Carolina Press, 1954); Frederick Lewis Allen, *The Great Pierpont Morgan* (New York: Bantam Books, 1956), 203–207; Ron Chernow, *Titan* (New York: Random House, 1998), 542–545; Ron Chernow, *The House of Morgan: An American Banking Dynasty and the Rise of Modern Finance* (New York: Simon and Schuster, 1990), 121–130; Jean Morgan Strouse, *Morgan: American Financier* (New York: Random House, 1999), 573–596.

27. *Commercial and Financial Chronicle*, January 28, 1908.

28. 1961 Reprint (New York: Harper and Brothers), 137.

29. Quotations from Fels, *American Business Cycles* 190; Friedman and Schwartz, *A Monetary History*, 128.

30. Quotations from 133–134 and 218. Contraction of 1893: Charles Hoffmann, *The Depression of the Nineties: An Economic History* (Westport, CT: Greenwood, 1970); Charles Hoffman, "The Depression of the Nineties," *Journal of Economic History* 16 (June 1956): 137–164; Samuel S. Rezneck, "Unemployment, Unrest, and Relief in the United States during the Depression of 1893–1897," *Journal of Political Economy* 61 (August 1953): 324–345. Panics of 1873 and 1907: Fels, *American Business Cycles*, 98–102; Friedman and Schwartz, *A Monetary History*, 156ff.

4

Labor and Its Fruits

It may be questioned whether in the existing state of society any method can be devised for doing away with labor disturbances.
                                                —William Buck Dana, October 17, 1894

The rise of an industrialized economy posed insistent challenges during the years that William Dana edited and published the *Commercial and Financial Chronicle*. Many of these tested his convictions and his mental powers to the limit. While others commanded greater attention, what contemporaries termed the "labor question" easily ranked among the most difficult.

Alternating cycles of prosperity and depression generated wide swings in the demand of employers for labor. When a business contraction prompted layoffs and pay cuts, frustrated, angry, and suffering wage earners tended to fight back with the only weapon that they possessed: the strike. Occasionally, they persuaded workers in other lines or trades, or sister businesses in their own venue, to boycott products of employers with whom they were locked in combat. Laborers were also aware that a return of prosperity contained opportunities. Good times meant a greater demand for workers. This demand could incite labor unions to walk out as a means of forcing a restoration of wages to former levels.

Employers for their part naturally resisted. They regarded setting the terms of work as an inherent right of management. They could and did combat strikes and boycotts. They locked out known union leaders and members, replacing them with unorganized workingmen as they might wish. They blacklisted union leaders and strikers, circulating names of offenders to other employers to ensure that those listed got no new jobs in their industry. Where they could, they sought the protection of the courts.

Initially, they claimed that strikes or boycotts were illegal combinations of labor to stop work and thus injure property. The ancient common law of conspiracy, they argued, forbade such combinations. The Sherman Anti-Trust Act provided an additional potential weapon, if courts could be persuaded that strikes—especially walkouts hitting bankrupt firms in receivership under court protection—constituted illegal combinations in restraint of interstate commerce.

Complicating the scene was the fact that the growing size and importance of large corporations threatened to turn cherished popular beliefs into fiction. Important currents of opinion held that labor and capital, if gainfully and lawfully employed, shared in a harmony or community of interests. Both worked. Both, pursuing gain, benefited society through the goods and services they produced for consumption. Master and worker had bargained as equals regarding wages and other conditions of employment. Only the morally vicious, the criminal, the mentally defective, and to a degree women and children because of their comparative physical weakness were excluded from this idyllic notion of the workings of the labor market. But now everything was changing. How could a single, independent workingman bargain in any meaningful way when seeking a job, higher wages, shorter hours, or better working conditions from a giant corporation? Was there any room at all left for the notion that employer and employee in a free-market environment were in any sense equals? Did the interests of capital and labor still converge, or amid new conditions had they diverged?

All of these questions, and others, tore at the fabric of society and the nation. All, because of their connection with the flow of commerce, directly affected business conditions. All repeatedly summoned comment from the *Chronicle*. As the emerging order matured, certain of William Dana's attitudes changed and others hardened. His comments, if representative of the views of his readers, may serve as a compass by which to discover something of the course of opinion among the country's most important business leaders.

For the *Chronicle*'s editor the teaching of classical economics that all property and wealth originated in labor was axiomatic. So much so as to be self-evident and rarely worthy of direct comment. He instead usually implied acceptance of the labor theory of value more obliquely, in comments about other subjects. For example, in an 1871 editorial on the eruption of mob action in connection with an anthracite strike in the coal fields around Scranton, Pennsylvania, he expressed hope that the struggle would soon end. The effects of such contests were not limited to their participants. They extended to "the interests of all orders of the community." In explaining how this was so, he appealed to the nineteenth-century American faith that everyone willing to work hard enough might rise to become the owner of a business. The expenditure of effort generated value, and made saving and accumulation of wealth possible on the parts of both wage earners and businessmen. As he developed this argument, it displayed, unintentionally, features that bore a curious resemblance to some of the things that Karl Marx wrote about the effects of business depressions. Strikes hit poorer firms harder than they hit affluent rivals. As a result, "the more opulent establishments" tended "to swallow up the poorer ones." The gap between rich and poor widened. Opportunities for individuals to rise from the ranks of wage earners to those of masters shriveled up. The number of employers shrank; that of employees grew. Finally, successful strikes artificially forced up wages and, thus, the prices of homes and other products where labor costs loomed large. This condition invited foreign enterprise to compete here, posing a further possibility that American laborers might lose their jobs.[1]

As prosperity returned at the end of the 1870s, Dana found occasion to comment on a speech given by reformer Parke Godwin to a Workingmen's Lyceum at New York's Cooper Institute. His remarks premised two prominent themes in nineteenth-century American popular thought on the fundamental belief that all property and values originated in labor. These themes, complementary to one another, were that there was a harmony of interest between capital and labor, and that wage earners through diligent effort could become independent business owners. He conceded that this country resembled the more mature nations of Europe in that it harbored "some really rich men," but comparatively only a few, and these could not be compared to the "bloated" bondholders on the other side of the Atlantic. Few wealthy Americans were "inactive or non-producing." "The man who works with his pen, or keeps busy half a dozen secretaries and twice as many telegraphic operators" was "quite as truly a workingman as he who hammers on the anvil or he who carries the hod." It was the "distinct feature of American life that we have no privileged and no idle classes." Americans were not divided into two classes, "the one offering labor for money, the other offering money for labor. On the contrary, in the great mass of cases, labor and capital are represented in the same person. The man who works is the man who owns." Likewise, the man who owned a bond worked and earned the interest. Americans were all "either now or expecting soon to be, bondholders or landowners." They were as a result as firmly opposed to "riot and revolution" and as firmly resolved to "maintain order and preserve the peace" as any person of wealth in Europe. It was a failure to remember the radical distinction between conditions here and those across the Atlantic that led so many "who ought to know better" to say and do so many foolish things about alleged economic injustice in the United States.[2]

Apparently wage earners in the late 1870s were not too easily persuaded of the truth of Dana's message. Speaking before the American Bankers' Association, he suggested that there was a need to begin a concerted effort to win the American worker over to the view that he shared in a harmony of interest with capital. What was required was to educate industrial wage earners to revitalize their confidence in the idea. There were positive developments to which the *Chronicle*'s editor thought it was possible to turn to help make the case. He discerned in the "action of natural forces a constant improvement going on in the condition of labor" and cited the recent experience of the cotton textile industry to show how this was so. Labor, analysis showed, received six cents a pound in wages for finished cotton cloth. Manufacturers, in contrast, received but one-and-a-half cents per pound in profits. (Dana acknowledged that this amounted to an 8 percent return on invested capital, but refrained from saying whether this was a generous return.) Given the imbalance, on a per-pound basis, between the benefits that labor and capital respectively received, mill owners had constantly to invest and reinvest in order to increase efficiency and the productivity of labor. As they did so, some of the results flowed to workers in the form of higher wages.[3] As we might put it today, a rising tide lifts all ships.

Dana's conviction that common interests united capital and labor, and that these grew out of the creation of value through the efforts of both, persisted for the balance of his life. They were evident through the troubled 1880s, the riotously-violent work stoppages of 1894, and the intractable anthracite strike of 1902, which was finally resolved through the intervention of President Theodore Roosevelt. Recurring strikes sorely tested that conviction and no doubt contributed to a decline in the frequency with which he expressed it. Remarks about a 1902 proposal from Harvard University president Charles William Eliot to reform labor relations indirectly approached the subject through reference to modern business practices. In these comments Dana generally agreed with Eliot that business cycles and their attendant unemployment and labor troubles were the result of bad legislation. He rejected Eliot's suggestion that the remedy lay in enacting remedial laws. There were already too many laws perturbing trade.

Turning to the problem of business depressions, he also denied the Marxian claim that it was "capitalist production" that drove the "periodical rise and fall of trade prosperity, in movements culminating in what we call 'booms' and crises." Instead, in a wonderful *non sequitur*, he blamed the problem on a "phenomenon inherent in the modern economic system [which was, of course, capitalism]. It may be modified; but to remove it would, we fear, require the remodeling of human nature." As long as farmers, manufacturers, merchants, and financiers were led by their hopes "to overdo things in a period of real prosperity, we do not see how alternate periods of reaction can possibly be avoided." The vagaries of weather and unpredictability of harvests and their effects on the capacity of the nation to consume complicated matters further. They constituted influences on demand and opportunities for labor that were beyond human control. It is fair to observe here that if labor was the source of value, and if there was a harmony of interest between labor and capital, Dana's reflections still carried an important qualification. Conditions might not provide *enough* demand for labor fully to employ it and stimulate sufficient consumption to maintain prosperity.[4]

We may turn to a 1907 book review in the *Chronicle* for a final illustration. True to form, Dana agreed wholeheartedly with the author's thesis that while the present industrial system contained some genuine causes for labor discontent, no rival scheme held any real prospect for improvement. Put bluntly, "radical means and radical ends can only work harm and mischief." Moderation was the only prudent course to pursue in attempting to improve conditions for wage earners. It would pay to remember that neither capital nor labor alone was sufficient to bring about prosperity. Each depended on the other. Without an accumulation of capital, humanity would still be living in caves and grubbing up roots. Labor created value, and it added value to capital. It received this added value in the form of wages. But capital was the mother of invention, and capitalists were thus entitled to compensation for their own risk, investment, and effort. "Labor," Dana agreed, "is entitled to such wages as the capitalist, allowing for his risk, can afford to give." A strike was a legitimate means of forcing such a wage, but if labor forced a higher wage it would break a trade. There was every reason to treat labor as a commodity and let the market set its value, since capital was only the fruit of labor accumulated through the operation of the market. After all, the market set the value of all forms of labor—that of capitalists, professionals, artisans, and so on. If there were no demand for this or that sort of labor, the market would set a zero-wage rate. Labor owned the right to organize, but not to monopolize. Monopolies abridged the rightful liberties of all men. Radical antibusiness rhetoric, meanwhile, fostered "class hatred" and created an immense insecurity of property that would stifle enterprise if carried too far. It followed that the safest course was to acquiesce in the present industrial system and work to improve relations between capital and labor in a peaceful manner.[5]

There was nothing new in what appeared in the *Chronicle* about labor as the source of value and property, or the supposed harmony of interests between labor and capital. Dana drew heavily on what he had learned at Yale, from classical economics, his experience, and current popular sentiment.[6] If there was anything notable about what he wrote, it was his tenacity amid changing conditions. That tenacity extended beyond the ideas we have just considered to his more general views regarding strikes and the rights of workingmen. In these cases, greater suppleness of intellect might have served him better. Novel circumstances collided head-on with old beliefs, considered to be truths discovered by economic science, that were hardening into an unyielding ideology. As they did so, they shared in a broader stiffening of opinion within the business community that became an increasingly powerful obstacle to reforms for which the need was growing ever more urgent.

Behind the ideas explored above lay a major change. The half century after the Civil War saw the birth of the country's modern labor movement. It was a difficult delivery by any measure. There is need here for only a brief summary, to provide a context for the remaining key themes in Dana's thought about labor.

The four railway brotherhoods (engineers, firemen, conductors, brakemen) formed in the decade after 1862. Shoemakers replied to mechanization by organizing in 1867, a year behind the advent of a movement for an eight-hour workday. Soon there were thirty national unions with 300,000 members. Depression in the 1870s cut these respectively to nine and 50,000.

Hard times brought unprecedented industrial strife. When police charged a radical labor meeting in Tompkins Square, New York, on January 13, 1874, a riot flared. In fall 1875 striking members of the Ancient Order of Hibernians met defeat in an effort against the Philadelphia & Reading Railroad. Using evidence collected by the Alan Pinkerton Detective Agency, prosecutors won death sentences for ten union leaders convicted of murder, and prison terms for fourteen others. Beginning on July 17, 1877, with a walkout against the Baltimore & Ohio Railroad to protest wage cuts, a general railroad strike spread rapidly to other lines on both sides of the Mississippi River. Riots shook Baltimore, Chicago, and St. Louis. President Rutherford B. Hayes sent federal troops to restore order after the militia failed to do so at Martinsburg, West Virginia, and Pittsburgh, Pennsylvania. In the latter, a mob tore up tracks, burned down shops and the Union Depot, and caused $10 million in damages after twenty-six men were killed in a pitched battle with militiamen.[7]

The Knights of Labor originated in 1878 as a secret industrial order open to wage earners of every sort. An appealing ritual and advocacy of an eight-hour workday, of boycotts and arbitration instead of strikes, of a progressive income tax, and of consumer cooperatives attracted members. Although unsupported by national officers, successful strikes and boycotts by Union Pacific and Southwest System shop men in 1885 and on the Wabash a year later helped spur membership to 700,000 by 1886. Then Jay Gould, owner of the Southwest System, by cutting wages provoked and then crushed a strike (March 1–May 1886). Demoralized by the defeat, K. of L. members defected in masses reducing the organization to a mere remnant.[8]

Meanwhile, on May 4, 1886 police broke up an anarchist meeting at Haymarket Square in Chicago. Afterward, a bomb exploded in their front rank, killing seven and injuring sixty-seven. They opened fire. Casualties in the crowd are unrecorded. The bomb thrower was never identified. Trials ended in August, with seven death sentences and one prison sentence. The incident did much to discredit the labor movement.[9]

At the end of the same year, a group of autonomous unions of craftsmen meeting in Columbus, Ohio, joined as the American Federation of Labor and at once set out to destroy the remaining lodges of the Knights of Labor. By the end of the decade the latter had effectively faded away. Depression in the 1890s hit American Federation of Labor membership hard. The return of prosperity spurred union growth from 265,000 members in 1896 to 1,676,000 in 1904.[10] The ten years beginning with 1892 contained the fiercest battles yet between business and unions. Strikebreakers crushed unionists at the Carnegie Steel Company plant in Homestead, Pennsylvania, in July of that year after the militia intervened to impose order in the wake of a gun battle between strikers and 300 Pinkerton detectives employed to protect two company barges being towed up the Monongahela River. Concurrently, pitched fighting between strikers and substitutes precipitated a proclamation of martial law and the dispatch of federal troops to protect silver mines at Coeur d'Alene, Idaho.[11]

Industrial warfare raged across the country in severely depressed 1894. Cripple Creek, Colorado, silver miners struck for an eight-hour work day in February. The United Mine Workers followed on April 21 with a general strike in the bituminous coalfields, two weeks after coke workers at Connellsville, Pennsylvania, had gone out. Nearly every mine in Colorado, West Virginia, Pennsylvania, Alabama, and the Midwest shut down as 170,000 men left their places. Public opinion inclined to sympathize with labor until violence flared. The effort failed in June, and United Mine Workers membership plummeted 75 percent to 20,000. An April strike against the Great Northern Railroad fared better. As the coalfields calmed, Gogebic, Michigan, iron miners went out for higher pay. St. Louis carpenters walked off their jobs. Omaha packinghouse workers; Patterson, New Jersey, silk weavers; New York shirt makers; New Mexico miners; and New Bedford, Massachusetts, textile workers walked off. Manufacturers in turn locked out 5,000 textile workers in Fall River, Massachusetts.

The industrial army movement was but a short-lived bubble on the surface of this churning maelstrom. In reply to prolonged unemployment, Jacob Sechler Coxey of Massillon, Ohio, adapted earlier ideas to present needs. He proposed that state and local government be empowered to deposit up to $500 million in noninterest-bearing bonds in the Treasury. In return they were to receive $500 million in fiat currency, to be expended on public works. The projects, mostly road building, were to employ all willing workers at $1.50 per eight-hour work day, thus stabilizing wages and hours. Persuaded by Carl Brown, a dreamy California labor agitator, Coxey began on Easter Sunday, March 25, a march of the jobless to Washington, DC to petition Congress to enact his plan. As many as forty ragtag groups of the unemployed from across the country began to advance toward the capital. While they met considerable popular support in the West, their movement struck fear into the propertied interests of the East as some 6,000 men walked, begged for food, and in some instances commandeered trains to aid in their passage. Coxey reached Washington with about 500 footsore companions on April 30 and was arrested the following day for walking on the grass as he attempted to reach the Capitol steps to speak. Troops evicted the rump of his company from Washington in July. Long before then, arrests and summary justice had put the other contingents out of business. Kansas Populist Senator Alfred A. Peffer's bill to enact the Coxey program received a peremptory burial in the upper house of Congress.[12]

The greatest labor upheaval by far was the railroad walkout of June–July. It began when George M. Pullman, owner of the Pullman Palace Car Company, cut wages but refused to reduce rents that his employees had to pay for housing in the company town of Pullman, Illinois. Rebuffed in attempts to gain a measure of justice, the shopworkers asked the American Railway Union, of which they were members, for aid. When no agreement could be reached, the union's response was to refuse to handle Pullman cars. Rather than negotiate or accommodate, the officers of twenty-four railroads constituting the General Managers' Association resolved to crush the union. They ordered that Pullman cars be attached to all trains serving Chicago. American Railway Union members in turn refused to move the trains. By the end of June railroads to the Windy City were paralyzed, with 125,000 men on strike. Pro-business U.S. Attorney General Richard Olney had 3,400 special deputies sworn in to keep the trains running. He believed that the union's action was an illegal conspiracy to restrain commerce between the states and to prevent shipment of the U.S. mail. Although Illinois Governor John Peter Altgeld said that the militia could maintain order, President Grover Cleveland ordered units of the army to Chicago as violence erupted. On July 2, a federal court enjoined the union and its officers from interfering with the movement of mail and interstate shipment of goods. The union's president, Eugene Victor Debs, went to jail for contempt. The combined forces of management and the federal government broke the strike and destroyed the American Railway Union.[13]

The last decade of Dana's life saw another anthracite strike and a nettlesome hatters' boycott at Danbury, Connecticut, both in 1902. The United Mine Workers went out on May 12, when intransigent owners rejected arbitration of a dispute over wages and union recognition. In the fall, with the approach of cold weather, President Theodore Roosevelt acted. Managers and the union agreed on the creation of a mediation commission. The operators, dead set against union recognition, absolutely rejected inclusion of a labor representative. Facing the likelihood of drastic federal action if the strike were not settled before winter arrived, they bowed when Roosevelt appointed E. E. Clark, head of the Brotherhood of Railway Conductors, to the commission as a sociologist. The miners won a 10 percent wage increase but not recognition. They returned to work. The hatters' struggle ended up in the Supreme Court.[14]

William Dana's response to this unhappy history of wrenching struggle as capital and labor attempted to define a workable relationship was mixed. Initially, much of it was moderate in tone. At the end, it did him little credit as a progressive, or even a flexible, social thinker.

In the years immediately after the Civil War, Dana had condemned strikes of ship caulkers and of building tradesmen demanding a reduction from ten- to eight-hour workdays. He likewise disapproved congresses of laborers whose "passion for combination," he wrote, exceeded members' capacity to compel capital to offer more liberal pay. Instead of such confrontational tactics, which opposed industrial harmony, he favored a "spirit of cooperation" such as the medieval guilds had represented. Through these, members together had obtained raw materials and cooperated in production. In an 1868 warning against work stoppages, he noted that they aimed to check industry just when high output was needed to pay the cost of the Civil War.[15]

During Pennsylvania coal strikes in 1872, the *Chronicle*'s editor acknowledged that the men in the pits "ought to earn the full value of their labor," adding the qualification that their "labor is unskilled or nearly so." The miners were overreaching themselves by asserting that low wages were the fault of the operators. Management, they charged, refused to limit production to permit an increase in prices and wages, "because it is to their interest to bring as much coal to the market as possible." The miners' outage, Dana wrote, went beyond the question of wages to hit directly at the chief prerogative of management: the question was whether those who had invested $300 million of capital in the industry would control it. Dana foresaw that only voluntary arbitration could restore peace. Meanwhile, the mines' output, crucial to national well-being, was lost.[16]

Our writer's response to the violent railroad conflicts of 1877 was remarkably balanced for the time. He found fault with both capital and labor. Many railroads were in financial trouble. Too often, though, this was because they were "trying to keep up dividends on watered stock, and in doing so have been grinding down their employees." The real extent of corporate abuses could be ascertained only through careful study when calmer conditions returned, but people who dismissed assertions that labor was suffering genuine hardships were speaking "flippantly." Scanty pay and scarce work were realities, "and we can feel commiseration for the hard case of the men without qualifying condemnation for their riotous actions." The current talk of corporate oppression, even given the reality of suffering, came "down to the inveterate prejudice against corporations. The only injustice a railroad can inflict upon its men is to neglect paying them, and that was not inflicted in the present case; the only thing it owes them is payment for services rendered, but it does not owe them employment." Still, it was already possible to draw some lessons. One was that violent labor struggles "work nothing but harm to those engaged in them." Destruction extended to their towns and their homes. Another was that an "outbreak" such as the rail strikes of 1877, while "deplorable," was "not an unnatural thing in times like the present, when everybody is coming down and everyone engaged in a legitimate occupation feels his income diminished." Fortunately, frenzied outbursts were short-lived. Even in Pittsburgh, Pennsylvania, peace would have been restored quickly if the authorities had delayed action until sufficient force was available.[17] Weeks later, the *Chronicle* returned to the theme of voluntary arbitration as the optimal way to resolve industrial strife.[18]

William Dana's response to strikes remained moderate, if pro-business, into the depression of the 1880s. Writing of contests that broke out in July 1881, he conceded that wage earners then confronted high prices for life's necessities, especially food. Unfortunately, labor rarely saved, even in good times. Now, a bountiful harvest promised to bring food prices down. But business growth appeared to be slowing. While railroad construction continued, it centered on completion of projects already begun. Manufacturers were looking to cut production. Imports were lagging. The country had "overtraded," and an adjustment loomed. The present, then, was "plainly no time for raising wages." Adding to costs would prolong recovery from the developing contraction. At the moment the "common interest" of labor and capital was "in preventing the check on enterprise which enterprise is suffering under from becoming worse."[19]

As business worsened, Dana's editorials sharpened. In 1885, he chided authorities for their "strange timidity or . . . disposition to keep on the right side of men [engaged in unruly strikes] who, defiant of the law as they may be today, will have votes to give not long hence." Even at that, his tone remained largely optimistic. He wrote that the future would undoubtedly produce more demagogues and more industrial warfare. But thoughtful people had come to recognize that there was a need for "constant" study of the labor question. There was already evidence of a desire to deal effectively with both "the exaggerated pretensions and relieve the just demands of labor as they arise." One could see a growing willingness to "provide for the improvident in their special days of trial." Given such progress, was it not "the glory of our day" that it showed a "wider recognition of the responsibilities of capital" than prevailed in less enlightened times?[20]

Not even the great Missouri Pacific strike that raged from mid-March through mid-May 1886 dampened the *Chronicle* editor's generally hopeful view of prospects for improved labor relations. He assigned that battle to the work of a few "hot heads." While regarding it as "very unfortunate," he wrote that the only real danger lay in making too much of it, or yielding to it, or violently stopping it. Simply keep property from destruction so far as possible and let the struggle run its course "like an old sore." Public opinion did not support the strike, which must fail because it was based, Dana claimed, on no real grievance.[21]

While our editor's pen scratched out bolder comments for a time after the Haymarket Square riots, his tone remained surprisingly temperate until depression brought the great industrial struggles of 1894. He acknowledged in the aftermath of the Haymarket tragedy that the eight-hour movement was continuing to attract new recruits. Their strikes were idling large numbers of men. Yet, there was scant evidence of general support for the "cowardly," murderous "socialist outbreak" in Chicago. He hoped that justice would be "so quickly and severely administered" to those responsible "that their entire following will become convinced of the unsuitableness of America as a camping ground for Anarchists."[22] A little more than a year later he asserted that American workingmen were neither socialists nor nihilists, so there was little reason for excessive fear of organized labor.[23]

Contemporaneously, conflicts between capital and labor extended their influence to the contents of the *Chronicle*'s editorials treating the annual reports of the U.S. Commissioner of Immigration. As a rule, William Dana held that immigration was good for the country. It added "to the wealth-producing capacity of the nation."[24] A temporary loss of enthusiasm for immigration crept into his remarks in 1887, however. Then, he wrote that some change, nothing radical, in our immigration and naturalization laws, would be desirable. The disappearance of a previously "boundless and inexhaustible" unsettled public domain argued for some restriction on the flow of new arrivals from abroad. The shift in the chief sources of immigrants from northern and western to southern and eastern Europe, bringing to these shores aliens "of distinctly inferior quality" to that of their predecessors, did as well. Most important, "almost every [present] danger to the organization of society" originated with foreign arrivals who had taken advantage of our liberal immigration laws and imported "socialism and anarchy . . . the worst evils that have come to us from abroad."[25]

From 1887 through 1890 Dana regularly addressed the threat of radicalism introduced from overseas. His position was not atypical for a key business figure. He offered mildly worded calls for revision of immigration laws to exclude polygamists, anarchists, socialists, and aliens who intended to work here for only a time and then return home with their savings. Afterward, references to the menace of foreign radicalism slipped from sight. He was unpersuaded that it would be practicable to enforce strict prohibitions concerning the political views of foreign arrivals. The "distinct deterioration in the character of immigrant arrivals in recent years" re-mained a cause for concern, though. That concern pointed toward national origins and low skills rather than to ethnicity. Nothing in the *Chronicle* suggested sympathy for the wave of nativism that overtook the country between 1887 and 1894, when the anti-Catholic and antiforeign American Protective Association grew from 70,000 to 500,000 members. Long before the opening of the twentieth century, the paper was extending recognition to the contributions even of Italians as productive workers.[26]

In the context of the times, racism was not a prominent feature of Wil-liam Dana's thought. There was no hint of anti-Semitism in the pages of the *Chronicle*. It clung to views first expressed when the last federal troops were withdrawn from the former Confederate States in 1877. Then, it had inveighed against efforts to pit Whites against Blacks. Two years later Dana wrote, "Densely ignorant . . . superstitious," and credulous, "but a child cast in the mold of man," the Black must nevertheless work out his own problems without intervention from real or would-be friends. The implication was that he could. In the meantime, the South was the "best country for the negro. His work is there, and there his labor is needed, and his removal would be disastrous to the country and to him." He could "endure exposure to sun when the white is struck down." "If the negro cannot live safely and happily in the Southern States of the North Amer-ican continent—a proposition which we do not admit for an instant—there does not seem to us any place for him in the world."[27] Nor did Dana abandon in later years views he had expressed ridiculing an 1879 proposal in Congress to make it a misdemeanor for the master of any ship to take on board at any foreign port more than fifteen Chinese with the intent to bring them to the United States. In supporting the bill as state elections neared, both major political parties were pandering to the anti-Chinese prejudice of Californians. It violated treaty obligations of the United States. It was unenforceable since U.S. jurisdiction did not extend to ships taking on passengers in foreign ports. Worse, it was "a direct insult" to China, and would "act as a check" on trade with China. Dana hoped that in time common sense would "put down" cries against the Chinese, "as in former years" it had "put down the not less unreasoning cries against the Irish and the Germans." Not long afterward he averred that there was "as yet room here for the Chinaman and everyone else who wants to come." Only time was needed to allow the nation to adjust to its new inhabitants and they to it.[28]

Condemnation of the conduct of unionists at Homestead in 1892 primed Dana to lend strong editorial support to business when the opening fusil-lades announced the outset of the industrial warfare of 1894. He branded the work stoppage at the Great Northern as "indiscreet" at a time when three of the five transcontinental railroads were in receivership. He roundly criticized the rash of other "little strikes" then breaking out. He blamed them on a "surprisingly radical" federal court decision to restore former wages on the Union Pacific Railroad. In contrast, he pronounced the use of an injunction to prevent strikers from interfering with property of the Toledo, Ann Arbor & North Michigan Railroad a "very ingenious device" for placing the road and strikers under federal control.[29] In this troubled scene, Coxey's industrial army movement was but a minor feature. Dana thought it among the "least noteworthy, because most trivial and transient," of the bubbles then afloat in American politics. While a few "honest fanatics" had inspired it, its popularity had developed solely among the "dead beats" of society and out of the facts that it promised food, transportation, and "a visit to the East, all for nothing." After the venture collapsed, the *Chronicle* satisfied itself with a call for "the most extreme punishment" of all industrials involved in stealing trains. It was time to make an example of them. The law-abiding public had wearied of the farce.[30]

The Pullman strike solidified Dana's opposition to strikes to the point of complete hostility. Belittling the laborers at Pullman, he reported: "It seems as if some men working for Mr. Pullman in his shops near Chicago had a difference with their employer and struck." Omitting any reference to the issue of rents in the company town, he depicted Pullman as a sympathetic businessman who docked wages rather than shutting down his plant and throwing his men out of work in a period of profound depression. The ensuing boycott of Pullman cars was, for our editor, a welcome event. Labor could not have made a less wise decision, as the outcome would show. The contest would be brief. There had never been a better time for railroads to "try the issue" of control, given the availability of an army of the unemployed to take the places of strikers. The American people would willingly endure the struggle rather than support a compromise "with men engaged in an attempt to enforce such a gross wrong." The strike was a part of what had become a general practice of making the railroads a "national grindstone."

This was strong stuff, shared no doubt by many leading men of commerce. But it is important to note that not even Ohio industrialist and U.S. Senator Marcus Alonzo Hanna went so far. The architect of William McKinley's successful 1896 presidential campaign and caricatured by many as the archetypical big businessman, Hanna had no use for Pullman's obtuse refusal to negotiate. Whatever his failings, Hanna understood wage earners and exploded: "The damned idiot ought to arbitrate, arbitrate, arbitrate! ... A man who won't meet his men half-way is a God-damn fool!"[31]

After the crisis Dana abruptly dismissed proposals to employ compulsory arbitration to settle labor disputes. While there was much to be said for voluntary arbitration, compulsory arbitration was a contradiction in terms. The very idea of arbitration depended on mutual consent. Nor was there any equitable way to enforce the findings of an arbiter where the process was compulsory. If the arbiter found for capital, there was no way to compel workingmen to accept the award. The employer could be driven from business if his men walked out. If the arbiter found for labor, a generous award could again drive the employer from business.

The November 1894 report of the commission appointed to investigate the strike elicited a round of castigation from the *Chronicle*'s editor. Commendably, the commission had stayed within its $5,000 budget. Far from being impartial, though, its report was highly prejudiced against Pullman and the General Managers' Association. It alleged that Pullman had maintained absolute control over wages, rents, and working conditions to the point of doing everything in his power to prevent unionization of workingmen. His provision of services of a physician and surgeon was designed not to provide care for laborers, but assure prompt settlement of any claims arising from job-related injuries. The General Managers' Association had no legal standing in the Pullman dispute. Labor had conducted itself throughout the struggle with undeniable dignity. Judging from the contents of the report, and if measured by the usefulness of the commission's services, Dana snidely concluded that the cost of its work would have been dear "even if the expenses had been limited to a thousandth part of the amount given."[32]

The Supreme Court's 1895 decision affirming a year's imprisonment for Eugene Debs for contempt of court brought more of the same. William praised the court's sweeping affirmation of national power over interstate commerce as incorporating the authority to cast aside obstructions to the free movement of traffic and the mails. It was especially appropriate that the ruling came on the anniversary of the strike "out of which the [legal] proceeding arose." Noting that Debs disliked the decision, Dana commented further with untypical acerbity: "Poor man, he posed as a hero and a martyr while destroying other people's property and trampling on other people's rights, under the claim that he had wrongs to redress and chose to redress them in that unlawful way; now he wakes up to find that he has no recourse but in abuse of the Court."[33]

The years following the Pullman strike saw the pages of Dana's *Chronicle* continue from time to time to acknowledge that labor and capital shared a community of interests. There were occasional references to the rights of labor, as well. The old commitment to the ideal of voluntary arbitration never entirely disappeared. But in the main, antiunion and antistrike sentiments found their way more and more often into print. Labor in the 1902 anthracite strike was likened to a highwayman willing to destroy the mines if it could not control their pay practices.[34] A year later William Dana greeted as "plain old common sense" the proposition of U.S. Commissioner of Labor Carroll D. Wright that since labor was free to quit, management could discharge workers at will except on grounds of union membership.[35] Meanwhile, he wrote that conceding that a union was orderly did not necessarily mean it was incapable of evil.[36] When the National Association of Manufacturers (NAM), founded in 1895 to promote foreign trade, shifted to an antiunion mission in 1903, Dana moved with it. As early as that year he congratulated it on its success in opposing eight-hour workday bills and bills to limit the use of injunctions against strikes.

Much more important, Dana wrote: "Organized labor is particularly denunciatory of trusts, but what greater trust is there than itself? It is the grand trust of the times. It is the muscle trust, the trust of men who make their living by manual labor. . . . If any institution needs to be exposed to the limelight, it is certainly trades-unionism."[37] Perhaps the definitive statement of his final position on labor unions and strikes resided in a 1910 editorial treating damages awarded to employers in the Danbury, Connecticut, hatters' case. He took entire satisfaction in rejecting the unsuccessful argument of one of the defendant hatters. The hatter had contended that anyone who believed that every man had a right to sell his own labor as he chose must grant unqualified support to labor unions. This was so because single individuals had no chance when bargaining with employers. The unorganized worker was but a helpless cog in a machine. Bargaining alone must reduce the general standard of living as it would always result in low wages. It was only through union membership that individuals secured any freedom of labor or power to contract. Accordingly, individuals should submit to unions, and if they did not then the union must compel submission. Dana abruptly dismissed this view as a "distorted notion of personal liberty, to be attained through 'collective action of the power of labor.' "[38]

The crosscurrents of Dana's thought as explored above leave us with a last, difficult question. Given his ideas about a natural harmony of interest between capital and labor, and the convoluted evolution of his thinking about the relations of capital and labor in general, what effective rights remained with labor? The answer is fairly straightforward, if not very satisfying. A few paragraphs should suffice to state it.

William Dana's understanding of the rights of labor grew, as did his general approach to industrial relations, out of his commitment to free-market principles. Economic individualism stood at the center. As free members of a society governed on republican and libertarian principles, workingmen enjoyed rights common to all citizens. These included freedom of belief, expression, and assembly. They also comprehended liberty of contract and the right to acquire, hold, and dispose of property (which incorporated their bodies and work). Given as much, Dana could not but concede the right to form unions, however strongly he might dislike them. Nor could he flatly deny a right to strike. We have already seen him occasionally acknowledge that some employers ground down their hired hands, and that workingmen deserved the "full value of their labor."[39]

There were limits to the right to combine in unions and to walk off the job. Union membership must be entirely voluntary, if it were to be consistent with the principle of personal liberty. So must participation in strikes. There could be no union action that involved coercion of workingmen, destruction of property, or lawlessness. Dana doubted, given his view of human nature, that society would ever be free of industrial conflict. He hoped, though, that a growth of goodwill might bring a time when capital and labor would turn more frequently to voluntary arbitration to settle their differences. Legislation was a dubious instrument for dealing with labor relations, for it interfered with the freedom on which an efficient market depended.

Our editor's most extensive and explicit comments on the rights of labor appeared in an 1887 article. The growing tendency of organized labor to seek preferential legislation, increasing governmental regulation of business through such measures as the Interstate Commerce Act of 1887, and the generally increasing assertiveness of unions provoked him to offer spirited comments on industrial relations in the country. He reminded readers of the continuing validity of the old principle that every man possessed a right to sell his labor "or as much of it as he pleases" and that "an employer has an equal right to employ whom, and as many or as few persons as he wishes, and that the terms of employment are simply matters of agreement between the employer and *each person* [author's italics] employed." We should note here that this view freed management to make it a condition of employment that applicants not join unions. It mocked the notion that individuals actually negotiated their own working arrangements. Dana deplored the fact that the country had departed so far from this notion. Ten-hour workday-laws limited the times of factory operation. Trade unions used strikes and threats of strikes to dictate whom businessmen would hire, that all would receive equal pay regardless of the quality of their work, and that only union men would be given jobs.

The only thing that could be said in favor of this trade union "tyranny" was that it was preferable to legislative meddling with business. It was unfortunate that it "put all men who submit to it on the dead level of mediocrity" It allowed no worker to rise above his peers, discouraging the development of skills. Even so, it retained a "small amount of manly independence." This remaining scrap of manliness was lost when unions sought protective legislation and won it. The *Chronicle*'s editor recognized that some few people needed the protection of government: "The paupers, the insane, and the physically defective. Children who have no natural or no discreet guardians need it. In certain matters women need it; and even all men against fraud and violence." Government that went further exceeded its proper bounds and injured, rather than helped, labor. If labor could not presently perceive this truth, the country must await the appearance of men who could.[40]

Dana stuck stubbornly to the belief that individual laborers could and should bargain with employers in an open market. The latter in turn should retain discretion regarding hiring, wages, and so on. He did grant, by 1889, that some reforms were necessary in the railroad industry. Laborers should be freed from the threat of arbitrary dismissal, enabled to participate in company insurance plans, and receive technical education for those of their children who wished to follow them in their careers. However, all of this was to be accomplished voluntarily and cooperatively, without force of law.[41] Five years later this moderate tone gave way to twisted logic when he characterized unflinching firmness of city police in dealing with a streetcarmen's strike in New York City and Brooklyn as "merciful to the laborers themselves." Vigorous enforcement of the law and suppression of disorder had kept them out of harm's way.[42] Use of the militia to suppress violence during bloody coal and gold miners' strikes in Colorado in 1904 stirred him to praise that contained a similarly perverse turn. He commended the governor for "protecting those willing to take the place of strikers."[43]

The notion of the right of the individual wage earner to "bargain freely" with a business, no matter its size, reached its logical conclusion when Dana swung to an unyielding defense of the open shop. By 1904 he was claiming that it was "at the base of our form of government." A year later he welcomed the NAM's allocation of $500,000 to fight what he termed the "illegal and improper tactics or methods of labor unions." The NAM's advocacy of "the right of every man to work where, when, and for whom he pleases, and be protected in that right, and the employer's right to run his own business and employ whom he pleases and be upheld in that right as long as he does not infringe on the rights of others" was beyond question. He offered his last and strongest word on the subject in 1909, when the American Federation of Labor solicited contributions to assist in organizing the workers at United States Steel. The employees of the steel company were neither oppressed nor aware of any wrongs requiring outside help. While the sensational elements of the press continued to crow about the rights of labor, he exclaimed: "It is needless to say again—what cannot be made bolder or clearer by argument—that the open shop issue is fundamental and vital. It cannot be surrendered, since the surrender of it would yield everything and set up an oligarchy within and even superior to what is nominally recognized as government by the people."[44]

Taken as a whole, Dana's comments about labor, its functions, its relationship with capital, and its rights do not present an attractive picture. We may applaud his hope that voluntary arbitration would one day become the norm for resolving industrial disputes. We may also credit his generally liberal views regarding immigration, his recognition of the rights of labor to fair compensation, to be exempt from arbitrary dismissal, to combine in unions, and (in principle, at least) to strike. Against these positives stood several negatives. His faith in a harmony of interest between capital and labor directly contradicted his championship of the open shop. It also depended on a mythic view that society included only two groups: all who were gainfully employed in whatever capacity and who were therefore "producers," and the rest, who were parasites or worse. His assertions that the labor market operated in some sense as a place of open, free, relatively fair bargaining between capitalists and wage earners rested on ideology rather than fact. While recognizing that combinations of labor, and strikes, were a part of the scheme of things, as Adam Smith had acknowledged, his comments were prejudicial where Smith's had been coolly analytical. They were, in the final analysis, closer to the stern moralism of Francis Wayland and the heartlessness of Social Darwinism than they were to Smith. They were closer yet to the spirit of rampant capitalism that triumphed and then stirred a wave of reform during and after his lifetime. They represented Dana very much as a man of his time and class. They were, in important respects, as Stow Persons wrote in *American Minds: A History of Ideas* "a convenient rationalization of the prevailing modes of economic activity." Where he would stand today on the question of industrial relations is impossible to say. There is at least some reason to believe, though, that he would be among those who during and after the 1950s bent the American people, including even wage earners, against labor unions.

NOTES

1. *Commercial and Financial Chronicle*, April 8, 1871.
2. *Commercial and Financial Chronicle*, June 4, 1879.
3. *Commercial and Financial Chronicle*, August 9, 1879. Classic treatments of the notion of a harmony of interests between capital and labor, and on America as a land of incipient capitalists include Henry Nash Smith, *Virgin Land: The American West as Symbol and Myth* (New York: Vintage Books, 1957), 138–304; Merrill D. Peterson, *The Jefferson Image in the American Mind* (New York: Oxford University Press, 1962), 67–87, 467–472; Richard Hofstadter, *The Age of Reform: From Bryan to F. D. R.* (New York: Alfred A. Knopf, 1955), 23–60; Charles Greer Sellers, *The Market Revolution* (New York: Oxford University Press, 1991), esp. 346–395; and Bray Hammond, *Banks and Politics in America from the Revolution to the Civil War* (Princeton, NJ: Princeton University Press, 1957).
4. *Commercial and Financial Chronicle*, May 21, 1887; June 30, 1894; November 1 and 29, 1902; quotations from November 29, 1902 edition.
5. *Commercial and Financial Chronicle*, May 18, 1907.
6. For the labor theory of value, see Adam Smith, *An Inquiry into the Causes of the Wealth of Nations*, with a new Preface by George J. Stigler (Chicago: University of Chicago Press, 1976), 1:7–25, 34–52, 72–160; Francis Wayland, *Elements*

of Political Economy, 4th ed. (Boston: Gould and Lincoln, 1860); and discussion in Chapter 1.

7. See especially Fred Albert Shannon, *The Centennial Years: A Political and Economic History of America from the Late 1870s to the Early 1890s* (Garden City, NY: Doubleday, 1967), 200–240, 342–343; Robert V. Bruce, *1877: The Year of Violence* (Indianapolis: Bobbs-Merrill, 1959); Gerald N. Grob, "The Railroad Strikes of 1877," *Midwest Journal of Political Science* 6 (Winter 1954–1955): 16–34.

8. Douglas Steeples and David O. Whitten, *Democracy in Desperation: The Depression of 1893*, 50, 89, 90–92, 103, 120, 146–147, 176; Kim Voss, *The Making of American Exceptionalism: The Knights of Labor and Class Formation in the Nineteenth Century* (Ithaca, NY: Cornell University Press, 1993); Robert E. Weir, *Beyond Labor's Veil: The Culture of the Knights of Labor* (University Park: Pennsylvania State University Press, 1996); Terence Powderly, *The Path I Trod* (New York: Columbia University Press, 1940).

9. Shannon, *The Centennial Years*, 237–240, 317; Henry David, *The History of the Haymarket Affair: A Study in the American Social–Revolutionary Labor Movement* (New York: Farrar and Rinehart, 1936); Ray Ginger, *Age of Excess*, 2d ed. (New York: Macmillan, 1975), 57–60, 366.

10. Leo Wolman, *The Growth of American Trade Unions, 1880–1923* (New York: National Bureau of Economic Research, 1924).

11. Paul Krause, *The Battle for Homestead, 1880–1892: Politics, Culture, and Steel* (Pittsburgh, PA: University of Pittsburgh Press, 1992); David P. Demarest, Jr., *"The River Ran Red": Homestead 1892* (Pittsburgh, PA: University of Pittsburgh Press, 1992); and Robert Wayne Smith, *The Coeur d'Alene Mining War of 1892*, 2d ed. (Corvallis: Oregon State University Press, 1961).

12. For a summary, see Steeples and Whitten, *Democracy in Desperation*, 88–94, 103 n.19, n.20; Donald LeCrone McMurry, *Coxey's Army: A Study of the Industrial Army Movement of 1894* (Boston: Little, Brown, 1924); and Carlos Schwantes, *Coxey's Army: An American Odyssey* (Lincoln: University of Nebraska Press, 1985).

13. Stanley Buder, *Pullman: An Experiment in Industrial Order and Community Planning, 1880–1930* (New York: Oxford University Press, 1967); and Almont Lindsey, *The Pullman Strike: The Story of a Unique Experiment and of a Greater Labor Upheaval* (Chicago: University of Chicago Press, 1942, 1964), treat the main issues and sources. See also Steeples and Whitten, *Democracy in Desperation*, 94–96, 104.

14. William Henry Harbaugh, *The Life and Times of Theodore Roosevelt*, new rev. ed. (New York: Oxford University Press, 1975), 165–179, 504–506, is still authoritative for Roosevelt. For an important perspective on the role of financier J. P. Morgan in settling the strike, see Ron Chernow, *The House of Morgan: An American Banking Dynasty and the Rise of Modern Finance* (New York: Simon and Schuster, 1990), 106–108.

15. "The Strikes," "The Eight-Hour Strikes," "Labor Congresses at Home and Abroad," respectively *Hunt's Merchant's Magazine* 55 (July 1866): 63–65; 59 (August 1868); and quoted 59 (October 1868): 292–295.

16. *Commercial and Financial Chronicle*, August 15, 1871.

17. *Commercial and Financial Chronicle*, July 22, 1877.

18. *Commercial and Financial Chronicle*, October 18, 1877.

19. *Commercial and Financial Chronicle*, July 8, 1882.

20. *Commercial and Financial Chronicle*, August 1, 1885.

21. *Commercial and Financial Chronicle*, March 13, quoted March 20, and March 27, 1886. Dana here drew a fine distinction between complaints regarding wages and hours and those concerning union recognition and membership.

22. *Commercial and Financial Chronicle*, May 8, 1886.

23. *Commercial and Financial Chronicle*, October 8, 1887.

24. *Commercial and Financial Chronicle*, August 19, 1882; July 21, 1883; July 21, 1886; September 5, 1891; August 22, 1903; and July 21, 1906.

25. *Commercial and Financial Chronicle*, May 22, 1887.

26. *Commercial and Financial Chronicle*, May 5, 1888; February 2, 1889; and August 13, 1887. The most useful introduction to nativism during the era remains John Higham, *Strangers in the Land: Patterns of American Nativism, 1860–1925* (New York: Atheneum, 1963), 35–87; also John Higham, "Anti-Semitism in the Gilded Age—a Reinterpretation," *Mississippi Valley Historical Review* 43 (March 1957): 559–578. See also, Morrell Heald, "Business Attitudes toward European Immigration, 1890–1900," *Journal of Economic History* 13 (Summer 1953): 291–304; Steeples and Whitten, *Democracy in Desperation*, 97–100, 105; and for a stimulating but derivative view, Richard Hofstadter, *The Paranoid Style in American Politics and other Essays* (New York: Vintage Books, 1967), 145–162; and Hofstadter, *The Age of Reform*, 71–93.

27. *Commercial and Financial Chronicle*, April 28, 1877; quoted June 14 and September 6, 1879.

28. *Commercial and Financial Chronicle*, February 8, 1879; and November 8, 1880; quoted April 8, 1882. The Burlingame Treaty of 1868 guaranteed to Chinese nationals the same rights of immigration in the United States as those enjoyed by citizens of other nations.

29. *Commercial and Financial Chronicle*, April 21 and May 5, 1894.

30. *Commercial and Financial Chronicle*, quoted April 28 and May 12; see also May 5, all 1894.

31. *Commercial and Financial Chronicle*, June 30, 1894. For Hanna quotation, see Thomas Beer, *Hanna* (New York: Alfred A. Knopf, 1929), 132–133.

32. *Commercial and Financial Chronicle*, quoted June 30; and November 17; arbitration, October 27, all 1894.

33. *In re Debs* (158 U.S. 564), 1895; *Commercial and Financial Chronicle*, June 1, 1895.

34. *Commercial and Financial Chronicle*, January 7; November 1; and quoted June 7, 1902.

35. *Commercial and Financial Chronicle*, September 1, 1903.

36. *Commercial and Financial Chronicle*, November 29, 1902.

37. *Commercial and Financial Chronicle*, April 13, 1903; Albert Kleckner Steigerwalt, *The National Association of Manufacturers, 1895–1914. A Study in Business Leadership* (Ann Arbor: University of Michigan Press, 1964).

38. *Commercial and Financial Chronicle*, February 12, 1910. For the Danbury hatters' decision, see *Loewe v. Lawlor* (208 U.S. 274), 1908.

39. Quotation from *Commercial and Financial Chronicle*, April 18, 1871.

40. *Commercial and Financial Chronicle*, August 20, 1887. For the likely recurrence of strikes, October 17, 1894.

41. *Commercial and Financial Chronicle*, April 13, 1889.

42. *Commercial and Financial Chronicle*, October 17, 1894.

43. *Commercial and Financial Chronicle*, July 23, 1904.

44. Quotations from *Commercial and Financial Chronicle*, May 14, 1904; May 25, 1907; and December 18, 1909. See also, Steigerwalt, *The National Association of Manufacturers*; and for developments at the middle of the twentieth century, see Gilbert J. Gall, *The Politics of the Right to Work: The Labor Federations as Special Interests, 1943–1979* (Westport, CT: Greenwood, 1988).

5

Property and Its Rights

The first maxim is a respect for vested interests, and for the security of private property
—William Buck Dana, April 5, 1873

William Dana's ideas about the rights of property were an essential link connecting his convictions about the natural order of things, labor relations, and the role of government in the evolving American economy. As these other links, they were forged on the anvil of his education and experience. They likewise bound his thinking to intellectual currents that had been prominent in the English-speaking world since at least the Glorious Revolution of 1689 when William of Orange and Mary displaced James II as reigning monarchs. Given full and systematic explication by Adam Smith and passed on through Francis Wayland at Yale,[1] Dana's fundamental understanding fell within the limits established by three statements. The first was the quotation heading this chapter.

The second appeared in the *Commercial and Financial Chronicle* in 1895, in an approving editorial about a recent address by U.S. Supreme Court Justice Henry C. Brown. Brown had spoken about capital and labor in an era when the scale of business enterprise was growing rapidly. He identified business consolidation and the growth of large corporations as forces driving national progress and prosperity, and as sources of the labor tensions that constituted the great social problem currently challenging the country. To this problem there was no easy solution. Certainly, socialism was no remedy. It flourished only in primitive societies, removed all incentive to work, and would idle all who wished to labor to provide luxuries for the rich. "The fact is," Brown had said with Dana's subsequent editorial endorsement, "the whole fabric of society is built upon the sanctity of private property. Were the foundation to be taken away the structure would crumble into ruins."[2]

The third appeared in the *Chronicle* a decade later, when its editor took a slightly different tack in returning to the same general theme. Considering the likely consequences of the newly passed Hepburn Act (extending federal regulation of interstate transportation, the Meat Inspection Act, and the Pure Food and Drug Act), he sharply criticized the abridgement of property rights that such legal intervention entailed. The great wave of reform reshaping the United States was moving too far, and too quickly. Measures such as these propelled the country into unfamiliar and dangerous territory. Formerly, the rights attaching to ownership of property had been clear and unmistakable. Holders could acquire, manage, and dispose of property as they saw fit, so long as they did not abridge the legally recognized rights of others. Now a gray area was emerging in which government was encroaching on and qualifying the rights of owners. Their new boundaries were not clear, although the growing appetite of the public and of government for regulation indicated that these limits were contracting. Expanding regulation was eroding cherished property rights. The result was a violation of sound and long-settled principles: "Whatever a man owns he owns absolutely, and ... the free play of competition is the only regulator which is possible in this imperfect world. ... The man owns his body and brain, to start with, as capital or tools for his own support or benefit; we all admit this as an inalienable right," even though labor unions, some ill-informed members of the clergy, and growing sections of public opinion were questioning it.[3]

Dana wrote most of what appeared during his lifetime in the *Chronicle* respecting the rights of property in reply to one or both of two sea changes that were transforming the business, social, and political environments of the United States. The most visible of these was the replacement of an economy in which small-scale enterprises predominated with one in which increasingly large companies held sway. Insatiable needs for capital for construction made railroads early leaders among large corporations. Breakneck expansion pushed them, and later other burgeoning industries, to chaotic and often ruinous competition. Industrialists attempted various devices to mitigate internecine warfare in the marketplace. Beginning in the depressed 1870s, and continuing through the business downturns of the 1880s and 1890s, railroad managements formed regional pools, usually called traffic associations, to apportion traffic and receipts among rival lines within their territories. These were inherently fragile, lacking the stability of either corporate structure or practically enforceable contracts. By nature they carried incentives to seek larger market shares or revenues by cheating. They were particularly vulnerable to business downturns, which often precipitated rate wars as debt-burdened railroads attempted to raise cash to meet fixed obligations. Pools were attempted in other lines of industry, as well, notably bar iron, wire nails, steel billets and beams, and Bessemer steel. The results were usually no less unsatisfactory.

In 1881 John Davison Rockefeller bent an old legal device, the trust, to a new use as a mechanism for combination when he created the Standard Oil Trust. Soon the device was in wide use in other lines of business. The second sea change occurred with the appearance of a new form of business concentration in 1888. In that year New Jersey legislated to permit formation of holding companies under general incorporation statutes rather than through special laws, and several other states quickly followed suit. The holding company promptly became the preferred means of combination. A wave of large consolidations, much of it centered in manufacturing, swept across American enterprise before the onset of severe depression in 1893. Harold Underwood Faulkner recorded that "forty-six" corporations with a capital of at least $1 million each were formed "in the years between 1890 and 1893 representing [a total of] over $1.4 billion in capital." The largest in manufacturing, all with at least $10 million in assets and all aiming at oligopoly, were United States Leather Company ($80 million), National Lead Company ($31.2 million), American Cotton Oil, Diamond Match, American Sugar Refining, Chicago Gas Trust, and Distillers' and Cattle Feeders' Trust. Joining them were Procter & Gamble, Illinois Steel, Carnegie Steel, Western Union, and other exemplars of concentration.[4]

The depression of the 1890s and the ensuing recovery brought a second, much larger wave of major corporate consolidations. The collapse had forced "an unprecedented number of railroad failures," necessitating the reorganization of railroads operating one-sixth of the country's trackage. Bankers, of whom J. P. Morgan was the most prominent and active, led in the task of reconstruction. They combined competing lines, abandoned weak branches, and worked to replace the old pattern of destructive competition with communities of interest. They simplified capital structure, often converting securities bearing fixed charges into contingent obligations with noncumulative charges. Distribution of additional preferred or common stock compensated holders of new junior securities. Since fixed charges were pegged to earnings, common stock promised little prospect of dividends. Bankers commonly ensured their continued control of the railroads by creating voting trusts that they dominated. One writer has aptly called this process "morganization," because of Morgan's preeminent role in it. In 1894 his leadership created the Southern Railway on the ruins of the former Richmond & West Point Terminal Railway and Warehouse Company. Within five years it controlled thirteen smaller railroads, owned an additional fifty-eight, and constituted a 9,000-mile system. In November 1895 Morgan reorganized the Erie, and then the Reading, 1896–1898. He combined forces with James Jerome Hill of the Great Northern to over-

haul the Northern Pacific in 1896. Two years later these two men participated in financial reconstruction of the Baltimore & Ohio. Concurrently,
other capitalists reconstituted the Union Pacific and the Santa Fé in 1895,
and the St. Louis & San Francisco a year later.[5]

While the railroads set the pace in the concentration of corporate power,
the process sped in parallel in other sectors of business. Between 1895 and
1904, 319 major business combinations formed in the United States. The
yearly average between 1898 and 1902 was 301, with 1,028 firms being
absorbed through consolidation in 1899 alone. Of the 319 new major combinations, 86 percent involved holding companies and only 14 percent outright acquisition. More than one-third of the new industrial giants aimed
at monopoly control. They came close: 319 firms controlled 40 percent of
all manufacturing assets in the U.S. In each of fifty industries, a single
company accounted for 60 percent or more of production. Of the firms
ruling American business in the mid-twentieth century, twenty came into
being between 1895 and 1904. These included United States Steel, American Tobacco, International Harvester, DuPont, Corn Products, Ana-
conda, and American Smelting and Refining. DuPont, General Electric,
Pullman, Westinghouse, and American Tobacco ranked among the sixteen
companies that generated at least 85 percent of the output in their lines
of trade. The growth of huge enterprises created vastly expanded needs
for credit and large issues of securities to finance them. Further concen-
trations of capital followed, through the formation and expansion of investment banks to meet these requirements. By the turn of the century
these, as lenders and as underwriters of securities issues supporting the
process of combination, were the financial nerve center of the nation. The
new reality struck directly at a venerated social memory. How accurate
this recollection actually was is less important than the fact of its existence.
What had been remembered as a nation of small artisans, manufacturers,
and shopkeepers with myriad opportunities for anyone willing to seize the
moment and work hard seemed to have disappeared.[6]

The sheer size of emerging and newly dominant enterprises posed insistent social questions. How could there even *be* a self-regulating market
that through the "invisible hand" of competition, best met social needs,
when a few gigantic entities (or even a single monopoly) exercised hegem-
ony over entire fields of commerce? If the new dispensation meant that
the market was no longer an effective mechanism, how could it be reconciled with a free-market ideology? Would it become desirable or necessary for government to intervene, to ensure that there was competition
and to protect consumers? Would intervention, if it occurred, be consistent
with the preservation of property rights? Or would it compromise security
of ownership, freedom of exchange, and the sanctity of private contracts?
What of the preservation of managerial discretion if a regulatory environ-

ment evolved? Could commerce thrive if the ability of management to decide freely were circumscribed by governmental action rather than by market forces? What did the developing order mean for the future of individual opportunity? What, if anything, did it portend for the span of economic options available to average citizens? Did it carry promise, or dangers, for the maintenance of a free society in which the ideals of liberty and equality (at least among adult white males) were deeply ingrained?[7] Did it contain hidden prospects or dangers? As a spokesman and advocate for business, Dana turned repeatedly to seeking reassuring answers to these and kindred questions.

William Dana struggled with the implications of the growing scale of enterprise for decades before arriving at what seemed to him a workable position. Since large corporations first became dominant in the railroad industry, he initially focused his attention on it. Because pools had proven ephemeral and ineffective, stability began to settle in within the railroad sector only with the reorganizations and combinations that occurred in the 1890s. Meanwhile, sensitive to the role of the railroads as our greatest collective corporate interest, the *Chronicle*'s editor consistently championed efforts to end rate wars. This did not mean that he wished to grant railway companies license to do anything they cared to. Writing early in 1882 of a rate war among the trunk lines between Chicago and Baltimore, Philadelphia, and New York, he warned that any resolution disadvantaging the metropolis was unacceptable. "Peace between railroads is of course desirable, but if communities and their business connections must be sacrificed to attain it, better we say, a hundred times better that the war should continue." He wrote with such force on the point, he continued, because the railways' "disregard" of New York's interest was placing an unbearable burden on its commerce and driving even its conservative merchants to consider legislative remedies that tasted "strongly of communism" We should note that this degree of solicitude for mercantile and shipping interests was rarely, if ever, in evidence when the concerns of other cities, and small interior communities, were at issue.[8]

A year later, our editor expressed satisfaction with what he perceived to be a growing public recognition of the value of pools. A comparatively modern device, he believed that they were likely to continue in use as long as business affairs remained as then constituted. Here a new note crept in, reflecting a change in thinking about the operation of the market. Put bluntly, his faith in free competition was beginning to weaken. "Competition if carried full length," he wrote, "can end only in destruction— the weaker must succumb—and this being so, the usefulness of pooling cannot be impeached." Pools grew out of such urgent needs that, while they might eventually give way to some better replacement, their elimination through legislation or otherwise was inconceivable. They assured returns to investors in railroads, and shippers, equal treatment with their peers. In thus sharing advantages, they balanced their service to social needs.[9]

Over time, the *Chronicle*'s pages expressed increasing sympathy for the railroads. By the mid-1880s they distinguished between the "old idea that a pool is a selfish, grasping monopoly, intent upon devouring everything within its reach," and a new, more benign view. Pools were now recognized to be instruments "of self-protection, designed simply to avoid the evils of reckless competition. Enlightened self-interest has been the stimulating cause; there has been no desire to assume the aggressive as against other departments of industry, but rather an attempt to avoid self-destruction." This was the difference between a pool and a monopoly, which was vicious in having designs on the property of others rather than merely seeking to protect its own property.[10] Primed, thus, to embrace new protections for business as they might appear, Dana welcomed the Supreme Court's 1886 decision that a corporation was a "person" in the sense of the Fourteenth Amendment to the Constitution and thereby entitled to due process and to the equal protection of the laws.[11]

Never enthusiastic about state attempts to regulate railroad rates, William Dana reported with satisfaction the Wabash Decision (also of 1886), by which the Supreme Court reserved to the federal government exclusive authority to regulate interstate commerce and invalidated any state rules affecting it.[12] The result, of course, was to rule out state regulation. Commenting a month later on a Mississippi case, he qualified what had seemed an unbending hostility toward state oversight of interstate businesses. He wrote that it was not "that State supervision in itself was undesirable or necessarily harmful, but that the claim of absolute [state regulatory] authority often led to an excess of zeal and abuse of power which interfered with both trade and vested [property] rights."[13] This remark proved to be a bit deceptive. His zeal to protect railroads from all forms of governmental interference was actually growing steadily. He greeted the 1887 Interstate Commerce Act with open opposition. Passage of the new law was an important turning point, injecting the federal government into the regulation of railroad rates and conduct. It prohibited pooling among interstate lines. It forbade rate discrimination, rebates, drawbacks, and imposing higher tariffs on short hauls than on long hauls on the same lines. It required ten days' notice of proposed rate changes, and public posting of rates. It created the Interstate Commerce Commission (ICC), the first federal regulatory agency. The ICC could receive and act on complaints arising under the law, summon witnesses, compel testimony, force railroads to produce their books, and impose on railroads a uniform system of accounting. It received power to invoke equity proceedings in courts to enforce its findings.

For the next quarter century, Dana steadfastly called for legalization of pooling. He no less strongly resisted efforts to widen federal regulation of business. When the Supreme Court in the Trans-Missouri Freight Association case of 1897 and subsequent cases ruled that the Sherman Anti-Trust Act prohibited all pools, the *Chronicle*'s reaction was to complain that the decisions went so far beyond the intentions of the Interstate Commerce Act to ensure reasonable rates as practically to make the railroads "wards of the government."[14]

As Congress continued to consider extension of regulation of the railroads and to supervise other interstate carriers, Dana repeatedly took up his pen in defense of business. He closely monitored court, Interstate Commerce Commission, and congressional rulings and deliberations interpreting the long–short haul clause and proposals to amplify it. He sharply criticized successful federal efforts to dissolve the Northern Securities (Holding) Company and thereby avert a union of the Northern Pacific, Great Northern, and Chicago, Burlington & Quincy Railroads during the period 1902–1904. He had opposed passage of the 1890 Sherman Anti-Trust Law. He criticized approval of three new national anti-trust measures in 1903, one creating a Department of Commerce and Labor, one bearing the name of Senator Steven B. Elkins of West Virginia that tightened enforcement of prohibitions against rebates in interstate rail shipments, and one intended to expedite court hearings in cases arising under the Sherman Anti-Trust Act. When the 1906 Hepburn Act was under consideration, he attacked granting rate-setting powers to the Interstate Commerce Commission and making its findings *prima facie* evidence as to fact in any court proceedings arising from its actions. Taken as a group, these measures all amounted to "persecution" of railroads.[15]

We have already encountered two of the reasons that William Dana advanced for opposing governmental interference with property rights. One was that all free institutions depended on security of property. The other, was that owners of capital were both bold and timid. Any action or event that was unsettling could impair or shatter the confidence of capitalists, reducing or shutting off the flows of investment and commerce. There were other reasons, as well.

Of these the most important was Dana's changing understanding of the nation's business environment. His defense of pooling as a form of combination reflected the beginning of an apprehension that the nature of the market was changing. There were instances in which competition could become destructive. Combinations for defensive purposes were therefore legitimate. All of this begs the question whether a genuinely free-market economy implies perfect or near-perfect ease of entrance into *and exit from* a field of enterprise. Dana set that issue aside. He was embarked on an intellectual voyage into new waters. The course he pursued is as revealing as it is interesting.

His 1886 observations that the changing character of competition warranted pooling as a defensive measure broadened by 1888 to include a defense of trusts. Hoping, he wrote, to provide a balanced discussion on a subject that typically provoked comments from "one extreme or the other," he rejected out of hand the view that trusts were the result of commercial conspiracies. He granted that they entailed "some almost necessary evils and a great many possible dangers." But they were a natural outgrowth of modern business conditions. Here he ventured beyond classical free-market theory. They were "inevitable," because the "effect of competition on regulating the price of manufactured articles" was not, even at its best, "wholly satisfactory." Prices fluctuated very widely. Individuals entered businesses when prices were high, and found themselves engaged in a life-and-death struggle to survive when prices fell. Competition, instead of setting "one natural or normal standard of prices" resulted in "two distinct ones. One, which includes all the elements of cost, determines when new capital will come in; another, which includes operating expenses in the very narrowest sense, determines when old capital will be driven out."

To a certain extent it served the public interest to preserve firms that would be needed in prosperous times. Combination was a means of doing so. Monopoly lurked as a possible negative consequence of concentration. If it existed, it could restrict output and maintain artificially high prices, but only at the risk of inviting competition. The other danger it posed was that it removed the incentive for innovation and efficiency. In offering these reminders of the dangers that monopoly posed, Dana returned to the teachings of classical economics. He added, as an accurate observation of his own, that Standard Oil was unique as a virtual monopoly in setting its prices low enough so as not to invite competition.[16]

During the last decade of his life, tendencies of thought that had begun to become evident earlier became more prominent in William Dana's writing as an apologist for business concentration. In 1900, commenting on the report of the U.S. Industrial Commission on the progress of concentration in manufacturing, he could note that the word "trust" as popularly used no longer reflected reality. Holding companies and other instruments of combination had replaced trusts. He then chanted for his readers the litany of advantages that the commission ascribed to giant enterprises. These outweighed such "obvious possibilities of evil as discharge of superfluous employees, arbitrary advance of prices and control of discriminatory freight rates." They included (here he unwittingly contradicted himself regarding release of unneeded workers) the ability to close superfluous or less well situated plants. They extended to operating the remaining plants continuously and at full capacity. They comprehended savings from the elimination of duplicate facilities, shipping from the plants nearest to markets, and use of the most suitable patents.[17]

Three years later, Dana moved toward the position he held until his

death. When Massachusetts Senator George Frisbie Hoar introduced a
new antitrust measure in 1903, he was ready with a response. He wholly
rejected Hoar's contention that trusts and other large corporations held
great and unnatural advantages. The senator had described companies as
artificial beings or persons in the eyes of the law, immortal, lacking in
conscience, and so powerful as to have become the greatest threat facing
the nation. Where Hoar saw a Hydra, the *Chronicle*'s editor saw only a
fiction: that trusts or huge corporations were evil and unnatural. He contended that no class of enterprise could "grow up into a lusty body,
everywhere, throughout such a vast country as this, without having good
as its main object, and evil, if evil it has, as a mere incident." Natural law
had given the combination of capital its development, and any effective
antitrust laws must accordingly be designed to "guide with a gentle hand,
and not roughly to suppress." Dana added that large combinations were
business endeavors that had "evolved from the necessities of the case to
accommodate the conduct of business to the changed conditions of the
present time." In any event, combination did not necessarily mean monopoly. "As a matter of experience," his own investigation had shown that
large combinations set lower prices than many smaller, geographically remote firms in the same line of trade. When a huge corporation approached
becoming "a monopoly new capital seizes the opportunity for new establishments and competition again appears. Our people do not long neglect
to improve a good opening for a profitable venture."[18] Such remarks carried a heavier burden of meaning than is at first obvious. They reflected
a grasp, which was contrary to prevailing popular opinion[19] and which will
be treated later, of the actual effects of monopoly on prices and markets
in the United States. And they contained the germ of ideas that would by
the middle of the twentieth century ripen into the concepts of monopolistic
and oligopolistic competition.

In 1906, William Dana filled in the missing pieces of his argument on
behalf of the new corporate order. In doing so he settled on a position
that seemed, to him at least, to reconcile the ideal of a free market with
the fact of an economy under sway of corporate behemoths. Just as he
had moved from a rejection of Social Darwinism in writing about labor
relations in 1874 to an acceptance of the notion of "survival of the fittest"
in 1893, he found the key in a word he used to discuss Senator Hoar's
1903 antitrust bill: *"evolution."*

In a sympathetic review of a recently published book on social conditions Dana warmly agreed with the author that currently developing social
and economic conditions were not really new. Instead, the country was
"proceeding in an orderly evolution," and things were the same as they
had always been, "differing in degree, indeed, but not in kind." Differences in birth, heredity, and environment had always led to "inequality of
condition, unequal distribution of wealth and opportunity." But progress

through the centuries had resulted in growing equality of opportunity. That was as far as things could go: no human law could "contravene natural law" and enforce "equality of life and condition." Society could neither roll back the advances of the last hundred years and enforce economic competition, nor impose socialism. The only practical socialism, Dana agreed, was "industrial socialism, and that is what is now being evolved in the economic life of the nation."

Contrary to folklore, a century earlier there were few opportunities in the United States for enterprising young men. Small firms, partnerships, and sole proprietorships conducted most business, restricting prospects for ownership and fortune. With the large corporation came an enormous capacity to generate wealth and multiply chances for an ordinary man to own a share of it. That was the meaning of industrial socialism. The United States had progressed and prospered through the operation, at least until recently, of the free market. This advance, climaxing with the arrival of the age of giant companies, was not an accident but a "natural evolution." It would be folly to abandon the principles upon which the country had thrived.[20] Had the *Chronicle*'s editor been J. P. Morgan himself, he could not better have expressed the ideology that had become a commanding presence among the leaders of American enterprise. They still offered pious and respectful nods to the old ideal of a self-regulating market. Their public statements and actions increasingly showed that they strongly preferred stability and order to the unpredictability that competition brought.

On another occasion that same year, the *Chronicle* appreciatively summarized an address, entitled "Some Results of Economic Evolution," delivered by the general agent of a major railroad. Giant corporations, the speaker maintained, were best understood as representatives of associative effort—"the doing collectively what the individual would find it impossible to do singly. Moreover, the corporation is an outgrowth of necessity—is the process of evolution." While granting that the theme of the address was not new, Dana praised it for the original illustrations it employed. He found particularly striking the comparison of corporations, as instances of cooperation, to beehives and anthills. Singly, bees and ants could not achieve large results. Associated in communities, as were people in corporations, they could. In business as in nature, the "great law of natural evolution, or in other words the adaptation of abilities to needs," had produced the large corporation as the entity that best performed needed functions and therefore survived. Although the railways were the speaker's primary illustration of these principles, they could be applied to all forms of business. It was also the case that the railroads must be servants of the communities through which they passed, for modern competition was so fierce that if they failed to serve they would lose out. They could not relocate, so their prosperity depended on that of their communities. The modern corporation, then, had evolved naturally to meet present needs.

Itself an institutional expression of cooperation, it had to behave as a servant if it were to thrive.

It remained only for Dana to add an emphatic coda to his strenuous defense of the emergence of the giant corporation. This he did in 1909. In a story reporting the appointment of J. P. Morgan, Jr. to the board of directors of United States Steel, Dana wrote of the younger Morgan as heir to one of his father's greatest creations. In a panegyric to corporate bigness he characterized this largest of the world's industrial corporations as "the most perfect type of an industrial organization—every department organized in accordance with the highest skill and the best practice, and fortified by the use of the most advanced devices and appliances, with every modern improvement in tools, machinery, &c." It exemplified, as well, the best financial management, greatest achievement of economies of production, the fullest publicity of corporate affairs, and "sane and sensible plans for enlisting the interest and promoting the welfare of employees."[21]

One can scarcely conceive of higher praise for management, and for pure size.

The preceding pages have dwelt mainly on William Dana's evolving ideas about and defense of the emergence of big business. Corporate behavior, although a major element in shaping popular opinion about large firms, has to this point received relatively little attention. It is somewhat artificial to separate the question of behavior from that of size, since size (as well as circumstances) may itself enable or rule out certain types of action. Yet, the distinction is a useful one, for present purposes. It permits greater clarity in treatment of issues than would otherwise be possible. We turn now to consider how Dana's defense of property rights responded to the growth of modern, mildly interventionist governmental attempts to regulate business conduct. The railroads will again figure prominently. Other industries, and questions such as the distribution of wealth, will also receive attention. Here, as with consideration of the growing size of enterprise, it will become evident that William Dana expressed views containing insights that would mature a generation or two after his death into conceptions of monopolistic and oligopolistic competition. It will also become clear that he correctly saw in the emergence of these new forms of rivalry novel conditions that frequently brought lower prices, rather than higher prices as many reformers claimed.

The abuses that the Interstate Commerce Act sought to address were nevertheless real. They were part of a broader complex of problems. Scale could offer genuine savings in the cost of operation. But it remained true that shippers in interior points, especially on noncompetitive routes, often paid higher tariffs than those who were more fortunately situated. This distinction extended to payment of higher charges for short rather than for long shipments on the same routes. Farmers often paid increased storage rates for crops in areas that lacked competing grain elevators or warehouses, as well as those where a single rail carrier owned or held an exclusive contract with the local storage facility. There were also instances of fraudulent downgrading of grain, with resulting cuts in prices paid to farmers. In the South, comparable conditions often obtained with respect to cotton gins and warehouses. In many Middle Border, Great Plains, and Southern states, angry agriculturists banded together to combat real as well as imagined mistreatment.

Beginning with the formation in 1867 of the Patrons of Husbandry (Grangers) and of the Farmers' Alliances a decade later, agrarians began to unite. Both movements sought, and in many instances won, passage of laws creating state commissions to regulate the rates and conduct of railroads, elevators, gins, and warehouses. Corporate interests almost immediately challenged these laws and the decisions of the state commissions in court. The *Chronicle* followed these developments closely. While at first it predicted that the new statutes were unlikely to cause as much harm as some hysterical business interests feared, it nonetheless invariably sided with the railroads and their corporate allies. In 1873 Illinois adopted a "Granger law" creating a state commission empowered to fix maximum grain elevator storage rates. Dana's displeasure with the statute turned to disgust when the U.S. Supreme Court four years later upheld it on grounds that elevators so vitally affected the state's interests as to be legitimately subject to its police power to pass laws protecting the public welfare and safety.[22]

The Wabash ruling reserving exclusive federal jurisdiction over interstate commerce came as a welcome change of direction. The passage in response to it of the Interstate Commerce Act was equally *un*welcome, as we have seen. Dana took heart in an 1890 Supreme Court decision striking down an 1887 Minnesota law that granted final rate-setting authority to a state commission without permitting court review. The high bench found that this limitation denied affected parties due process of law. Dana had regarded it as particularly objectionable, because in effect it suffered "the lawmaker to become the arbiter of the constitutionality of the law that he had made." With another handed down the same week, this judgment had, he wrote, prevented "our great carrying interests" from being "irrevocably embarrassed by Socialistic legislation." The importance of the questions involved was so great that the two decisions marked, he concluded, "an epoch in the industrial and constitutional history of the country."[23] His pleasure was even greater when the court in 1894 actually struck down a ruling of the Texas Railroad Commission. In that instance the justices held that the commission's action set arbitrary and unreasonable rates. As such, it violated due process of law as guaranteed citizens of the states by the Fourteenth Amendment to the Constitution. State regulations that arbitrarily reduced carriers' rates amounted to unconstitutional takings of property.[24] The decision incorporated the notion of substantive due process into American constitutional jurisprudence. It also reserved to conservative federal judges, many of them former railroad attorneys, the capacity to determine which regulations and rates were reasonable and which were not.

Dana's criticism of the expansions of the Interstate Commerce Act embodied in the Elkins and Hepburn Acts, respectively of 1903 and 1906, was simply a renewed manifestation of deeply held convictions. He waved aside ICC complaints that limitation of its authority to issuance of cease-and-desist orders against carriers that illegally granted rebates left it with insufficient power to act. He harrumphed that the commission possessed adequate authority and should itself "cease and desist" from its tiresome requests for the ability to revise tariffs. Nor, when the Hepburn bill to grant the ICC such authority was under consideration, did he concede that there was any need to do so. The agency already held, he maintained, all the force it needed to correct "the evils arising from the granting of rebates and unlawful preferences to favored shippers." Despite these and other objections, the measure was approved. It extended ICC jurisdiction to include revision of rates of interstate railroads, oil pipelines, ferries, terminal facilities, express and sleeping car companies, and bridges. Pending court decisions, its orders governing carriers were to be binding, thus placing the burden of proof on carriers. It sharply restricted the granting of free passes—a favorite means of currying lawmakers' favors and *quid pro quos* from other businesses—and forbade railroads from transporting goods that they produced, save for timber and other materials necessary for their operation. It expanded the ICC's membership from five to seven. After the bill passed, he added to his other objections to it the prediction that its complexity and internal contradictions would lead to endless litigation regarding its meaning. It went without saying that the new law involved an unprecedented invasion of the most cherished prerogative of property and management: the right to set prices and determine the terms of trade.[25]

William Dana's advocacy of business led him to resist attempts to regulate the behavior of big firms in interstate manufacturing and other sectors of commerce as strenuously as he defended the interstate railroads. As early as 1886 he condemned the governor for instructing the attorney general of Pennsylvania to begin legal action to dissolve a pool among anthracite producers as "uniquely" groundless. Long locked in competitive price slashing, mine operators had confederated in late 1884 to stabilize their market. Their pool, he wrote, did not meet the definition of a monopoly on several counts. First, anthracite prices had actually fallen until July 1886. Second, pools in other businesses, including manufacture of steel rails and of cotton goods that were formed for the same reason, had not stirred protests. Last, several members of the anthracite combination had joined reluctantly, driven to overcome their objections by the "law of self preservation."[26]

The editor of the *Chronicle* adapted his arguments and advocacy to meet changing conditions as time passed. In 1889 his paper applauded an Iowa federal court order forbidding a receiver to close a bankrupt railroad. The ruling, he wrote, protected businesses depending on the line. It also guarded the railroad, for the judge went on to say that it could be sold with the proceeds to go to creditors. Then, in a curious turn and contradiction of his earlier reference to the rights of businesses dependent on the branch, Dana added that any new management clearly owned the right to close it.[27]

Attempts of pools, syndicates, trusts, and holding companies to control markets drew Dana's attention repeatedly, and usually with the remark that passing laws to prevent predatory business practices by such groups was not necessary. The 1889 failure of a syndicate to corner the copper market and manipulate prices was a case in point. The effort had failed "solely because the laws of supply and demand were too strong for it to contend against." A trade combination "must make prices low enough to encourage consumption." One that could "seriously restrict output in any given line is in danger from every quarter"—from new entrants within the industry as well as from rivals without.[28] Soon after, our editor lambasted new Texas and Missouri antitrust laws. They were so extreme as to be a "joke," even though it was true that combination could involve dangers that warranted regulation of business conduct in instances in which competition had become "practically obsolete."[29]

William Dana took little notice of the Sherman Anti-Trust Act before federal courts began to interpret it. His reactions to Supreme Court decisions regarding its applicability to interstate railroads and organized labor have received some previous attention. The union of the American Sugar Refining Company, E. C. Knight Company, Franklin Sugar Company, Spreckels Sugar Refining Company, and Delaware Sugar House, creating a combine that refined 95 percent of the country's sugar, provided another occasion for comment. The Justice Department brought suit to dissolve the combination on the grounds that its market domination and ability to set prices constituted an illegal combination in restraint of commerce among the states under the Sherman law. The *Chronicle* reported the resulting 1895 Supreme Court decision without comment, implying agreement. The justices' finding and reasoning were stunningly obtuse. The law, they decided, pertained to interstate commerce. It did not apply in the present case, which involved only acquisition (by a national combination) of a company in a single state, Pennsylvania. Besides, the statute applied to commerce, and the present issue was manufacturing, an entirely separate question.[30]

The organization of United States Steel, with a capital of $1.4 billion, in 1901 was a turning point by any measure. The new holding company brought together Carnegie, Federal, and National Steel, and American Tin Plate, American Wire & Steel, American Steel Hoop, National Tube, American Bridge, and American Sheet Metal in a single entity that immediately controlled between 60 and 70 percent of the domestic market. The new industrial titan depended heavily on the power and genius of J. P. Morgan, Sr. for the successful negotiations and financial arrangements that gave it birth. Dana greeted the new arrival on the corporate scene warmly. He granted that its sheer size might stir public hostility but believed that no opposition strong enough to be harmful could develop unless the company acted against the public interest. He thought there was slight risk of its taking such a step. United States Steel had formed in large part to avert the outbreak of potentially disastrous product and price competition. Its creators had brought it into being for defensive purposes, rather than to force increases in the prices of iron, steel, and products made of these materials. It was clearly to the advantage of the company, he continued with a now-familiar refrain, to maintain low prices. Experience had "shown that even moderate prices stimulate a production larger than the country can consume." The wisest policy must be to hold prices to the lowest point that would "return a fair profit."[31]

Months later an assassin ended President William McKinley's life, and Theodore Roosevelt succeeded to the presidency. Dana's paper initially reflected cautious hope that the new president would pursue a conservative course. In this its editor was soon disappointed. Sometime during the early winter of 1901–1902 the new chief executive began to prod the Justice Department to action. The attorney general launched an antitrust suit against the Northern Securities Company in February 1902. This step marked the beginning of serious efforts at the national level to enforce the Sherman Anti-Trust Act. It left the financial world in shock. Up to this point the Sherman law had seemed to be pretty much a dead letter, and holding companies had appeared to stand beyond its reach.

Throughout and beyond these developments, Dana repeated familiar arguments. A summer 1903 address by Stuyvesant Fish, president of the Illinois Central Railroad, elicited strong praise. Fish predicted continued combination in all areas of business. In time the country's 800 railroads would be consolidated into twenty or thirty systems, but they would never fall under control of a single individual. Combination eliminated destructive competition while permitting efficiencies and economies of scale. Standard Oil, Fish noted accurately, had continually reduced oil prices, increasing its profits through a growing development and sale of by-products. The tendency of the times was to use everything possible. The Armours, for example, "utilize everything but the squeal of the hog. We think that this is the correct view to take"—concentration was the result of the "inexorable logic" of the times. "[Political] affairs in the country will have to be conducted so as to be brought in harmony with it."[32]

Just months earlier, Congress had created the Department of Commerce and Labor. It contained a Bureau of Corporations. Directed by a Commissioner of Corporations, the Bureau was empowered to require standardized annual reports from and investigate and report on the operations of interstate corporations, excepting carriers that fell under the jurisdiction of the ICC. They were subject to the same degree of oversight as the ICC exercised over carriers, and to the same standards of financial accountability as those applying to national banks. This turn of events earned no plaudits from our editor. In December, upon hearing rumors that Standard Oil or some other large firm might test the constitutionality of the law by refusing to submit the required annual report, he suggested that such a test was very much needed.[33]

After Roosevelt won the presidency in his own right in 1904, the character and extent of his commitment to Progressive reform became increasingly, and more alarmingly, clear to William Dana. More vigorous enforcement of the Sherman Anti-Trust Act, as through the successful effort to dissolve the Northern Securities Company and the initiation of other suits, were profoundly disturbing. Resounding public and press accusations of price fixing, insanitary conditions, adulteration of products, and sale of worthless medications, in the meatpacking, food, and drug industries provoked mounting pressures for congressional action as 1904 gave way to 1905. Roosevelt responded with a call for an investigation of the so-called beef trust, consisting of the country's six biggest beef processors: Armour & Company, Swift & Company, Morris & Company, National Packing Company, Schwarzschild & Sulzberger Company, and Cudahy. The resulting report, submitted by Commissioner of Corporations James R. Garfield, amounted to a complete whitewash of the packers. An angry Roosevelt forwarded it to Congress on May 4, 1905. Dana welcomed it. He wrote that its contents brought "a good deal of surprise," given that public opinion regarded the trust as "heinous . . . odious in the extreme." The *Chronicle* unreservedly accepted the finding that there was no monopoly in beef packing. While the trust controlled 98 percent of the kill in eight western cities and 75 percent in New York City, the national figure for the preceding year was only 45 percent. Using Garfield's figures, Dana showed that meat brought in only $39.26 of the $51.28 per head that packers paid for cattle. The by-products ($5 or $6 of that sum from hides) accounted for all profits, which amounted to but 1.8 to 2.3 percent of sales. This modest figure even took into account profits of 17 or 18 percent that resulted when the packers' private stock cars were used to transport cattle to the stockyards. The beef packers were accordingly "open to criticism only so far as amounts offered them by railroads for use of their private cars were excessive. On this last point we are without adequate facts. . . .

[If] the packers are treated more favorably than other shippers, the discrimination should be removed," even though a slight increase in beef prices would result. There was no basis for legislation or antitrust prosecution against the packers.[34] We should note here that calculating profits as a percentage of sales strongly favored the packers. Had Dana figured annual return on invested capital, the result would likely have made it far more difficult to defend them.

There things might have remained, for Roosevelt was preoccupied with passage of the Hepburn railroad bill. Conversations with his personal physician, Department of Agriculture chief chemist Dr. Harvey Wiley, and others finally persuaded him to incorporate into his December 5, 1905, annual message a call for "federal regulation of interstate commerce in misbranded and adulterated foods, drinks, and drugs." Rhode Island's powerful Senator Nelson W. Aldrich managed to bury the resulting bill in committee until the following February, when he suddenly relented. Probably the publication in *Collier's Magazine* of articles exposing dubious practices of the patent medicine industry, threats by the American Medical Association to carry the issue into the partisan arena, and a personal appeal from Roosevelt figured in the reversal. Roosevelt's authoritative biographer, William Henry Harbaugh, speculates that Aldrich may also have wanted to sweep aside obstacles to a showdown debate of the Hepburn railroad measure. Even so, the food and drug bill might have died in the House except for the publication in February of Upton Sinclair's novel *The Jungle*, which provided a graphic and gruesome indictment of the meatpacking industry. Intended to turn readers to socialism, it instead turned their stomachs.

Unhappily for the packing industry, one of the stomachs turned was Roosevelt's. The president ordered an investigation of Sinclair's charges through the Department of Agriculture, bypassing the Bureau of Corporations. He personally appointed social worker James B. Reynolds and Commissioner of Labor Charles P. Neill to determine whether Sinclair's accusations were true. It turned out that many of them were. He also confided in Indiana Senator Albert Beveridge, who had for some time been aware of conditions in the packinghouses. The latter prepared a meat inspection measure, which passed the Senate on May 25, 1905. The House sat on the bill, as the packers arrogantly worked for one crippling amendment after another. As a result Roosevelt decided to send to the lower chamber, and make public, the report of Neill and Reynolds. Dana fumed at this turn of events. He termed the new report prejudicial in the extreme, its authors charged only to verify criticisms of the packing industry rather than conduct an impartial survey. It promised further to compromise overseas sales of American beef, which had already fallen off as a result of declining foreign confidence in the cleanliness and wholesomeness of the product. If the conditions it described actually existed, how, he asked, could it be that workers in the industry had not come forward to report them? If the meat inspection bill and the pure food and drug act passed, where would government interference with the conduct of business end? Despite such objections, the meat inspection, pure food and drug, and one other regulatory measure passed at the end of June. Dana's world, in which the rights of property were broadly defined and protected, was arguably, if obstinately, passing away.[35]

After passage of the several federal regulatory laws of June 30, 1906, William Dana settled into a mixture of anger and gloom. In imposing new curbs on the use of property, the measures tabooed once-accepted economic truths, overrode long-understood individual rights, and aimed to correct "evils in chief part imaginary." They created new classes of crimes. They

take possession of some of our largest industries (as, for instance the railroad rate law), transfer their management from the officials elected by owners to commissioners who are made regulators of the companies' business (although having no property interest in the concerns)—transfers made with the express purpose of reducing the net revenue of these organizations, notwithstanding stock in them has furnished up to this time the chief instrument for the investment of the public savings. The point of greatest concern, however, is that the country just now is about to face a period during which these high-handed laws are to be put into operation . . . with not a little virulence [toward corporations].

It was strange to say, amid such conditions, that only isolated voices here and there spoke out clearly in defense of the old truths and against the new policies. It appeared that the country no longer had a conservative political party, the "radical view" having swept aside ordinary partisan differences. One dangerous spirit advanced under a banner inscribed with "every economic error afloat in any land."[36]

Roosevelt was not finished with big business, however. His antitrust campaign continued. Shock waves radiated in all directions when Judge Kennesaw Mountain Landis in the summer of 1907 fined Standard Oil $29 million for some fourteen hundred separate violations of the Elkins Act. Uneasiness edged toward panic in the financial markets. The president refused to change course until October, when bank speculators unsuccessfully tried to corner the copper market with drafts from their own unstable firms and a leading New York bank. Within days the institutions involved had closed, credit tightened across the country, Westinghouse went into receivership, interior banks called for more and more money from New York, and the Trust Company of America tottered at the edge of failure. At this point, Roosevelt returned from a hunting trip in Louisiana and met with officials of United States Steel and his confidant and Secretary of State Elihu Root. The United States Steel representatives persuaded the president that acquisition by United States Steel of financially troubled Tennessee Coal and Iron, even at a somewhat inflated price, would prevent the latter from failing and restore confidence. Roosevelt assented, and affairs calmed. The incident helped solidify the president's maturing convictions that the Sherman Anti-Trust Act should be amended so as to place all interstate businesses under federal supervision. Giant enterprise was here to stay; it should be regulated, not dissolved. He followed with intensifying attacks on predatory great wealth and on members of the judiciary who protected trusts.

William Dana, who had cheered the resolution of the panic of 1907,[37] resisted Roosevelt's advanced ideas as strongly as Roosevelt advocated them. He was beside himself when the president inspired the introduction of an amendment to the Sherman Anti-Trust Act intended to grant the national government broad new authority. The amendment would, if passed, require the registration with the federal government of *all* corporations engaged in interstate commerce as a condition of immunity from prosecution under the Sherman law. The catch was that registration could be obtained only by filing with the Commissioner of Corporations a written statement as to the formation, organization, financial condition, contracts, and proceedings of a corporation *"as may be prescribed by general regulations from time to time to be made by the President."* The president would also enjoy the power to revoke or alter regulations, while the Commissioner of Corporations was to have authority to approve or disapprove of business combinations entered into by registered corporations after deciding whether or not *"in his judgment"* such a combination would constitute an unreasonable restraint of trade or commerce among the states or with foreign countries. Dana agreed in principle that amending the Sherman law was desirable. The current proposal superficially appeared to relax federal authority, by limiting application of the Sherman measure to unreasonable combinations. In fact, it sought "in a most insidious manner" to extend national power beyond interstate carriers to all interstate corporations and give to the executive branch the capacity to determine when combinations were unreasonable. All in all the proposal was an assault on property and Roosevelt's speech supporting it was "intemperate ... radical and extreme," a source of "sorrow and pain."[38]

Given what we have just seen, it comes as no surprise that the *Chronicle*'s editor obdurately criticized efforts of urban Progressive reformers to address some of their greatest complaints. These included the use of bribery to obtain from state legislatures or municipal governments the rights to exclusive franchises and special privileges for public utilities, such as tax advantages, sometimes for negligible fees, for periods of as long as ninety-nine years. They often and predictably extended to excessive or unreasonable charges for services, and at times to poor or even unhealthy service. Angry reformers worked to subject utilities to municipal control or, worse from Dana's perspective, ownership. Studies and reports concerning municipal socialism both in Europe and in various American cities received extended treatment in the *Chronicle* where their deficiencies were invariably exposed. Whenever cities attempted to operate street railways, water and sewage systems, electrical power generation and grids, and the like, dire results were, Dana's paper reported, inevitable. Here as elsewhere, the only safe course was to guard private property rights and let natural market forces correct any deficiencies.[39]

It is possible to offer many more illustrations of William Dana's resistance to efforts to regulate corporate behavior and his defense of the rights of property through the end of Theodore Roosevelt's presidency and until Dana's death while William Howard Taft occupied the White House.[40] However, doing so would add nothing of substance to the discussion to this point. A brief turn to two further themes will suffice to complete our consideration of William's notion of property rights.

When the Congressional battle over the Hepburn bill was approaching its climax in the spring of 1906, Roosevelt lashed out in anger at the individual and corporate "malefactors of great wealth" who resisted efforts to compel responsible business conduct. For the next year and more, the *Chronicle*'s editor returned frequently to the theme of wealth. He steadfastly disagreed with the notion that accumulating wealth was one of the strongest inducements to productive human activity: one's enterprise could not succeed unless work and the possibility of accumulation continued to be associated with it. To separate those at the top of society and industry and punish them would not injure idlers, but it would eliminate a country's actual innovators and leaders and leave a "nation of pygmies." Imposing limitations on fortunes would have the same effect as cutting off at the knees everyone who had reached the legal limit of height.[41]

After the death of New York financier Russell Sage in July 1906, Dana wrote that Sage's departure had little effect on business. This was for two reasons. First, Sage had carefully arranged his affairs. Second, he had never been either a constructive or a destructive influence, only an accumulator of wealth. Unlike such "Captains of Industry" as "J. P. Morgan, E. H. Harriman, and James J. Hill," who had "been prominent in the business activities of the nation" and "the development or advancement of the country," Sage had been nothing more than an example of a "man of large wealth living in a plain and unostentatious way."[42]

Dana returned to the theme of wealth in his editorial response to Roosevelt's December 1906 state of the union message. Terming its length "repellent," he found in it little to praise save for its lofty moral tone and a generally praiseworthy literary style. The president's criticism of lynchings of Negroes and denunciation of speakers and muckraking writers who stirred up class hatred evinced a proper moral posture. But the "familiar determination to govern and repress capital" was still evident. A case could be made for an income tax as a source of revenue. Regrettably, Roosevelt's view of it as "semi-punitive" (of great fortunes) placed it squarely in conflict with the right of property as affirmed in the Declaration of Independence.[43]

The implications of this statement became clearer a week later when Dana reflected on a recent session of a meeting of the National Civic Federation. There, Andrew Carnegie had advocated that half the estates of the wealthy be given to the community when their owners died; his debating opponent called for confiscating those estates. Dana countered that if the estates were left in the hands of competent heirs they would benefit society more through productive employment than if they were distributed. If not left in able hands, the proverb that there were only two generations between shirtsleeves would again be validated, as was the one that "dirt is good and God rolls every third generation in it." Besides, William added, it was "a sign of upward progress that there is a growing acceptance of the doctrine that wealth is a trust, morally speaking." Consequently, "wealthy men are more and more endowing charities and other institutions for social betterment. But the public cannot expect to both take by confiscation and receive by free gift." It was, therefore, he concluded, inexpedient to "check this growing liberality of disposition by threatening to seize and divide."[44]

In 1907, as Roosevelt traveled down the Mississippi River and reiterated his explosive message about wealth, the *Chronicle* adopted an uncharacteristically derisive tone. It reported that the president in "rasping" speeches of "great vehemence" was asserting that corporations must "go to the wall" when their conduct conflicted with what was right. His call for the courts to construe the Constitution so as to grant broad regulatory authority to the federal government was deeply dispiriting to business. Add to this his "constant declarations against 'swollen fortunes' and 'predatory wealth,' " his support for a "graded income tax and a progressive inheritance tax," his wish "to see the law of master and servant [industrial relations] changed," and his magnetic capacity to induce politicians to follow his lead, and the "whole country" was "engaged in an anti-railroad, anti-corporation, and anti-capital crusade." At the end of the year, for good measure, Dana added the charge that the president had incorporated into his state of the union message attacks on corporations and wealth based on two "unsound" premises. The first was that wealth and accumulation were intrinsically dangerous. The second was that government possessed the wisdom, infallibility, and incorruptibility not found in the people who created it and could therefore safely and responsibly regulate commerce and great fortunes.[45]

The remaining element of property rights to which William Dana directed an unceasing defense brings us full circle back to the question of the rights of labor. However much an abstraction, theory, or even convenient rationalization for the *status quo* it might be in the new corporate environment, he doggedly held fast to the view that labor's right to contract freely was an essential aspect of the right of property. It was, then, no less sacred than any other form of property. It followed that nothing should be allowed to impair the liberty of laborers to bargain individually and free of coercion for the best terms of employment that they could obtain. Coercive interference with nonstrikers or strikebreakers, and most forms of governmental intrusion into labor relations, were to be prevented. What this meant for the proper role of government in industrial relations will be addressed in the next chapter, which considers what William Dana thought to be the legitimate functions of public authorities.

We need here to illustrate Dana's position only briefly. His reactions to three 1908 Supreme Court decisions fairly reflected his stance. On February 4, the high court invalidated Section 10 of the 1898 Erdman Act. The offending passage prohibited interstate carriers from requiring as a condition of employment an agreement (known as a "yellow dog" contract) by workers not to join a labor union. The decision denied the applicability of the Constitution's commerce clause to regulation of the conduct of interstate carriers in setting the terms of employment for their labor force. This domain fell entirely outside the definition of the term "commerce." It therefore violated the freedom of property and contract rights guaranteed by the Fifth Amendment to the Constitution. Further, federal regulation of commerce could not contravene any fundamental right secured by other provisions of the Constitution, including the rights to freedom from compulsion in hiring and/or accepting jobs. Our editor argued that all defenders of liberty, including proponents of unions, must agree with the ruling. "Next to life itself, the highest privilege possessed by the citizen is personal liberty, and the right of freedom of contract."[46]

Four days later came a decision that closed litigation arising from an American Federation of Labor secondary boycott instigated against their employers by striking hatters in Danbury, Connecticut. The justices unanimously ruled that a secondary boycott by a labor union violated the Sherman Anti-Trust Act and awarded $80,000 in damages to the employers. The judicial determination was ironic in the extreme. A law intended to prevent interstate combinations of business from conspiring to restrain trade was, and for the first time, turned against labor unions. Dana not only endorsed the decision but added that the Sherman law should be amended so as explicitly to apply to both capital and labor. He added that the amendment should not stigmatize unions. Instead, it should "permit combination, but . . . make the acts of such combinations dependent wholly upon their merits." His statements appeared to be fair-minded; but in view of his strong commitment to the principle of the open shop, they should perhaps be accepted with caution.[47]

At month's end the Supreme Court in *Muller v. Oregon* upheld an Oregon measure that limited the hours of work for women to a maximum of ten per day. Counsel for the state, Louis D. Brandeis, departed from usual practice in the lengthy brief that he presented. He did not depend on citations of legal precedents. Instead, he argued on the basis of masses of sociological, economic, historical, and statistical information to show that Oregon had acted properly to protect the health, safety, and welfare of its employed female citizens in passing its ten-hour law. Rejecting the view that the statute impaired women's liberty of contract as guaranteed by the Fourteenth Amendment, the justices found for the state. Dana, in an extended and tortured exposition, wound up agreeing with the decision. *Muller*, he said, was very unlike the 1905 *Lochner v. New York* finding in several important respects. *Muller* limited its protection to the weaker sex. *Lochner* had not differentiated between the sexes or different sorts of work and their health effects in setting maximum hours of work for bakers. There were instances in which health considerations and the differing physical and mental endowments of the two sexes ought to be taken into consideration. The Oregon law had properly done so. It did not, then, unconstitutionally impair women's freedom of contract.[48]

Taken as a whole, William Dana's body of writing about the rights of property shows important tendencies. It displays a move over time away from rigid adherence to the free-market economics that he had learned at home and as a college student and young man. He never quite abandoned references to the operation of the market. This was especially the case when the issue was government interference with what he considered to be the rights of property owners freely to acquire, use, and dispose of their holdings so long as doing so did not impair the rights of ownership of others. He held to an individualistic notion of freedom of contract for workingmen and workingwomen to the end of his life. Nevertheless, he tempered it with recognition that protections could be extended to classes needing it, such as women, children, and (as we saw in an earlier chapter) persons with disabilities. In these respects he remained a child of the America of sole proprietorships, partnerships, and small companies in which he had grown up.

At the same time, Dana's thinking about property rights and the market evolved in important ways. He came to believe that completely free competition carried too high a price. It meant excessive instability and disorder, price wars, and expensive and avoidable business failures. He reconciled his faith in free markets with the rise of big business, monopoly, and oligopoly by the beginning of the twentieth century through recourse to the idea of evolution. The country had advanced to a new condition, in which association and cooperation were replacing the erratic old free-market economy with a new regime of greater order and stability. Through agreements among gentlemen (for example, in pools) or new forms of organization such as trusts and holding companies, the United States had traveled far beyond the more primitive conditions of the previous century.

Big business, meanwhile, meant more rather than less individual opportunity, for the growth of large corporations brought greater possibilities for enterprising young men to share in ownership of property (through stock purchases) than had ever been the case in the era of small businesses and cutthroat competition. Large enterprise also brought efficiencies and economies of scale. At the same time, it did not portend victimizing a helpless public through ruthless and extortionate pricing. When prices passed a certain point, competitors would always come in to a given line of commerce, or rivals in other lines would be able to offer substitute goods. Moderate prices, experience had shown, brought wider markets and greater profits than any other arrangement. In sum, Dana's understanding, if it still held some elements that seem today to be contradictory, nevertheless accurately gauged the character of monopolistic and oligopolistic competition. In some respects it anticipated what economist John Kenneth Galbraith would one day call "countervailing power." In these terms, it was forward looking, perhaps prophetic, even if future realities on occasion seriously betrayed William Dana's optimistic expectations.

NOTES

1. Adam Smith, *An Inquiry into the Causes and Nature of the Wealth of Nations* with a new preface by George J. Stigler (Chicago: University of Chicago Press, 1976), 1: 136ff; and Francis Wayland, *Elements of Political Economy*, (4th ed. (Boston: Gould and Lincoln, 1860), 19ff.

2. *Commercial and Financial Chronicle*, June 29, 1895.

3. *Commercial and Financial Chronicle*, June 30, 1906.

4. Harold Underwood Faulkner, *Politics, Reform, and Expansion, 1890–1900* (New York: Harper, 1959), 75; Luther Conant, Jr., "Industrial Consolidations in the United States," *Quarterly Publications of the American Statistical Associations* 8 (March 1901): 207, 226; Edward Chase Kirkland, *Industry Comes of Age: Business, Labor, and Public Policy, 1860–1897* (New York: Holt, Rinehart and Winston, 1961), 225–230, 216–236; and Douglas Steeples and David O. Whitten, *Democracy in Desperation: The Depression of 1893* (Westport, CT: Greenwood, 1998), 19, 25.

5. Edward Gross Campbell, *Reorganization of the American Railroad System, 1893–1900* (New York: Columbia University Press, 1938), 145–201; Henry Varnum and Henry W. Poor, *Poor's Manual of Railroads, 1900* (New York: Henry Varnum and Henry W. Poor, 1901), lxxix, 136; for "morganization," see Ron Chernow, *The House of Morgan: An American Banking Dynasty and the Rise of Modern Finance* (New York: Simon and Schuster, 1990), 66–70; Peter Tufano, "Business Failure, Judicial Intervention, and Financial Innovation: Restructuring U.S. Railroads in the Nineteenth Century," *Business History Review* 71 (Spring 1997): 1–40; Steeples and Whitten, *Democracy in Desperation* 75–76.

6. Of special value for the concentration of economic power, see Fritz Redlich,

The Molding of American Banking: Men and Ideas, Part 2: *1840–1910* (New York: Hafner, 1951), 359–397ff; Ralph L. Nelson, *Merger Movements in American Industry, 1895–1916* (Princeton, NJ: Princeton University Press, 1959), 71–169ff; Naomi R. Lamoreaux, *The Great Merger Movement in American Business, 1895–1904* (New York: Cambridge University Press, 1985); Stuart Bruchey, *Enterprise: The Dynamic Economy of a Free People* (Cambridge: Harvard University Press, 1990), esp. 340–344; Robert Higgs, *The Transformation of the American Economy, 1865–1914* (New York: Wiley, 1971); Victor S. Clark, *History of Manufactures in the United States*, 3 vol. (New York: McGraw-Hill, 1929), 3:29, 43–44, 87–89, 92–96, 220–249, and passim. See also Joseph Allan Nevins, *John D. Rockefeller: The Heroic Age of American Enterprise*, 2 vols. (New York: Scribner's, 1940), 2:365–402 and passim; Ron Chernow, *Titan: The Life of John D. Rockefeller, Sr.* (New York: Random House, 1998); Chernow, *The House of Morgan*; Vincent P. Carosso, *The Morgans: Private International Bankers, 1854–1913* (Cambridge: Harvard University Press, 1987); Campbell, *Reorganization of the American Railroad System*; David O. Whitten, *The Emergence of Giant Enterprise, 1860–1914: American Commercial and Extractive Industries* (Westport, CT: Greenwood, 1983); and Steeples and Whitten, *Democracy in Desperation*, esp. 75–82, 115, 198.

7. Robert H. Wiebe, *Self-Rule: A Cultural History of American Democracy* (Chicago: University of Chicago Press, 1995).

8. *Commercial and Financial Chronicle*, January 7, 1882; and quoted January 28, 1882.

9. *Commercial and Financial Chronicle*, September 18, 1883.

10. *Commercial and Financial Chronicle*, September 4, 1886.

11. *Santa Clara Co. v. S.P.R. Co.* (118 U.S. 394), 1886; *Commercial and Financial Chronicle*, September 18, 1886.

12. *Wabash, St. Louis & Pacific R.R. Co. v. Illinois* (118 U.S. 557), 1886; *Commercial and Financial Chronicle*, November 27, 1886.

13. *Commercial and Financial Chronicle*, November 27, 1886, commenting on litigation between the receiver of the Vicksburg & Meridian Railroad and the Mississippi Railroad Commission.

14. *Commercial and Financial Chronicle*, April 3 and 17 and June 12, 1897; February 12, March 28, and October 29, 1898, regarding *U.S. v. Trans–Missouri Freight Association* (166 U.S. 290), 1897; *Commercial and Financial Chronicle*, November 25 and December 16, 1899, regarding *Addyston Pipe & Steel Co. v. U.S.* (175 U.S. 211), 1899.

15. *Northern Securities Co. v. U.S.* (193 U.S. 197), 1904; *Commercial and Financial Chronicle*, January 25–December 20, 1890; November 26, 1898; November 18, 1899; April 25, 1903; January 2 and 30 and March 12, 19, and 26, 1904; January 27; April 14, 21, and 28; June 23 and 30; and July 7, 1906; and January 18, 1908. For a general study, see Gabriel Kolko, *Railroads and Regulation, 1877–1916* (Princeton, NJ: Princeton University Press, 1965).

16. *Commercial and Financial Chronicle*, July 28, 1888; Wayland, *Elements of Political Economy*, 114–118; Smith, *Wealth of Nations*, 1: 69, 147, 165, 278.

17. *Commercial and Financial Chronicle*, March 10, 1900; U.S. Industrial Commission, "Trust and Industrial Combinations," *Report of the United States Industrial Commission*, 19 vols. (Washington, DC: Government Printing Office, 1900).

18. *Commercial and Financial Chronicle*, January 10, 1903.

19. Agrarian radicals, labor activists, and a range of social reformers led among those who stereotyped trusts, or big business generally, as entities that preyed on shippers, consumers, and competitors through enforced rebates, jacked-up prices, and underselling, to mention but a few offenses. For illustrations, see John Moody, *The Truth About the Trusts* (New York: Moody, 1904); Charles E. Edgerton, "The Wire-Nail Association of 1895–1896" and other selections in *Trusts, Pools, and Combinations*, rev. ed., ed. William Zebina Ripley (Boston: Ginn, 1916), 16–17 and passim.

20. *Commercial and Financial Chronicle*, May 19, 1906, reviewing William Morton Grinnell, *Social Theories and Social Facts* (New York: G. P. Putnam's Sons, 1906).

21. *Commercial and Financial Chronicle*, May 29, 1909.

22. *Munn v. Illinois* (94 U.S. 113), 1877; *Commercial and Financial Chronicle*, July 19, 1873 and March 3, 1877.

23. *Chicago, Milwaukee & St. Paul R.R. Co. v. Minnesota* (134 U.S. 418), 1890; *Commercial and Financial Chronicle*, March 20, 1890.

24. *Reagan v. Farmer's Loan & Trust Co.* (154 U.S. 362), 1894; *Commercial and Financial Chronicle*, May 27 and June 2, 1894.

25. *Commercial and Financial Chronicle*, January 27, February 3 and 10, March 3, April 14 and 28, and June 23 and 30, 1906.

26. *Commercial and Financial Chronicle*, October 9, 1886.

27. *Commercial and Financial Chronicle*, November 2, 1889.

28. *Commercial and Financial Chronicle*, March 23, 1889.

29. *Commercial and Financial Chronicle*, June 8, 1889.

30. *U.S. v. E. C. Knight Co.* (156 U.S. 1) [June 21] 1895; *Commercial and Financial Chronicle*, June 26, 1895.

31. Quotation from *Commercial and Financial Chronicle*, March 2, 1901. For an incisive brief treatment that places the formation of United States Steel in context of the rise of big business, see Alfred D. Chandler, Jr., "The Beginnings of 'Big Business' in American Industry," *Business History Review* 33 (Spring 1959): 1–31. For the emergence of monopoly and oligopoly competition, see note 6 above and Alfred D. Chandler, *Giant Enterprise: Ford, General Motors, and the Automobile Industry* (New York: Harcourt, Brace and World, 1964) Alfred D. Chandler, *Strategy and Structure: Chapters in the History of Industrial Enterprise* (Cambridge: MIT Press, 1962); Alfred D. Chandler, *The Visible Hand: The Managerial Revolution in American Business* (Cambridge: Harvard University Press, 1977); Alfred D. Chandler, *Scale and Scope: The Dynamics of Industrial Capitalism* (Cambridge: Harvard University Press, 1990); Ralph W. Hidy and Muriel E. Hidy, *Pioneering in Big Business, 1882–1911*, vol. 1 of *History of Standard Oil Company* (New York: Harper, 1955); and John Kenneth Galbraith, *American Capitalism: The Concept of Countervailing Power*, rev. ed. (Boston: Houghton Mifflin, 1956). Quotations from *Commercial and Financial Chronicle*, March 2, 1901.

32. For early hopes, persisting through 1902, see *Commercial and Financial Chronicle*, December 7, 1901, and December 6, 1902; for the address of Stuyvesant Fish, see *Commercial and Financial Chronicle*, August 22, 1903; for Northern Securities, William Henry Harbaugh, *The Life and Times of Theodore Roosevelt*, new rev. ed. (New York: Oxford University, 1975), 157–162, passim; and note 15 above.

33. *Commercial and Financial Chronicle*, December 5, 1903.

34. Harbaugh, *The Life and Times of Theodore Roosevelt*, 247–252; *Commercial and Financial Chronicle*, April 15, 1905, and quoted May 11, 1905. For further information on the meatpacking industry, see Mary Yeager, *Competition and Regulation: The Development of Oligopoly in the Meat-Packing Industry* (Greenwich, CT: JAI Press, 1981); Whitten, *The Emergence of Giant Enterprise*, 89–109 and passim; and Margaret Walsh, *The Rise of the Midwestern Meat Packing Industry* (Lexington: University of Kentucky Press, 1982).

35. Harbaugh, *The Life and Times of Theodore Roosevelt*, 247–252; *Commercial and Financial Chronicle*, April 21 and June 9, 23, and 30, 1906; Upton Sinclair, *The Jungle* (New York: Doubleday and Page, 1906). The third measure was the Immunity of Witnesses Act, which required corporation officers to testify to company operations and conduct without invoking the plea of immunity. Dana, of course, challenged its constitutionally under the Fifth Amendment of the Constitution.

36. *Commercial and Financial Chronicle*, June 30, 1906.

37. For a summary, see Harbaugh, *The Life and Times of Theodore Roosevelt*, 253–259, 320–329; *Commercial and Financial Chronicle*, November 9, 1907.

38. *Commercial and Financial Chronicle*, January 18; February 15, 22, and 29; May 23; and quoted February 1 and April 18; all 1908.

39. For examples, see *Commercial and Financial Chronicle*, January 13, 1906; and March 23 and April 6, 1907. The most provocative introduction to the origins of urban Progressivism during the depression of the 1890s is David F. Thelen, *The New Citizenship: Origins of Progressivism, 1895–1900* (New York: Columbia University Press, 1972). Also H. Roger Grant, *Self-Help in the 1890s Depression* (Ames: Iowa State University Press, 1983); John Rogers Commons et al., *The History of Labour in the United States*, vol. 2 (New York: Macmillan, 1918), 509–513. Contemporary material may be found in the *St. Louis Post-Dispatch*, January 20, 1893; *Philadelphia Public Ledger*, February 6, 1894; *San Francisco Chronicle*, July 22, 1894; *Seattle Post-Intelligencer*, July 22, 1897; Richard Theodore Ely, "Natural Monopolies and the Workingman: A Programme of Social Reform," *North American Review* 147 (March 1894): 294–303; American Federation of Labor, *Report of Proceedings of the American Federation of Labor* (Bloomington, IN: American Federation of Labor, 1893, 1894, 1895), respectively 31–41, 336–342, 65–69.

40. For examples, see *Commercial and Financial Chronicle*, 1908–1910, passim, for numerous editorials about antitrust prosecutions, attempts to extend regulatory measures and impose progressive income and inheritance taxes, and efforts to address imbalances in relations of capital and labor.

41. *Commercial and Financial Chronicle*, April 21 and May 12, 1906.

42. *Commercial and Financial Chronicle*, July 28, 1906.

43. *Commercial and Financial Chronicle*, December 8, 1906.

44. *Commercial and Financial Chronicle*, December 15, 1906.

45. *Commercial and Financial Chronicle*, quoted October 5 and December 7, 1907.

46. Quotation from *Commercial and Financial Chronicle*, February 8, 1908, referencing *Adair v. U.S.* (208 U.S. 191) 1908.

47. *Commercial and Financial Chronicle*, February 8, 1908. *Loewe v. Lawler* (208 U.S. 274) 1908 ended litigation dating back to a boycott initiated in 1902.

48. *Muller v. Oregon* (208 U.S. 412) 1908; *Lochner v. New York* (198 U.S. 45) 1905; *Commercial and Financial Chronicle*, February 19, 1908.

6

The Role of Government

The sturdy farmer of the revolutionary period would have resisted the idea that he was unable to protect himself . . . that he needed a large measure of government to help him out.
     —William Buck Dana, September 10, 1887

September 10, 1887, marked the beginning of two years of celebrations in the United States. It was the 100th anniversary of the close of the six-week debate during which delegates to the Constitutional Convention in Philadelphia had hammered out agreements regarding the structure and powers of the new national government that they were devising. The approval of the final draft of the manuscript occurred a week later. Ratification by the people of the required nine states, acting through specially elected conventions, was accomplished in 1789. As commemorative activities began, William Dana took advantage of the occasion to publish in the *Commercial and Financial Chronicle* a special editorial entitled "THE CENTENNIAL OF THE CONSTITUTION." The piece offered a fuller statement of his political philosophy and view of the proper role of government than any other single essay that he wrote.

Dana foresaw that the celebrations then beginning would be useful in reminding Americans of the sagacity of the Constitution's authors. They would highlight the capacity of the great organic law to meet the needs of a society that had quickly evolved from a few millions of farmers scattered along the East Coast to one of tens of millions of people spread across the continent from the Atlantic to the Pacific Oceans in an industrializing and urbanizing regime. The festivities promised another value, too. They would remind all Americans of the aims that the frame of government embodied. Calling on anarchists and communists to embrace this sacred guarantor of American rights or leave the country, our editor added, "there has during the last score of years grown up a disposition to construe [the Constitution] less rigidly. . . . For instance," he asked in a wonderfully anachronistic reference to a mode of travel unavailable in 1787, "who would have supposed that the clause 'to regulate commerce among the states' would ever be made to cover the supervision and management of the details of railroad management?" Which of the Founders would not have "started," he continued with a comparably untimely disregard for resort to paper currency during the American War for Independence, to discover that the federal government had used the provision empowering it "to coin money" to justify a "forced" issue of paper currency during the Civil War?

"Then," Dana went on, there was the "growing tendency to paternalism in government. Government is asked to remedy all the evils that afflict mankind." Instead of encouraging the old "habits of self reliance" the inclination was to look more and more to national and state legislation for relief from every problem. "The sturdy farmer of the revolutionary period would have resisted the idea that he was unable to protect himself in the ordinary, every-day affairs of life." "That was not his theory of government. On the contrary," our writer said as a faithful follower of Jeffersonian and Jacksonian principles, "his belief was that that government is best which governs least. . . . Accordingly, the powers granted [to the national government] under the Constitution are limited and specified." Centennial celebrations, he concluded, would exert their most positive effect if they rekindled among Americans an understanding of these fundamental Constitutional principles.[1]

This paean to the Constitution could, by and large, have come from the pen of Yale Chancellor James Kent. It was of a piece with Kent's reverence for the great document. It reflected his conception that humanity had never devised a greater plan for ordering society. It followed his determined adherence to the view that it conferred specific grants of power on the national authorities. It echoed his conviction that the instrument of government aimed to defend the sanctity of property and individual rights, and created the judiciary as an essential protector of those rights against unconstitutional interference by public officials.[2]

Given William Dana's guiding ideas of the meaning of the Constitution, it would be easy to leap to the conclusion that his view of the role of government was primarily, if not almost exclusively, negative. Government was formed under the cover of universal moral law to protect the individual rights that nature itself ordained. These included personal liberty, and the right of property in all of its dimensions. The means of providing such protection lay chiefly in *not interfering* in the sphere of individual action or with the operation of the market or of natural law more generally. Of course, public authorities should avoid measures that threatened to disturb business confidence. Even maintenance of order and justice could be construed negatively. Both involved preventing interference with the natural liberties of individuals. Where authority was conferred on government, the applicable grant was explicit, specific, and to be narrowly construed. Congress' power to regulate commerce among the states and with foreign nations referred, apparently, only to trade rather than to any other form of business activity (until, after passage of the Sherman Anti-Trust Act, it could be extended to the conduct of secondary boycotts by organized labor). And at that, where interstate carriers were involved, it seemed to be confined properly—if we take the 1887 editorial at face value—only to modes of transportation available in 1787. The power to "coin" money meant exactly that. It did not include issuance of paper currency. With so many things apparently beyond the legal competence of government, it is fair to ask what, then, government—especially national government—could legitimately do. The answer turns out to be more complex, and to indicate greater suppleness of intellect, than these introductory remarks suggest.

There are ways in which William Dana's conception of the role of government calls to mind an unstable *ménage à trois* of ideas. The three parties to the arrangement were his notions of the American Constitution and federal system, economic laws, and morality. Deriving as they did from sources whose views overlapped, we would expect them for the most part to agree, or at least in general be mutually reinforcing. They were, although there were instances in which one or another seemed to be a bit out of joint. Frankly, sometimes they collided with one another. Considering that the *Chronicle*'s editor was human and given to emotional attachments as well as to principled convictions, it is to be expected that they could contradict one another and actual political, economic, and social conditions.

At the center stood Constitutional principles asserted at the opening of this chapter. Dana in political, economic, and social matters usually turned first to the Constitution, then to natural law or morality. Civil war, dashing his hopes for a peaceful resolution of sectional differences, dominated his first years of publishing. He expressed no doubt regarding the right of the United States to assert and maintain its integrity by resorting to arms. He did not contest federal authority to raise and support such forces as were required. He unquestioningly accepted the need for the government to take advantage of the patriotism of the people, report its financial needs honestly, and seek "[t]he amount of taxes required by the exigency of the case."

After the great conflict ended, Dana pleaded for a speedy restoration of the southern states to full partnership in the Union. He opposed Reconstruction through military occupation and flatly rejected the view that no other course would protect the rights of freedmen. He interpreted the impeachment of Andrew Johnson and other radical measures as congressional attempts to usurp control of the executive and judiciary branches of government. He favored compromise on the question of Negro suffrage. The vote should first be granted to Blacks owning land. If it proved successful, then all freedmen could be enfranchised. He welcomed the withdrawal of the last forces from the South in 1877, as troops finally marched out of Florida, Louisiana, and South Carolina. The war, he believed, had long since accomplished its goals of freeing the slaves and restoring the Union. He was pleased that a way had been found to stretch "our fundamental law" to ensure a peaceful settlement of the disputed presidential election of 1876. The compromise that ended the crisis (of which withdrawal of the army was one element) made Rutherford B. Hayes president, promised a cabinet post to a Southerner, and held out the prospect of federal subsidies for a Pacific railroad with a southern terminus. It also averted what could have become widespread civil disorder, since Hayes' rival Samuel B. Tilden was the actual victor.[3] These events ended a sorry chapter in our history, but they by no means eliminated questions as to the role of government.

During the Civil War, Dana had accepted as plausible the view that a federal subsidy to aid construction of the first transcontinental railroad could be justified as a war measure. Apparently unaware of its inclusion in the compromise of 1877, he greeted a congressional proposal to subsidize building of a southern transcontinental railroad icily. In general, government, and especially the national authority, ought not do for the people what they could do for themselves. The Constitution, he stated flatly, conferred on government no right to subsidize a railroad, "bolstering up private enterprises by guaranteeing bonds or credit in any form." For good measure, he drily recorded amazement that cities as varied in location as St. Louis, Memphis, Cincinnati, Savannah, and New Orleans all published maps showing that they sat on the thirty-second parallel in a direct line with San Diego, the proposed western terminus of the line.[4]

William Dana granted that the United States ought to possess a large merchant marine. He also believed that the Constitution allowed certain sorts of government actions that would help in developing a maritime industry. For example, Congress could remove the prohibition against American registry of foreign-built ships. A law that had originated to guard our flourishing shipbuilders had, after the Civil War, become an obstacle to American shipowners, since our own shipbuilding industry had sunk to unimportance. He came also to favor removing other barriers to American competition on the seas. These included consular fees, reduction of the tonnage tax, and elimination of the hospital tax. At the same time, he adopted a "wait and see" attitude about subsidizing mails dispatched on ships of American registry.[5]

While at various times a philanthropic contributor to public education, a school board member, and a supporter of Yale University, Dana believed that the Constitution restricted responsibility for public instruction to local governments and to the states. For that reason, while he thought that the high incidence of illiteracy in certain parts of the country was "alarming," he found an 1884 congressional proposal to provide national aid for public education even more so. It was "paternalism in its worst form . . . a bill to help those who will not help themselves." It was axiomatic for him that if people in states with high illiteracy rates wished to make education free and universal, "[t]hey could and would do it." Accordingly the bill should be rejected.[6]

Calls for other forms of governmental intrusion into the economy received equally short shrift. In an 1882 editorial about the growing popularity of the idea that the federal government should assume ownership of the telegraphic system, the *Chronicle* flatly rejected the scheme as ill-advised. If the government allowed the companies to set their own valuation before it bought them, it would be in effect supporting stock watering. If it set the valuation, the result would be to suppress the creation of new telegraph companies. In either event, the public ownership was "a trifle too autocratic or communistic for America." To look away from the market and to government for a remedy for all social problems would eliminate incentives for investment, and unwisely abandon old ideas about the proper role of public authorities. For emphasis, the editor added: "To fly to the Government for relief is flying into the arms of incompetency."[7]

Dana's resistance to public ownership or subsidization of enterprises properly left to capitalists extended to state and local projects as well. It is an amusing exercise to read his editorials condemning cost overruns for construction of the Brooklyn Bridge, and even for assisting in its erection. In one of his rare miscalls he wrote: "We have always thought the bridge enterprise a stupendous mistake . . . and have never been able to appreciate the logic of the conclusion . . . that when a large amount of money has been unwisely put into an enterprise, there is a necessity of putting in more." He predicted that the structure would offer slower transit than ferries and added that the bridge was a stellar example of "non-remunerative enterprises which are shunned by private capital but are deemed suitable for the money of the public." Criticisms continued through the opening of the architectural marvel in 1883. Then, Dana was still growling that it would benefit Brooklyn rather than New York, be subject to fog closures, return inadequate tolls, and had yet to complete important transit connections in Brooklyn. Even with a railroad deck the bridge remained a "Colossal wager." If the bridge's problems were solved, it would unify the metropolis and become "the wonder of the age, even," he skeptically added, "if the age learns to accept it as a matter of course and feels no wonder about it."[8]

Ideology appears to have triumphed over new realities in William

Dana's comments on other issues involving the role of local government, as well. He deplored agitation for and celebrated defeat of a proposal for municipal ownership of Chicago's street railways. He roundly condemned the election in 1910 of a socialist as mayor of Milwaukee, linking the result to an unhealthy tendency to extend "the function of government in all directions." Even a plan to issue municipal bonds to extend New York's subway system won no support from the *Chronicle*. Why not adhere, the editor asked, to "the good old-fashioned way of letting private capital come in and take the risk of present losses in return for the probability of future gains?" Doing so would both confine government to its proper role and free taxpaying property owners of an obligation that might extend for as long as forty years and jeopardize real estate values in the entire city.[9]

Speculation in securities, influence peddling by lobbyists, dishonesty in management—especially in banks, trust companies, insurance companies, and utilities vested with a public interest—posed an additional challenge to William Dana's conception of the proper functions of government. In principle, he accepted the necessity of some regulation, particularly at the state and local level. His view of federal authority over interstate commerce was, as shown in the previous chapter, even more restricted. In theory, he accepted the necessity of some forms of regulation; however, it is difficult to find a regulation of which he actually approved. He thought that legislation to restrict speculation, for example, would be no more effective than would laws "against the small pox or scarlet fever," and accordingly he did not favor it.[10] As he saw it, when banks speculated, or failed, the fault lay with officers, not directors. He deplored dishonest management no less than speculation. He rebuked the House of Representatives' investigative committee for pursuing only a halfhearted probe of the Crédit Mobilier scandal, which involved fraud and influence peddling in the construction of the Union Pacific Railroad. He championed publicizing corporate affairs so that investors would receive accurate information. State law could be an effective instrument for assuring adequate reporting of corporate conditions, he thought. He fully agreed with several state court rulings that directors could assume no responsibilities and liability beyond employing men of good reputation, and approving all important loans. It would be impossible to recruit good directors, who were typically men with many and varied interests, if more were asked of them. It was entirely infeasible to expect that directors would operate as detectives who would ferret out misconduct.[11] As for insurance and trust companies, they were legitimately subject to state supervision; but it should not be allowed to become so burdensome as to detract from the conduct of business.[12] The stock exchange should be left to reform itself, and Dana applauded it when it did so. He also pointed out that it expelled miscreants. Similarly, with respect to laws governing employers' liability in the event of injuries to workingmen, there needed to be a balance. Rather than placing the entire burden on the laborer, it should be divided between master and workingman through retention of the principle of contributory negligence. To abandon it in favor of a law that freed the laborer of all responsibility would be, rather than a "fair deal," a fraud.[13] The broad outlines of a philosophy of minimalist government intervention in the economy remain unimpaired through this review of Dana's views.

Two additional points deserve brief treatment here. The first is that the *Chronicle*'s editor unwaveringly opposed both relaxing bankruptcy laws and retaining usury laws, at any level of government. While such acts seem at first blush to deal with unrelated matters at opposite ends of the financial spectrum, they in fact involved converging principles and issues. Measures that prohibited usury tended to drive credit out of jurisdictions where they ruled, to jurisdictions that allowed the market in money free play. Elimination of usury laws was a means of encouraging lending, which was an important instrument of business growth. It was also, as we saw earlier, specifically authorized by the New Testament and therefore carried the weight of revealed divine sanction as well as of the natural laws of the market. Bankruptcy statutes that were too lenient regarding the rights of debtors likewise worked against market principles and morality. They could discourage even prudent lending if they appeared to be too one-sided in their provisions, for such an imbalance could drive capital into hiding. Meanwhile, people might be induced to borrow excessively, spend too liberally, conduct their affairs improvidently, or even enter bankruptcy fraudulently if laws governing bankruptcy sheltered them too much from the consequences of their actions.[14]

The second point requires a bit more elaboration. It is that William Dana steadfastly advocated economy and efficiency in government. This inclination figured in his strong opposition to the institution of a system of postal savings banks. Doing so would deepen the federal government's involvement in something from which it should divorce itself: banking. It would place the postal system in competition with the national banks. Even worse, it was not necessary. Existing national banks and savings institutions were sufficient for the wants of the country. Creation of postal savings banks would add to the expense of government without increasing its efficiency or serving some bona fide purpose. Such remarks about economy in government were of a piece, of course, with Dana's lifelong devotion to the classic capitalist virtues of industry, thrift, sobriety, and providence with respect to private as well as public conduct. Just five months before he drew his last breath he published one last editorial criticizing the extravagance of Americans in private no less than in public spending. Citing the comparative observations of an American banker who had just returned from a trip to Europe, he worried: "A large class of American people are running wild in useless extravagance. They are buying several hundred million dollars worth of automobiles annually," which would require further large expenditures for maintenance. Meanwhile, high crop prices of the last few years had induced typically conservative farmers to buy land on credit. There were even reports from the Hawkeye State of the "mad desire of Iowa farmers for automobiles" costing the state millions of dollars.[15]

The question of government efficiency inevitably raised issues of expense and function that loomed much larger than that of whether to create a postal savings system. By 1868 the *Chronicle*'s editor was calling for repeal of the Civil War cotton tax. It was, he wrote, draining the South of money that would aid in the rebuilding of the region's industry, and that would also enable it to buy northern goods. He was agreeable to continuing the income tax as late as 1870, providing it were capped at 3 percent so as to reduce the temptation to prepare fraudulent returns. But these were only minor sources of revenue, and they did not loom large.[16]

Customs duties held greater importance for the period under review. They were the principal source of revenue for the United States Treasury. During the period of consistent federal surpluses (1867–1894), they usually outran internal revenues by a ratio of 3:2 or even 2:1. Dana devoted far less editorial attention to them than to money and banking, the regulation of business, and, at the turn of the century, to the problem of overseas empire. Nevertheless, they were a matter of sufficient concern to warrant brief discussion. He believed that protective tariffs not only withheld money from the use of business, but that they also artificially increased the cost of living and, as Chapter 3 showed, the risk of business depressions. Free trade was not really an option for him. It was a fact that domestic industry in some instances could benefit from moderately protective duties. It was also true that his readership was varied and not united on the question of tariffs. Manufacturers, international as opposed to domestic merchants, financiers with business both here and abroad, and railroad management held differing interests that recommended a cautious editorial course, if only to protect the *Chronicle*'s credibility with its constituencies and their willingness to pay for subscriptions.

The several tariff increases of the Civil War and Reconstruction years had elevated duties to an average of 47 percent by 1869. A year later, William Dana called for an elimination of a tariff on the necessities of life, for which he thought that there was no need "except in the last emergency of government ... in the present condition of the Treasury there is no excuse whatever for maintaining any duties upon them." A majority in Congress apparently agreed, passing a bill that placed 130 items, mostly raw materials, on the duty-free list. A new measure in 1872 continued the downward trend, but the solons three years later restored most of the recent cuts. When iron and steel producers at the end of the decade declared that tariff protection was essential for prosperity, he rejoined that prosperity was the result of no single cause. Perhaps "some hidden law" accounted for the country's marvelous growth throughout the century. But assigning its growth to the tariff was the logical equivalent of blaming the presidential electoral commission of 1877 for the outbreak of yellow fever that followed in 1878. Attempts to reduce duties during the depression of the 1880s drew repeated comment. A law effecting minor reductions won approval in March 1883. Congress continued to struggle with the tariff question. Disappointed with the failure of a reform bill in the House of Representatives in 1884, Dana declared that the issue would not go away. It was in the interest of manufacturers to lead, "instead of oppose, the movement [to reduce imposts wisely]. No one aims or desires to harm vested interests." The country could and should move to "real" protection, say at 33⅓ percent of dutiable values, rather than maintaining oppressive rates. When President Grover Cleveland devoted his entire 1887 message to the surplus and tariff reduction, Dana again advised for moderate reform including provision for free raw materials.[17]

Our editor offered cautious criticism of the increases incorporated into the 1890 Republican McKinley Tariff. He closely followed the complex parliamentary maneuvering that followed the introduction in 1893 by House Ways and Means Committee Chairman William L. Wilson of a bill to enact significant reductions. The Senate gutted it by adding 634 protectionist amendments before its passage the following year. President Cleveland let the weakened measure become law without his signature. Malodorous revelations surfaced of influence peddling by the sugar trust and of senatorial speculation in its stock as the upper chamber struggled to adjust the sugar duty. Nonetheless, the *Chronicle* claimed that the new measure did well in admitting lumber, flax, hemp, indigo, wool, and some industrial chemicals and dyes to the duty-free list. Modest reductions in average duties for manufactures from 47.5 percent to 39.9 percent *ad valorem* would also, it noted, continue adequate protection for industry, and passage of the bill would end months of business uncertainty over the outcome of wrangling between the two legislative chambers. The incorporation into the tariff of a renewed income tax elicited an unenthusiastic response. Most of those who had "wanted a lower tariff law by no means favored the revival of the income tax.... Experience has taught chiefly that a tax of that character catches chiefly men with tender consciences and trust estates. That is enough to condemn it in the judgment of intelligent men, even if it had no other objectionable feature."[18]

A month after William McKinley's election to the presidency in 1896, the House Committee on Banking and Currency adopted the motion by Representative Marriott Brosius (R-Pa.) to invite commercial, industrial, and financial bodies to submit suggestions for reform of the country's currency system. In his final annual message, in December, Cleveland still defended the 1894 tariff, although he knew well that the central place of protection in the president-elect's program promised revision. Cleveland asserted that the 1894 tariff, fashioned mainly to provide revenue, would yield an adequate return if given a fair chance while business improved. Lower duties also promised a larger external market for American exports.

McKinley moved at once on the tariff, promising in his inaugural address to call Congress into special session to deal exclusively with that subject. Congress assembled on March 15, 1897. Maine Representative Nelson Dingley promptly introduced a bill, which he had prepared during the previous session. The House approved it on March 31. Senate protectionists padded it with 872 amendments. Anticipating this outcome, and a consequent delay in addressing other issues, Dana at the end of 1896 had written: "Those who voted for McKinley, whether Democrats or Republicans, cannot now object to a higher tariff; they voted for him knowing that protection was one feature of the policy he represented."[19]

The passage of the Dingley Tariff removed deliberations over customs policy from the agenda of Congress for a dozen years. When the federal legislature in 1909 enacted yet another protective measure, Dana's views had changed not one whit. He still favored only moderate protection of manufactures, and a scheme of duties that kept raw materials and foodstuffs as inexpensive as possible. He was displeased that a proposed Constitutional amendment threatened to extend a federal income tax to individuals. He was also unhappy that a corporate income tax, while it had been reduced, had been retained. He believed that the chief result of passage of the bill would be a sense of "relief that a [legislative] process so inevitable disturbing to business calculations has reached its end."[20]

Our writer's relief at the end of the special session of 1897 was typical. He generally regarded adjournment as "the most welcome act" of a session. His objections went beyond matters of expense to include matters of process, as well. He was a particularly harsh critic of the fact that Congress could consider as many as 15,000 private bills, applying to single individuals, in a session, while acting on only a dozen measures of public importance. He thought that prioritizing the congressional agenda was essential. He believed that a streamlining of congressional parliamentary procedure would bring an improvement. In particular, it made no sense to him that a bill passed in the Senate and sent to the House could not receive consideration in the lower chamber unless it were reported out by the proper committee. If the committee bottled it up, the approval of the Speaker and a two-thirds majority was required to bring it to the floor. It made no more sense that conference committees of the two houses formed to reconcile two different versions of a bill might report an entirely different final version. Congress was, he believed, subject to a tyranny of committees; and Congress should begin its first session the December immediately following November elections, rather than thirteen months later. The second session and presidential terms should begin the following July 4, close to the July 1 beginning of the fiscal year. Strikingly, while he favored economical government, William also endorsed paying to high federal officers salaries sufficiently large to attract men of the best quality to seek office or service on the bench. In this regard he stood in the tradition of Adam Smith. While he challenged the usefulness of information gathered through responses to some of the questions that the Bureau of the Census added from time to time, and its growing corps of clerks, in the main he found the decennial census to be a valuable tool of commerce.[21]

All things considered, William Dana saw a restricted, but important, role for government. When we turn to the largest issues of his times, that role turns out to have been much more important than what we have seen thus far. It was, in fact, crucial.

For purposes of discussion, we can identify in William Dana's thinking two different primary streams of editorial concern regarding government while he was an editor and publisher. While both were evident for the entire period (1861–1910), one predominated before the election of William McKinley to the presidency in 1896. The other occupied center stage afterward. In the former period, Dana devoted the greatest part of his editorial attention to the struggle between proponents of paper currency and silver inflation and advocates of a gold standard and conservative, or "sound," money and banking policies. In the latter, chiefly during the first decade of the twentieth century, his foremost concern was increasing government interference with property rights through attempts to extend regulation of business. Chapter 5 has already considered this subject at length.

Dana's ideas about money, as other economic subjects, depended heavily on his study of classical theory as framed by Adam Smith and transmitted through Francis Wayland. Since convenience, Wayland wrote, would have prompted society to abandon barter for the use of money as a medium of exchange with or without governmental action, the appropriate role of public authorities with respect to money was quite limited. As the agent of society, government held but a single proper monetary function. That was to increase the convenience that money brought. Society could employ government to denominate precious metals as legal tender, meaning that the debtor need offer nothing else in payment. If government did designate a substance as legal tender, it should require that it was of uniform purity, divided into conveniently sized portions, and prepared so as to display its face value. There was no further official role with respect to money. Precious metals, as far as their values were concerned, were like any other commodity and subject to the same laws of trade.

Wayland, as Smith before him, reserved the creation of paper currency to private banks. Different sorts of banks circulated bills of exchange, non-promissory notes, and promissory notes payable in specie and on demand. Bank currency offered substantial advantages. A bill with a face value of 1,000 ounces of silver might cost only two or three cents to produce, saving the community a great sum if it accomplished what the silver would have. Replacing such currency was also less costly than replacing silver. Currency was far more portable than precious metals. And because note holders rarely, if ever all sought to convert their notes to specie (gold) at the same time or even in proximate times, Smith had pointed out, bankers could maintain reserves of precious metals equal in value to only a fraction of the face value of the circulating notes. This freed, for profitable employment, precious metal that would otherwise be locked idle in vaults. As with metallic currency, the function of government with respect to paper money was not to choose whether or not to employ it. That was society's choice. No community, however, would tolerate a worthless or a fluctuating currency. It followed that government inherited the task of making any paper currency reasonably secure, by establishing standards of liability for stockholders and directors of banks.

According to Wayland, government should also "take all reasonable means to diminish the *fluctuation* [in value]" of a paper currency. This was best done by maintaining—and here Wayland was more conservative than Smith had been—a very high proportion of specie to paper through the issuance chiefly of large-denomination notes. That would force a primary reliance on metal currency, fluctuations in the value of which depended chiefly on variations in international exchange rates. Wayland concluded his discussion of banks with some addenda that reflected the experience of the young United States. Government, he wrote, should neither oppress banks nor protect them from the consequences of their actions. There should be no banking monopolies. State legislatures should not create banks through special legislation, impose excessive fees for charters, nor levy unduly heavy taxes on financial institutions. Such conduct generally taught banks injustice. Wayland complained that state legislatures had largely ignored this advice, defending banks from the consequences of suspensions and allowing them to violate charter obligations. "The language of this conduct" had been, "simply . . . [let] us fleece *you* and *you* . . . the public."[22]

Having matured with such beliefs, Dana found, in the financial situation of the United States in the years following the Civil War, ample cause for worry. Financing the bloody conflict had forced the United States to extraordinary exertions. As early as August 5, 1861, Congress imposed a tax of 3 percent on all yearly personal incomes in excess of $300. The national legislature also increased customs duties several times and acted to raise revenue from a variety of excise, manufacturing, and sales imposts. For the first time, internal revenues surpassed customs receipts in importance as a source of federal funding. The income tax generated about 20 percent of government income; manufactures and sales charges another 26 percent. Issues of paper currency shared heavily in supporting the war effort. On December 31, 1861, the United States suspended payment of its obligations in specie, in order to direct commerce as well as public finance toward a greater reliance on paper instruments of exchange. In February 1862, Congress authorized the issue of $450 million in irredeemable legal tender notes, popularly called "greenbacks." The creation of a system of national banks afterward brought into being a further new form of currency, national banknotes. That these must be secured, by requiring nationally chartered banks to deposit with the Treasury a stipulated minimum sum of U.S. bonds and to maintain in the Treasury deposits of bonds equal in value to 90 percent of that of the notes they circulated, assured a market for the principal means employed to finance the war, loans. These were mainly in the form of bond issues, underwritten and sold through major bankers. The passage of a 10 percent yearly tax on note issues of state banks, on March 3, 1865, effectively drove them from circulation and protected national banks and their notes from competition by state-chartered institutions. Five months later, in August, the cost of the war pushed the national debt to a peak of $2.845 billion.[23]

Several problems associated with public finance drew repeated comment from Dana during the half century that he lived after the cessation of the sanguinary four-year struggle to restore the Union. None commanded more attention than money, and its close relative, banking. In some respects his notions reflected no progress beyond what he had learned through his formal education. In others they were merely commonplaces for persons of his time who frequented the business circles in which he moved. In a few significant regards, his grasp of money and banking placed him among the most progressive thinkers of his era.

The *Chronicle*'s editor understood very well that the government's suspension of specie payments and subsequent issuance of legal tender notes and creation of a note-issuing national banking system had installed a fiduciary monetary system in the United States. He viewed these measures as necessary responses to the exigencies of war. He knew that whatever exchange value the greenbacks or national banknotes possessed did not derive from their intrinsic worth. In the former instance, it derived from the fact that the legal tender notes were direct liabilities of the Treasury, although the Treasury bore no obligation to redeem them in specie. In the latter, it originated in the fact that national banknotes were indirect liabilities of the Treasury, which was required to maintain a specie reserve of 5 percent for redemption purposes.

To say that William Dana understood these things is not to say that he in any way liked them. He did not. He was pleased when the Supreme Court in 1870 decided by a five to three vote that the greenbacks were legal tender only in transactions entered into after Congress authorized their circulation. Their use in contracts concluded earlier violated those agreements, and thus abridged property rights. When the tribunal a year later, after the filling of two vacant seats with new justices, reversed itself and ruled five to four that the greenbacks were legal tender for all contracts, whether entered into before or after passage of the law providing for them, he described the decision as "wrong in law and pernicious in its practical" effects. It implied that Congress could literally define anything it wished to as money. In doing so it overturned, he warned with disgust, the constitutional principle that ours is a government of delegated and limited powers.[24] He never afterward wavered from adherence to the principle that irredeemable paper currency was an evil to be avoided at all costs. He believed that the continuing depression throughout the 1870s was largely a result of the business distrust caused by "currency agitation" of those maneuvering to obtain new issues of greenbacks.[25]

When the Supreme Court in 1884 upheld the constitutionality of an 1878 law prohibiting any new contraction of circulation of the Civil War notes, the *Chronicle* fired off an editorial fusillade. The earlier legal tender decisions had upheld congressional authority to issue paper currency on the grounds that doing so was an appropriate means of helping finance the late conflict. The new ruling was much more far-reaching. It maintained that circulation of the notes was a constitutional use of congressional power to establish and maintain a uniform system of money. Further, the power to coin money was an inherent and exclusive attribute of sovereignty. The Constitution did not deny to the federal government the power to circulate a paper currency. Hence, Congress held that power to the fullest possible extent. Dana warned darkly that this decision was nothing less than "a studied assertion of national power, going in some respects far beyond any former decision." It claimed a national authority to impair the obligation of contracts, to "debase the coinage and to force creditors to accept the degraded coin at its face value." There could be no more offensive a statement of federal power, nor was it any reassurance that the people controlled the government. They could on a whim change the standard of values. The decision was so sweeping as to give " 'centralization,' that bugbear of the [founding] fathers" its greatest victory. Now, our writer concluded, was the time for conservatives to join in a comprehensive effort to reform the currency and drive the inflationists from the field.[26]

The understanding of the *Chronicle*'s editor that money was "simply an instrument for measuring and canceling debts" was correct. He strayed into error in some of his other opinions about money. In 1865 and 1866, the government had gradually redeemed greenbacks, until the amount outstanding had fallen to $356 million. Pent-up demand and postwar economic expansion more than compensated for any dampening effect that this action might otherwise have produced. After Ulysses S. Grant was elected to the presidency in 1868, national policy swung to favor hard money. Every year the chief executive asked Congress to enact legislation providing for the resumption of specie payments. Congress obliged with the Public Credit Act in 1869. The measure mandated resumption of government payments in specie, but without requiring that the greenbacks be maintained at par with gold. Then a deadlock developed between congressional factions favoring and opposing the legal tenders, and resumption of specie payments at par. Depression pushed distressed farmers and laborers in 1873 to clamor for new issues of greenbacks. They argued that an increased circulation of money would stimulate gains in prices, incomes, a willingness and ability to purchase, and general trade. Near the end of the year Dana took sharp exception to these views. Since money was merely an instrument, new issues of paper currency would "only add to the volume, without adding to the value, of the whole circulating mass." It would not increase prosperity. Instead, it would further weaken confidence and damage business. In addition, adding to the quantity of legal tender notes in circulation would rob the "holders of our currency" by subjecting them to any loss resulting from its inevitable depreciation in value.

Readers with good memories must have appreciated this argument. The irredeemable legal tenders had fallen from par when they were first issued, in 1862, to thirty-nine cents in the spring of 1864. Postwar prosperity and redemption of $100 million of the notes had encouraged a rise in their circulating value, but it still fluctuated ten or more cents below par. Dana was not finished yet, though. He charged that the depreciation prompted by issuing more greenbacks would be a "pernicious form of indirect taxation . . . imposed upon the country without need, without justification, without the special authority of Congress, and under cover of war powers long ago extinguished [by the end of the Civil War]." Greenback inflation would, in a phrase, bring about "monstrous evils."[27]

In fact, as Milton Friedman and Anna Jacobson Schwartz showed in their classic monetary history of the United States the inflationists were on to something. Changes in tax rates, fluctuations in public spending, borrowing, paying down the national debt, and variations in the amount of currency in circulation could all change the stock of money. So could the leverage intrinsic to a fractional reserve, note-issuing, national banking system, where each dollar in reserve could give rise to several additional dollars in deposits, through lending. The volume or stock of money did and does matter. There was and is a positive relationship between its volume and its value. Measures changing the stock of money can and do encourage or discourage business.[28]

If Dana erred in one respect, about money, his grasp exceeded that of inflationists in another. In an 1875 editorial he maintained that it was chiefly a shortage of credit, rather than of currency, that created the tight monetary conditions blamed for contracting business. That the country had prospered in the years after the Civil War, while the Treasury was redeeming greenbacks wholesale, he offered as evidence in support of his contention. Whether valid or not, this was not his most important point. He went on to offer a telling criticism of inflationists that showed how fully he understood the new financial realities transforming the country. The greatest error of which the greenbackers were guilty was that they failed "to comprehend the great revolution which modern enterprise has effected in the use of substitutes for money [currency]. Cheques now take the place of cash, and hundreds of millions of debt are canceled and paid every week in this city [New York] without the use of a dollar in actual cash. The contraction of currency, so long as there is no contraction of credit," he wrote with all of the authority that he could muster, "will do little else than call into operation some of the thousand economies by which society in modern times economizes money."[29]

By the time William Dana wrote these words, the context and content of the national debate over money had changed significantly. Congressional wrangling over monetary policy proceeded throughout the depressed years of the 1870s. In April 1874, greenbacker influence won approval of a bill to increase the circulation of legal tender notes to $400 million. President Grant responded with a veto on the 22nd. In June, the legislative and executive branches agreed on a compromise. Dana characterized a newly passed law as the most significant currency statute since that of February 1862, under which the legal tender notes had originated. The measure provided for creation of a bureau to redeem greenbacks. Further, it authorized a slight increase in the volume of greenbacks, to a maximum of $382 million. In accomplishing these things Dana believed that it had at last settled the question regarding the legal limit on greenback circulation. More important, it had also ensured that henceforth Congress could only provide for retiring the notes, since their issue had depended on the constitutional authority of Congress to declare and provide support for waging war.[30]

Just months later the protracted struggle over the full resumption of specie payments climaxed. On January 14, 1875, after heated deliberations, Congress finally passed the Specie Resumption Act. It stipulated that on and after January 1, 1879, the Treasury was to redeem the greenbacks at par with gold. Greenback circulation was to be fixed permanently at $300 million. If there were not a sufficient federal surplus to accomplish the necessary redemption of notes, the law empowered the Secretary of the Treasury to sell at par 4.5 or 5 percent bonds to obtain the needed gold. Lawmakers threw a crumb to inflationists by including a provision permitting national banks to increase their note issues by $5 million for every $4 million in greenbacks that were retired. Dana had long campaigned for passage of a resumption measure.[31] He wasted no time predicting that it would speed the return of prosperity by improving confidence in the nation's money and in the security of property.

The *Chronicle* often repeated this refrain between the law's passage and its effective date. Its editor roundly condemned the continued opposition of inflationists to resumption. "Inflation and honesty are," he asserted on one occasion, "opposites." Worse, inflation invited "official extravagance, and . . . corruption."[32] He scorned demagogic predictions in Congress that resumption (by tightening the supply of money) would produce even worse business stagnation as a "deplorable war in Washington upon the public credit."[33] Americans would not be misled by such stuff. "Our people," he wrote hopefully, "are too shrewd to give a dollar for [a paper note worth] ninety cents."[34] Inflationists needed to change their thinking. A moderate, healthy contraction of the currency was in truth "a needful preliminary to specie resumption." It would lift confidence and thereby ease credit, which was the key to restoring prosperity. Dana illustrated the crucial role of credit by showing that England functioned as the financial clearinghouse of the world with a smaller volume of money than the aggregate stock of currency in the United States.[35]

Resumption may well have figured in business revival when it came in 1879. The coincidence of short crops overseas with bounteous harvests here was likely of much greater importance.[36] By that year, too, Dana's focus as a defender of stable values and sound money had shifted in reply to a new turn in the divisive contemporary political battle over monetary policy. The reasons are well-known to anyone familiar with the history of the period.

During the 1870s the leading commercial nations of Europe substituted gold for silver as the basis of their monetary systems.[37] One result was to reduce the demand for silver for monetary use. At the same time important new discoveries in the West pushed the United States to world preeminence as a silver producer during the period 1871–1915. Between 1870 and 1874, annual American output of the white metal jumped from 12.4 million to 28.9 million ounces. After a dip in 1875, the yearly yield shot up to 63 million ounces in 1892. For years before the 1870s, the prices of gold and silver had been relatively stable. The former sold for about $22 per ounce, the latter for $1.32. In 1873, rising American output and changing European policies brought an almost imperceptible decline in the price of silver to $1.297. On February 12, before the drop was noticeable, Congress passed a new coinage act with little discussion. The bill defined the metal, denominations, bullion content by weight, and degree of fineness (purity) of metals to be used in our coinage. That standard upon which all other coins were based was to be the gold dollar, at 25.8 grains nine-tenths fine. (The smallest denomination gold coin actually minted was the quarter eagle, which was worth $2.50.) The law ended minting of standard silver dollars (412.5 fine grains) for domestic use and continued that of "trade dollars" of 420 grains (378 fine) for international commerce. Its aim here was to force the lighter-weight 377.25 fine grains Mexican dollar from circulation in foreign trade, especially in the Orient where it was widely used. It also proposed to function as leverage, Dana reported, to secure the international adoption "of silver for the use of the civilized countries of the world." As an advocate of bimetallism to be achieved through an international agreement, and of conservative money policies, William endorsed the law.

The growing abundance of silver, discontinuance of the coinage of standard silver dollars, the onset of depression in 1873, the historic appreciation of silver and use of it as money, and objections of monetary conservatives to the greenbacks converged to encourage a shift in the strategy of American inflationists during the 1870s. Agitation for new issues of greenbacks never completely died out; but silver became the preferred vehicle for expanding the money supply. It gained support during the business downturn of the 1880s and became the commanding issue during the severe depression that devastated the nation during the 1890s. In retrospect, a coinage act that had drawn relatively little attention when it was passed came more and more to seem, to those agrarians and workingmen hardest hit by bad times, to have been the result of a conspiracy of great financiers. These unscrupulous operators had combined to monopolize the control of money and drive prices down. As prices for goods and services fell, the cost of money in terms of goods and services rose, profiting the financiers and oppressing producers and debtors. So was born the myth of the "conspiracy of 1873" to "demonetize" silver. Dana, who had worked so hard for specie resumption, had now to direct his attention toward a new menace: calls for increasing coinage of a metal rapidly falling in value. If silver enthusiasts won their way, declining silver prices placed the country at risk of coining silver dollars whose worth by weight fell increasingly short of their face value. Here was a new threat to monetary stability and security of property values. William Dana's defense of sound money and the role of government in assuring it entered a new, more urgent, phase.[38]

By the end of the 1870s, pressure to resume coinage of silver dollars was building up rapidly. Missouri Representative Richard Parks Bland introduced in the House a proposal to renew coinage of silver dollars in unlimited quantity at a weight ratio of 16:1 with gold. The lower chamber approved the proposal in October 1876, but conservatives blocked action in the Senate. On November 5, 1877, the House again passed the bill. The Senate concurred after incorporating a weakening amendment offered by William B. Allison of Iowa. The Bland-Allison Act became law on February 28, after Congress overrode a presidential veto. It required the Treasury to buy $2 million to $4 million of silver a month and coin it as standard dollars. Dana, as other conservative spokesmen for propertied interests, vigilantly opposed the legislation. At the beginning of 1877 he published a piece that likened governmental attempts to fix the price of commodities—in this case, silver—to King Canute's legendary effort to hold back the tide by royal order.[39]

The Bland-Allison measure was not the only bump on the road to a final resolution of the contest over inflation that would satisfy conservatives. It continued in operation after the resumption of specie payments. The government actually purchased only the minimum quantity of silver specified in the law. But the state of affairs satisfied neither inflationists nor their opponents. The former unceasingly pressed for free coinage. As an exponent of the view of the latter, William Dana resisted the coinage of *any* silver as dangerous in the absence of an international bimetallic agreement and of a sufficiently large Treasury gold reserve to meet redemption needs and the demands of international trade. Unending agitation for silver was, he believed, profoundly unsettling for business. In March 1881, upon learning to his surprise that Britain and Germany were not strongly supportive of an international bimetallic conference to be held in Paris in April, he expressed disappointment. He believed that only concerted action could restore silver to the old 15½:1 ratio with gold. After it became apparent during the following weeks that only French and American representatives favored an agreement, he reported that America's business classes had altered their views. Earlier they had been willing to give bimetallism the benefit of the doubt. Now, any agreement "must place the stability of [the price of] silver beyond question before we can enter into" it.[40]

When Britain and France seemed disinclined to join in a new bimetallic conference in Paris the following year, the *Chronicle*'s editor strongly counseled Congress against tinkering with the monetary system. It would be premature and unwise to do so after successfully concluding such strenuous efforts to get the country back on a gold basis. "The truth is," he warned, "the influence of vicious currency legislation is not open to sight, it is hidden and subtle, but breaks out at times," as it was doing at that time by prompting fearful investors to unload their notes and other holdings for gold and ship it overseas.[41] In contrast, he was pleased when Senator John Sherman offered a bill to establish a Treasury reserve of $100 million in gold, and later with its passage in the stead of competing proposals to create mixed reserves of gold and silver.[42]

Dana clung to his hope for international bimetallism for another decade. When depression in 1885 brought reports of renewed interest in France and Germany in reinstating silver coinage, he immediately weighed in with editorial endorsement. "All that is needed," he penned, "is for the United States to simply suspend coinage [of silver], and Europe, left thus to struggle with the [business] conditions its own [monetary] folly has produced, will speedily work a way out for all." He agreed with the writer of a letter to the *Chronicle* who wrote that circumstances had progressed beyond the point at which a single country could maintain a bimetallic system, although France's 70-year success with bimetallism showed that bimetallism was in principle workable. The main obstacle to international bimetallism was the stubborn determination of British banking interests to protect their preeminence.[43] He expressed similar interest in, but not much hope for, proposals in 1889 for yet another Paris meeting to confer about bimetallism.[44]

Meanwhile, Dana steadfastly stood against any moves to expand silver coinage in the United States alone. He just as determinedly argued that the country should abandon its dangerous flirtation with silver inflation and end minting of the white metal. He condemned the 1890 Sherman Silver Purchase Act because it obliged the Treasury to buy 4.5 million ounces of silver a month, issue against these purchases a new currency (the treasury notes of 1890), and mint the silver into dollars. The law was fiscally irresponsible, amounting to a subsidy that would take up the entire output of our silver mines. It would stir up enormous fears about the ability of the Treasury to maintain payments in gold. Enacted as a compromise between those favoring free coinage and those hoping to hold back the silverite tide, Dana believed that it was worse than free coinage. "Free coinage," he wrote, "no doubt would be an icy cold bath, for its operation would neither raise the price of silver nor flood the country with currency, so after a few weeks' experience it would be abandoned by its best friends." The Sherman law, in contrast, was more insidious. Its operation would weaken confidence, but over a much longer period of time. The resulting uncertainty could lead to currency redemption that would ultimately work great injury to business and force the country off the gold standard. With the failure of still another international bimetallic conference, in Brussels at the end of 1892, William Dana appears to have abandoned hope for international bimetallism. Thereafter, he moved to unyielding support for discontinuance of coinage and use of silver dollars, and to embrace a single gold standard of values.[45]

The wrenching depression of the 1890s made defense of the gold standard seem more important than ever. It put an entirely new complexion on political struggles over the money question. Around 1890 the Farmers' Alliances had drifted into politics, forming the People's Party. It quickly made impressive, or frightening depending on one's perspective, inroads in several Southern and Middle Border states. At its first presidential convention in Omaha in 1892, it adopted a platform that by the standards of the time was radical. There was a demand for the free and unlimited coinage of silver at a ratio of 16:1 with gold. The platform called for an increase in circulating currency to at least $50 per capita, and replacement of national banknotes with a currency issued by the government only. It asked for national ownership of railroads and communications, creation of a postal savings system, a graduated income tax, prohibition of alien ownership of land, direct election of U.S. Senators, adoption of the secret written ballot, introduction of the initiative and referendum, and an eight-hour workday. The party's candidate, James B. Weaver, polled 1 million of the 12 million votes cast in the presidential balloting. As the depression persisted, silverites captured the party and thrust its other issues aside. In 1896 they captured the Democratic Party as well, leading it to adopt a free silver platform and nominate Nebraska Congressman William Jennings Bryan for the presidency. Populists fused with the Democrats to increase prospects for a silver victory in the election of that year.

Meanwhile, depression placed the Treasury under siege. After a major London bank suspended payments to depositors seeking to make withdrawals in late 1890, British investors unloaded American securities to cover themselves. Gold flowed out of the Treasury and overseas in payment. Americans who held paper currency became increasingly distrustful of the ability of the Treasury to maintain a reserve adequate to meet its obligations as reduced federal revenues and increased expenditures began to erode the surplus after the 1890 Republican fiscal program took effect. They began to redeem their greenbacks and treasury notes in gold, drawing the reserve down further. An endless cycle of circulation-redemption began, as the Treasury attempted to place the currency back into circulation through payment of its bills, only to see notes redeemed again. On April 21, 1893, the gold reserve dipped below $100 million for the first time since its creation in 1882. On December 30 it was down to $80 million. At the same time silver dollars piled up in vaults, for lack of popular demand for them. Four times during the period 1894–1896 the government resorted to bond issues, totaling $262 million, to raise gold in order to prevent exhaustion of the reserve that would drive the country from the gold standard. Affairs did not settle down until William McKinley, running on a sound money platform, decisively defeated Bryan for the presidency.

William Dana was far from idle during these harrowing years. Literally every edition of the *Chronicle* from January 1893 through the end of 1898 contained at least one editorial defending sound money. Dana at first predicted that repeal of the 1890 silver purchase law would remove the uncertainty that had caused depression.[46] When prosperity did not promptly return after a special session of Congress voted voted for repeal on October 30, 1893, he blamed the continued agitation of advocates of free silver and resulting threats to the Treasury reserve. While his defense of sound money took many forms, one or two references will suffice to illustrate his now familiar views. In 1894 Representative Bland proposed coinage of the silver seignorage—that is, the profit the government made when it coined silver dollars whose face value exceeded their bullion cost. Dana scorned the plan as a "stupendous embodiment of ignorance" and was greatly relieved when Congress on April 4 sustained a presidential veto.[47] The following year he proposed "a thoroughly organized move-ment . . . to induce every [business] man to put his hand into his pocket and give what he is willing to give to defeat once and forever these [sil-verite] enemies of prosperity." He believed that the time was favorable to end the "free-silver lunacy," and the way to do so was to educate the people and provide "the means" to assure electoral victories of every promising sound-money candidate.[48] While the *Chronicle* did not abandon its nonpartisan tradition in 1896, neither did it conceal its continuing com-mitment to government guarantees of a stable, gold-backed money stan-dard. A hopeful Dana thought that he discerned the beginnings of business recovery immediately after the election. His worries about the federal money system did not end until Congress passed a definitive act on March 14, 1900. The new Currency (Gold Standard) Act reaffirmed that the gold dollar of 25.8 grains, nine-tenths fine, was the standard unit of value. It placed all forms of money issued by the United States at parity with gold. It provided authority to sell bonds to maintain a reserve of $150 million for redemption of legal tender notes. Better to serve rural needs, it also permitted chartering national banks, with a minimum capital of $25,000, in towns with less than 3,000 residents.[49] Dana could now turn from his long effort to win a government guarantee of sound money to his second great financial concern, banking. While complex, the issues to be ad-dressed require less extensive discussion than the subjects just treated.

The national banking laws of 1863 and 1864 had created a system of free banking by independent corporations. There was no provision for central coordination or reserves. To obtain a federal charter, incorporators need meet only a few general requirements. For example, the laws pegged minimum capital requirements to sizes of the communities in which the banks were situated. They provided that each bank must buy and deposit in the Treasury U.S. bonds equal in value to one-third of its capital. In addition, national banks were empowered to issue paper currency, the national banknotes. When they did so, they had to purchase and deposit in the Treasury U.S. bonds equal to 90 percent of the face value of the notes.

Prudent bank management imposed difficult, competing demands. De-posits had to be deployed so as to maximize both liquidity and profita-bility, "opposite poles in the banking universe," as the authors of the authoritative history of the depression of the 1890s wrote. A prudent port-folio was balanced between long-term (ten, fifteen, and twenty years), intermediate-term (three, five, and ten years), near-term (three, six, and nine months), and highly liquid, instantly redeemable (daily, weekly, thirty, sixty, and ninety days) investments and loans. Banks could readily place long-term money in business and real estate loans. Shorter-term loans had to be secured by collateral more easily liquidated than land and factories. Unfortunately, bankers in the nineteenth and early twentieth centuries enjoyed few opportunities for securely investing money that must be quickly available. Highly liquid, short-term debt instruments had no reliable market. Hence, the shorter a loan's term, the tighter the money market for it. Meanwhile, bankers confronted a conundrum. There were idle funds (short-term) in one account and a deficiency (long-term) in others.

The results were foreseeable. Real estate borrowers found it difficult to obtain loans, while short-term funds sat in vaults unused. Cities offered greater opportunities than rural areas, and the possibilities increased with the size of the city. New York, because its stock exchange had become the country's major equity market, offered the best prospects. Call loans to brokers made a lucrative, highly liquid market for New York bankers. Brokers secured these loans with stock, which could be liquidated quickly in the lively city stock exchange. Call loans secured by stock of sufficient value to provide a margin for normal market fluctuations were safe earning assets. Investors liked them, too. They let the buyer leverage stock purchases. When New York banks depleted their own short-term lendable funds, they turned to banks in other cities. These directed their own excess reserves, together with those of their country correspondents, to the metropolis. There, the stock market (in good times) made money for banks across the country. That the national banking laws allowed smaller bankers to place three-fifths of their mandatory reserves in the designated central reserve cities of St. Louis, Chicago, and New York added to the flow. The movement of funds from many country banks to a lesser number of city banks, then to central reserve city banks, and at last to New York, resulted in a triangle or pyramid, hence a pyramiding, of reserves.

The system worked and was profitable. If a bank anywhere in the pyramid needed its reserves, it sent a call up through the pyramid to the broker who had taken out the call loan. If the client who owned the stock given the bank as collateral could not produce the required money on call, it was sold and the necessary money was sent down the pyramid to the recalling bank. This was fine as long as there were only limited calls for repayment. If many banks called for funds at one time, the stock market could fall as a wave of stock sales to recover call loans struck it. In a falling market banks holding stocks as collateral for call loans watched closely. When the value of stocks offered as collateral for loans fell to approach the loans' value, they offered such stocks for sale. The prospects for a market collapse resulting from increasing sales of stock held as collateral grew, as the gap between the values of the stocks and loans narrowed. In periods of crisis, banks in major cities issued clearinghouse certificates to use in lieu of cash to settle interbank balances. The Treasury could ease currency stringency, too. As long as it operated at a surplus, it could repurchase outstanding federal bonds as a means of placing money in circulation. When the surplus vanished during the depressed 1890s it sold bonds, as shown above, to replenish its reserves. In either event, it was taking on functions properly reserved for a central bank. This complex of problems persisted into the twentieth century, when federal funds markets and Treasury bills replaced call loans as the principal highly liquid assets.

There was more. In financial circles profound criticisms of the banking system were gaining support in the last quarter of the nineteenth century. One was that the system lacked coherence. Another was that it failed to provide adequate security. A third was that national bank note circulation was inelastic. By this contemporaries meant that fluctuating seasonal requirements for money failed to stimulate needed adjustments to the currency supply. Note circulation contracted when demand for currency was high and forced interest rates up, and increased when the reverse was true: it did not expand and shrink in parallel with the needs of commerce. Inelasticity was, of course, an intrinsic quality of national bank notes because their circulation was pegged to deposits in the Treasury of U.S. bonds that member banks held. The problem was really much less serious than it seemed. William Dana, as we saw above, was well aware that the greater part by far of our commerce was carried on by use of checks.[50] But for inflationists, the focal question was the amount of circulating currency.

Dana was among the earliest, most persistent, and most prescient of advocates for banking and currency reform in his America. This role reflected significant changes in his thinking over the years. Initially, he had been skeptical of the creation of a system of nationally chartered banks with note-issuing ability. He feared that the institutions would be nothing more than a reincarnation of the infamous "pet" banks of the Jacksonian era. Further, if any profit attached to note issue, it should go to the government rather than to banks. Even as the Civil War was coming to an end, he began to plead for a return to specie payments. Not until 1870 was he persuaded that the national banking system was "no longer an experiment." While still imperfect, with a slow process of note redemption that at times resulted in redundant money, it had nevertheless "fully achieved the goals of its promoters and almost put to silence the cavils of its foes."[51]

Soon after, Dana began to sketch out ideas that in time ripened into a support for a broad range of banking reforms. In the winters of 1870–1871 and 1871–1872 he considered how the fall grain, pork, and cotton trades and April demands for money for temporary settlement of accounts subjected New York to seasonal outflows of money and monetary stringency. The remedy, he proposed, was a more elastic currency, perhaps to be provided by temporary issues of 3.65 percent Treasury notes.[52] When he heard reports that President Grant's 1873 message would address, among other monetary reforms, the problem of inelasticity, he responded with almost rhapsodic enthusiasm. "Elasticity," he said, "is the quality which compels the currency to shrink into conformity with the needs for it. When we see such a beautiful symmetry of alternate contraction and expansion achieved in other machines, why can we not insinuate it into the delicate mechanism of our currency?" Why could not the currency contract in the summer and expand in fall and winter? Was such a prospect hopeless? He thought not. Imagination and will could provide the solution.[53]

More was needed of national banks than an elastic currency. Because they were private corporations "intrusted with public functions" they owed "certain duties not only to . . . stockholders" and customers, "but also to the general public." Accordingly, the institutions ought never to lend to individuals, even long-time and large customers, who were attempting to corner currency, gold, or silver.[54] When popular opinion bristled at the accumulation of deposits in national banks during the depression of the 1870s, Dana pointed out that banks did not make their money through deposits. They earned their profits by lending; deposits were only so much "dead weight." Reports of bad loans, official misconduct, and poor management were sure to bring criticism. Because of their crucial economic role, William Dana believed that banks should be subject to frequent inspection by government examiners. Inspections uncovered poor management, inadequate reserves, and risky lending practices. They deterred dangerous or criminal conduct, improving safety and thus confidence.[55] Recognizing a need for coherence in the national banking system, our editor was, by 1876, wondering whether the American Bankers' Association might prove to be the mechanism that could provide it.[56]

Up until the beginning of the 1890s the *Chronicle* devoted relatively little attention to banking reform *per se* as Dana focused on the greenback and silver questions. When stirred to comment, he averred that he held "no attachment to our present national system that would prevent our accepting a better." He immediately backtracked, however, cautioning against any hasty or hostile legislation in the name of reform, reminding readers that such action "would rob us of the best banking system that any country has ever enjoyed."[57]

That all changed in the 1890s as the tidal wave of support for silver neared its crest. In July 1891, William Dana offered a succinct but comprehensive assessment of our national banking system that reflected the development of his thinking thus far. He observed that the United States could look to no other country for a model of how to meet its unique banking needs. Its vast expanse and rapid development called for an enlarged currency supply *and* one that would meet local needs. National banknotes and silver fell short on both counts. They gravitated toward New York. The country held three unmet needs regarding currency. These were, first, "a paper and not a coin currency." The second was "a currency that will not gravitate toward and accumulate in New York each summer."

The last was "a note which when out of use will have an unfailing tendency towards the home of the issuer, kept in readiness for any coming need."[58]

With the arrival of depression two years later, financial interests came to regard reform of banking and banknote issues with the same urgency that silverites attached to their agenda. Discussion naturally centered at the annual meetings of the American Bankers' Association (ABA), where financiers and economists presented papers and speeches proposing improvements to the banking system. Dana had attended regularly since his purchase of *Hunt's Merchants' Magazine*, so his was a familiar figure at these gatherings. Even with reform sentiment swelling rapidly, bankers remained divided over the best course to pursue. Conservatives desired to increase note issues to the full par value of bonds national banks placed in the Treasury, and special high-tax supplementary issues as a means to provide elasticity. More progressive bankers wanted to divorce note issues from the Treasury and adopt a currency secured by the assets of banks.

A major reform effort began at the October 1894 Baltimore meeting of the ABA. Alonzo Barton Hepburn (the most determined reformer of the time and president of New York's Third National Bank), Charles C. Homer (president of Baltimore's Second National Bank), and financier Horace White authored it. It proposed to substitute an asset-based for a bond-backed currency. Issues were not to exceed 50 percent of a national bank's paid-in, unimpaired capital and were to bear a 1.5 percent annual tax. Emergency issues were also to be allowed, up to an added one-fourth of a national bank's capital and subject to the regular tax, and to a special surtax to ensure prompt retirement when they were no longer needed. The U.S. government was to be absolute guarantor of the notes, the Treasury accumulating a guarantee fund of 5 percent through a yearly impost on notes outstanding. Dana applauded the intent and direction of the plan.[59] Somewhat altered, it became the core of the legislative program that the Cleveland administration submitted to Congress that December. As changed, it projected note issues valued at up to 75 percent of, and constituting a first lien on, the assets of national banks. Issues were to be secured through retirement from circulation and deposit in the Treasury of legal tenders, in lieu of bonds. The Treasury was to gain discretionary power to retire other notes as well. There was to be an annual tax on note issues, to redeem notes of failed banks. Legal reserve requirements were to be abolished. State banks complying with the plan's provisions were to be exempted from the 1866 punitive tax on their notes. The plan, reflecting Cleveland's (and Dana's) ideal of the complete separation of "[g]overnment from the business of banking" amounted to a restatement of Jacksonian free-banking principles. Congressional deadlock over money and banking doomed the proposal from the moment of its introduction, the House refusing on January 9, 1895, to set a date for its consideration.[60]

Dana's disappointment with the rejection of the Baltimore proposal and the 1894 administration proposals simmered until William McKinley won the presidency in 1896. Shortly after the ballots had been counted, the Indianapolis Board of Trade sent out invitations for a monetary reform meeting to be held in the Hoosier capital in January. Delegates representing business interests in 100 cities attended. Most were merchants, but there were noted bankers, too, including Charles Homer. Dana praised the convention for brushing aside "all nostrums and palliatives" and calling unequivocally for a sound-money system, retirement of the greenbacks, and a turn to an asset currency. McKinley, in his March inaugural address, bypassed the money question and declared that tariff revision was his top priority. At his bidding Congress met in special session weeks later. After legislators approved a new schedule of customs duties they adjourned hastily in July (because of obstructionist opposition) without addressing money and banking. Thus, the Indianapolis convention's call for congressional authorization of a commission charged to propose financial reforms went unanswered.

After the solons left Washington, leaders of the Indianapolis movement appointed an independent commission. At its head was noted economist and gold standard proponent James Laurence Laughlin from Chicago. Henry Parker Willis served as research assistant, gaining experience he would later use when he helped Laughlin and others frame the Federal Reserve Act. The reassembled Indianapolis convention in January 1898 promptly approved a preliminary report published earlier that month. It offered several recommendations. The most immediate was solidification of the gold standard. It also proposed granting the Treasury authority to sell bonds to protect the reserve, and creation of regional redemption centers. Treasury redemption and fiscal functions were to be separated. The United States was to move to an asset currency modeled on that proposed in the Baltimore plan. Dana followed these events attentively and endorsed the ideas of the Indianapolis convention.[61] McKinley withheld any action until after he signed the tariff into law, on July 24, on advice that raising the money question might jeopardize congressional support for the tariff. Then he appointed a three-member commission to seek an international bimetallic agreement, while working to broaden support for money and banking reform among businessmen here. The commission's errand failed, as Dana had predicted.[62] The administration's financial recommendations went to Congress in December in the annual report of Secretary of the Treasury Lyman J. Gage.

The administration's proposals essentially followed those of the Indianapolis plan, with additions to weaken the vicious cycle of redeeming greenbacks for gold by providing that they were to be recirculated only in exchange for gold. In addition, national banks were to be authorized to deposit $200 million of greenbacks in the Treasury as reserves, withdrawing them from circulation, and to circulate notes to par value of gold bonds received for the greenbacks deposited. Emergency, high-taxed asset notes, secured by a safety fund, would meet the need for elasticity. Dana assigned the scheme the "highest value." He was optimistic that the "sincere and intelligent thinkers" serving on the House Committee on Money and Banking would consider it on its merits, unobscured by such side questions as the "crime of 1873" and free silver. If they did so, they would produce a proper resolution of the money question and dissolve "the unnatural alliance between the agricultural South and the mining West" while meeting the needs of the country for an elastic currency.[63]

Inflationist sentiment was still strong enough in Congress to prevent approval. Then, the coming of war with Spain redirected attention away from money and banking. It was not until 1900 that an enlarged Republican majority could pass a revised gold standard act.[64] Legislative divisions were still too wide to bridge quickly on the question of money and banking. In 1903 Dana wrote that it would be easier to extract "sunbeams from a cucumber" than to secure passage that year of a bill creating "an automatic currency" supply-adjusting device. Reform sentiment born of depression in the 1890s continued to ferment, however. Congress saw the submission of new money and banking reform bills each session, and during each session William Dana continued to monitor and advocate their passage. Finally, pressure for change ripened into the Aldrich-Vreeland Act of 1908, a belated compromise response to the panic of 1907. This measure at last injected a degree of elasticity into the national currency system. In addition to notes based on deposits in the Treasury of federal bonds, it authorized national banks for six years to make emergency issues of currency based on municipal, county, and state bonds, and commercial paper. To ensure that the special circulation was withdrawn as soon as it was not needed, it bore a graduated tax of up to 10 percent.

The act still omitted any safeguards for the credit supply. This omission was not accidental. Rather, it reflected deeply rooted beliefs, in which Dana shared and for which he fought. As submitted the House bill that contained the kernel of the act included provision for the creation of a guarantee fund to protect bank deposits, and to be administered through regional associations of national banks. Whenever the balance in the fund exceeded $25 million, the excess was to be used on January 1 and July 1 to purchase and retire greenbacks. To Dana's mind, "any kind of guaranty for the deposits is wrong. Its tendency would be to lessen the inducement to efficient, careful and conservative management over imprudent, slovenly and hazardous management. In the estimation of the depositors, the good bank would have no advantage over the poor bank." All banks, however managed, would stand on the same level, irrespective of their capital, and with deposits guaranteed there would be slight inducement to acquire either a large capital or substantial reserves. Nor would depositors "be put on inquiry with reference to the character of the management or the standing of the institution." The cause of most bank failures was poor practices, not corruption. Consequently "even the most ceaseless vigilance" could not perfectly protect against the tendency of poorly managed banks to make imprudent loans. The result would be to require sound banks to make good the losses of poorly managed peers. And instead of reducing the threat of runs, the guaranty fund might actually increase it. If a "couple of dozen medium-sized institutions (say carrying 25 to 20 million resources each) throughout their country close their doors," it might easily happen that confidence in the whole structure would be impaired and "general runs be started," endangering the solvency of a great many institutions. Such an argument assumed, it would seem, that depositors as a matter of course would ordinarily enjoy access to adequate information upon which to base their choice of banks, and, indeed, that they would *have* a choice. This was scarcely the case for masses of ordinary people, and for inhabitants of small communities. We would not be wrong to suspect that Dana did not foresee the rise of retail banking, with its implications for the applicability of his views.[65]

The most important provision of the Aldrich-Vreeland Act was establishment of a National Monetary Commission of nine Senators and nine Representatives to study and report on the banking and monetary systems of the United States and European countries. While they worked, William Dana remained firm in his beliefs about reform of our money and banking systems. His final editorial on the subject appeared at the beginning of 1909. One obstacle to shifting to an asset currency, he wrote, was to find a way to make it attractive to current holders of U.S. bonds. A proposal at the recent annual meeting of the American Economic Association held promise. Let the Treasury offer the option of converting existing bonds into new issues of bonds. The new obligations would bear a sufficiently higher rate of interest to allow them to sell at as high or at a higher price than current issues even after the privilege of issuing notes against them was withdrawn. This shift could be accomplished gradually, and it would be well worth the added interest expense to the Treasury. It would constitute "the best expenditure our Government could make," by eliminating an "impossible" monetary system that was "absolutely unresponsive to trade movements," not "worth preserving," "a burdensome machine at best," and "the antithesis of a Central Bank device." It is a pity that William Dana did not live to see the report of the commission that the Aldrich-Vreeland Act authorized. It contained much of which he would have approved and eventuated in passage of the Federal Reserve Act in 1913, three years after his death.[66]

William Dana in all likelihood would have preferred to confine his paper's attention to the purely commercial aspects of global affairs. News of steamship sailings, variations in demand for and prices of commodities in world markets, fluctuations in trade in money and in exchange rates, and various industrial and agricultural developments offered ample material. The increasing pace of communication, as the use of steamships grew and undersea telegraph and telephone cables multiplied made it easier, and more important than ever, to brief readers in the timeliest manner possible. But other events inevitably drew Dana's attention to the evolving international interests and role of the American government. The second great wave of European imperialism and colonialism surged during the latter half of the nineteenth century. Focusing on Africa, the Pacific islands, and Asia, it created novel conditions. These conditions confronted America's leaders with the need to adapt the nation's policies. It became impossible for the *Chronicle* to avoid commenting extensively on American foreign policy and questions of empire.

Our editor's views matured slowly. As they did, they offered scant evidence to support the hypothesis that a "new imperialism" based on control of sea-lanes and access to foreign markets was gaining broad support in the American business community. Quite the contrary. Dana was, if anything, a reluctant, even a balky, imperialist. Commenting on the purchase of Alaska, he wrote at the beginning of 1868: "We did not favor the acquisition, but now that it has been added to our domain . . . we trust our people will not be long in ascertaining what are its advantages and reaping benefit from them." He counseled in the same article against any acquisitions in the West Indies as naval outposts. These would be highly vulnerable in event of war, while "the people are not disposed to have their means squandered upon territorial acquisitions for which, to say the least, we have no immediate occasion." Better for the nation to take time to recuperate from the Civil War.[67]

Dana's writing continued in much the same vein until the close of the century. On several occasions he warmly endorsed international disarmament. In 1872 he observed that the cost of standing armies was an oppressive burden on European taxpayers, and the temptation was excessive to use the forces to destroy the very peace they were intended to protect. He accordingly hoped that popular demand would lead to arms reductions and settlement of international disputes by diplomacy. Seven years later he was keenly disappointed when the German Reichstag rejected a proposal to convene a European congress to consider the propriety of arms reductions, adding that he still hoped for "a general movement in favor of disarmament." The fact that the Reichstag had even considered a proposal for a conference he interpreted as encouraging.[68]

Growing international interest in building a canal across the Central American isthmus also elicited cautious comments. Dana dismissed the idea that construction by a foreign power jeopardized American interests, thought the cost of the project well beyond this country's means, and that therefore another country would build the waterway. He was sharply critical of an 1881 letter from Secretary of State James Gillespie Blaine to each of our ministers in Europe asserting that under the Monroe Doctrine and an 1846 treaty with New Granada (Colombia) the United States held an exclusive right to guarantee the neutrality of an interoceanic canal in Colombia. Colombia, he wrote, as a sovereign nation, could enter into any international agreements it wished. Besides, only by amending the Constitution could the federal government gain the power to build an isthmian canal and that was not necessary. "We have always taken the position," he added, "that we ought to wish the canal God-speed. Come from what source it might, by whomsoever managed, by whomsoever constructed, the harvest of profit would be ours. . . . If we will not take part in the work, let us not hinder it."[69] Meanwhile, in 1878, a comparable hesitancy regarding overseas territories surfaced, when the United States concluded a treaty through which its ships gained access to Samoan ports. William Dana opined that the arrangement would bring few near-term benefits. American trade with the islands was small, and the native population was dwindling. True, Pago Pago was the best harbor in the Pacific and en route to Australia. Given as much, at some future point the islands might assume greater importance.[70]

Through the 1880s, subscribers to the *Chronicle* read increasingly probing editorials addressing the implications of the growing interest of the European powers in gaining new colonies. In 1885 it dismissed German designs on Pacific islands as unrealizable, given Germany's lack of sea power. It continued to oppose American construction of an isthmian canal. It regarded the dispatch of an American representative to an international congress on the Congo as a turning point. The question of overseas possessions was becoming insistent. Since the acquisition of such territories would constitute a radical departure, William Dana believed that it was now "opportune to ask, what kind of government do our people want in the future?" There must be a full debate to take "the sense of the country," "before we are irretrievably committed to a policy" involving such radical change as would the acquisition of an empire.

A bit more than a year later Dana reported that Cuban deputies to the Spanish Cortés had, in the course of discussing a possible loan to the island, raised the question of home rule. He doubted that the loan would be forthcoming, since Spain valued the island precisely for its financial resources. But as to home rule, the "Cuban people command sympathy. They have been long and seriously misgoverned . . . bled for well nigh four hundred years" by Spain. Dana wrote that one day Cubans would win home rule. Little did he know how soon his prophecy would come true.[71] Still, for a long time he doubted that the United States should project its power beyond its borders. The question became urgent in December 1895 when President Cleveland, in his annual message, invoked the Monroe Doctrine in a sharp warning to Britain to settle peacefully a dispute over the boundary between British Guiana and Venezuela. Secretary of State Richard Gresham Olney underscored Cleveland's remarks with a stiff diplomatic note to Britain. For a few days the American public luxuriated in an outburst of jingoism and patriotic fervor. Dana, however, regarded Cleveland's utterances as being "in every way unfortunate." The United States, he wrote, had no clear interest in the matter. Besides, the Monroe Doctrine did not apply since the question was one of title and not of new acquisition. The business community agreed with Dana, the British ministry thought a peaceful outcome expedient, and Britain and Venezuela reached an agreement early in 1896.[72]

The revolution that Cubans launched in 1895 to win their independence was not so easily resolved. As early as February, the Senate adopted a resolution recognizing Cuban belligerency; the House followed in April. Only administration and Senate opposition forestalled action on more far-reaching proposals, including resolutions endorsing American intervention on behalf of the rebels. Opposing forces on the island settled in for a long, sanguinary struggle. Cleveland, in his last annual message, pointedly referred to American patience and peaceful intentions—while warning that intervention would become necessary to end bloodshed when it became clear that Spain could no longer control the island. Dana favored this restraint, as did the larger part of the business community, believing that the threat of war or the outbreak of hostilities would prolong uncertainty and delay the country's recovery from economic depression. After it became clear that on February 9, 1898, Spain's minister to the United States had sent an insulting description of President McKinley to his superiors in Madrid, Dana conceded that his resignation was necessary.

But when an explosion sank the battleship *Maine* in Havana harbor on February 15, William Dana's reaction was very cautious. He hoped, he wrote, that an impending investigation would put the presumption that the explosion was accidental "beyond question." A month later, still looking for a way to avoid war, he was pleased to report that the truth seemed to be that the "cause of the destruction was from within the ship and not without." As late as mid-March, he still thought it probable (and very desirable) that "some amicable and honorable way out of difficulty [with Spain] will be found." As war sentiment rose in the United States, stirred in part by press reports of Spanish atrocities, he appealed to readers to exercise patience and follow Christ's example of avoiding violence. He added, in the same early April 2 edition of the *Chronicle*, a second editorial emphasizing that the "Cuban disturbance, and it alone" had perpetuated business uncertainty and delayed the return of prosperity. When war came, he did not welcome it, but he did recognize it for the turning point that it was. For the first time, the United States would be waging "a foreign war of aggression," with a regular army rather than a militia, and "with the armament and resources of a first class military State."[73]

Dana came only slowly to accept that a war begun to liberate Cuba ended as a means of creating a far-flung American empire extending from Cuba to Puerto Rico, Guam, and the Philippines. He welcomed the end of hostilities and reports of Spanish peace overtures. The halt of fighting would, he believed, remove "the incubus of war . . . and so far as that is concerned the door to enterprise [business revival] is opened." On August 20, 1898, he wrote an editorial on the meaning of the war with Spain. Lavishing praise on the American naval forces who defeated the Spanish fleet in Manila harbor, he praised Admiral George Dewey for persisting until the port of Manila had fallen as well. He continued, wistfully and with deep irony, suggesting that he still held doubts about the country's new status as the owner of colonies.

It seemed a necessary event to round out Admiral Dewey's war services. It makes, too, the war itself more complete. No doubt the trend of opinion is heavily toward retaining those islands. Having already secured Honolulu, the Ladrones and Porto Rico, it was very easy for public sentiment to include Manila. After our old institutions had been thrown to the winds, what was there to restrain our people. . . . Having scaled the wall to pick off the poorest apple on the tree and found it good, why should we not hold up our hands to catch the more luscious fruit ready to fall into them?

A week later, Dana was less wistful about America's loss of innocence regarding colonial dependencies. He now rejected the possibility of returning the Philippines to Spain as something that would outrage the American public. He thought it absurd to hold only Manila while leaving the rest of the island of Luzon open to possibly hostile control. The "fact—for . . . it is a fact—that we have entered upon a colonial career" meant that the United States must govern Luzon as a dependent territory. It was only a short additional step to accept the December 1898 report of General Wesley Merritt that the Filipinos were "not now capable of self-government, because they are undereducated, ill-civilized and without even competent leaders." In February 1899, the Senate finally approved a peace treaty with Spain. Under its terms the United States paid Spain $20 million and retained the Philippines. By then, our writer believed that the Filipino movement for independence was not to be taken seriously. Insurgents in the islands had provided no assistance to the United States during the war with Spain, had won no battles. Led by Emilio Aguinaldo, they were "at best barbarians . . . the majority fighting, like the American Indians of a century and a half ago, with their aboriginal bows and arrows." American rule would be a civilizing influence.[74]

Dana's apprehensions about overseas colonies never really disappeared. When the European powers began to carve China into commercial spheres of influence, he described the development as "no misfortune to the interests of trade and civilization. China has proved itself incapable of real development on its own." What Americans needed at the moment was a "prompt and energetic defense" of their "treaty rights . . . in China and . . . the preservation and protection of their . . . commercial interests." Given as much, there was "every prospect" of enlarged trade with China without creating an American sphere of interest there. In fact, he wrote early in 1899, "[p]erhaps the most striking part of the so-called 'colonial movement' of the present time is that no one has yet demonstrated that from a trade standpoint the gain will equal the cost." He suspected that the contemporary colonial movement would prove to be a "mere episode of international politics" that would require considerable government subsidies. His caution extended to Hawaii, too. Although the Constitution did not provide for it and history showed that the majority political party admitted territories to statehood whenever the step would advantage them, he favored some sort of permanent territorial status. It was inconceivable that a group of Pacific islands might one day wield the balance of power in the Senate. It was no less so that the alien laborers constituting half the archipelago's population would be given the vote.[75]

There is no need to linger over Cuba. Dana was satisfied that the introduction of modern sanitation to Santiago de Cuba, hitherto one of the dirtiest cities in the world, was by itself a sufficient "historical justification for American intervention in Cuba." That the United States improved tax collections, brought disease rates down, bettered education, and protected the rights of Cubans were further benefits. Meanwhile, Cubans also received schooling in self-government that would repay them whether they decided in time to become independent or to "be joined to the United States as a colony." The *Chronicle*'s editor accepted Cuba's 1901 decision for self-government without demur. He strongly approved of the treaty, ratified in 1903, finalizing arrangements for Cuban independence.[76]

Dana's coverage of international affairs remained extensive in the following years. He continued to repeat familiar calls for reductions in spending on armaments, and in international tension.[77] Of the foreign policy questions that deeply concerned him, only one more requires consideration. That is his reaction to the events through which the United States gained the right to build a canal across the Isthmus of Panama. By 1903, when a U.S.-backed revolution detached Panama from Colombia, his views were very different from those of a few years before. He embraced the event, for it opened the door "to speedy action in carrying forward the Panama Canal project." Abandoning former constitutional qualms, he added: "Any supplementary legislation which may be needed to enable the administration to prosecute the work will no doubt be readily granted." In a separate editorial he justified the revolution and American intervention, despite the provisions of the 1846 New Granada treaty. Panama, he wrote, was remote from and but feebly connected to the rest of

Colombia, while the treaty's neutrality guarantees referred to external threats rather than to internal revolution.

Not long after, a controversy erupted over the propriety of the intervention of the United States in Panama. Charges of failure to abide by the 1846 treaty circulated furiously. At the beginning of 1904, Dana strenuously defended the action of the captain of the USS *Nashville* in landing forces whose presence effectively aided the rebels. President Roosevelt had recently introduced a vital new element into the picture with a report that Colombia had begun planning to build the canal itself and to double the price to be paid for it by this country, to $40 million. There were also indications that the government of Colombia had invited France to help suppress the rebellion. The conclusion was inescapable:

This seems too unanswerable to require amplification, for a neck of land which is in the path of mankind must be held to belong to mankind, not to the handful who happen to claim political ownership. We say again that the course of the Government in this matter seems to be more and more clearly right, and that the judgment of history will be emphatically in its favor.[78]

Lifelong, William Dana was a strict constructionist of the Constitution. He believed that it created a national authority with clearly specified and delimited powers, and that it balanced powers between the states and nation, all as means of protecting individual rights. This understanding led him consistently to oppose various forms of governmental regulation, intrusion into the sphere of private enterprise, and interference with personal rights. Repeatedly, it directed him to defend sound monetary and banking principles as he understood them. It established, as well, the boundaries beyond which the national authority could not go in international affairs. But Dana was neither foolish nor inflexible. He occasionally let ideology triumph over reality, but it is to his credit that this happened rarely. Given the extent to which the world changed during his lifetime, it is to his credit that this innately conservative, scrupulous, perceptive, and gentle man was able to adapt his views of the role of government as greatly as he did.

NOTES

1. *Commercial and Financial Chronicle*, September 10, 1887.

2. James Kent, *Commentaries on American Law*, vol.1, 12th ed., edited by Oliver Wendell Holmes, Jr. (Boston: Little, Brown and Company, 1873), passim.

3. "Federal Finances Examined" and "The Crisis of Reconstruction," *Hunt's Merchants' Magazine*, respectively 47 (December 1862), quoted 511 and 48 (February 1868), 121–124; *Commercial and Financial Chronicle*, November 11, 18, 1876; and January 20 and March 3 and 10, 1877. For the compromise of 1877, see Comer

Vann Woodward, *Origins of the New South, 1877–1913* (Baton Rouge: Louisiana State University Press, 1951) 24, 42ff, and passim.

4. *Commercial and Financial Chronicle*, March 23 and 30, 1878.

5. *Commercial and Financial Chronicle*, February 18, 1881, and July 12, 1884.

6. *Commercial and Financial Chronicle*, March 24, 1879.

7. *Commercial and Financial Chronicle*, December 2, 1882.

8. *Commercial and Financial Chronicle*, May 24, 1879; June 17, 1882, and May 26, 1883.

9. Municipal ownership, see *Commercial and Financial Chronicle*, April 7 and 14 and May 26, 1906; socialist mayor, April 9, 1910; subway bonds, January 23, 1909.

10. *Commercial and Financial Chronicle*, February 8, 1882, and March 30, 1907; for influence peddling, August 13 and 27, 1881.

11. Bank directors and Crédit Mobilier, see *Commercial and Financial Chronicle*, February 22 and March 1, 1873; and February 11, 1888; fraud, speculation, and morality, January 6, 1878; August 13 and 27, 1881; August 20, 1889; February 1, 1890, for illustrations; accurate information for investors, February 20 and September 20, 1879; and April 17, 1909. Provision of accurate information was, of course, the bedrock mission of the *Chronicle*.

12. *Commercial and Financial Chronicle*, May 5 and 12 and June 30, 1906; and February 6, May 1, and October 2, 1909.

13. Stock exchange, see *Commercial and Financial Chronicle*, miscreants, January 19, 1878, reforms, April 2, 1910; employees' liability, May 8, 1909; publicity for shareholders, September 20, 1879; March 16, 1889, and February 20 and April 17, 1909.

14. For illustrations, see usury, *Commercial and Financial Chronicle*, March 6, 1873; bankruptcy, November 5, 1877.

15. Postal savings, see *Commercial and Financial Chronicle*, February 10, 1910; quotation regarding automobiles, June 25, 1910.

16. "Repeal of the Cotton Tax," *Hunt's Merchants' Magazine* 58 (January 1868): 31–33; "The Income Tax," *Hunt's Merchants' Magazine* 62 (May, 1870): 321–326.

17. For federal receipts, see United States Bureau of the Census, *Historical Statistics of the United States: Colonial Times to 1957* (Washington, DC: Government Printing Office, 1960), 712; Joseph Allan Nevins, *Grover Cleveland: A Study in Courage* (New York: Dodd, Mead and Company, 1932), 367–402; Frank W. Taussig, *Tariff History of the United States*, 7th ed. (New York: G. P. Putnam's Sons, 1923), 155–250; quotations from *Commercial and Financial Chronicle*, March 10, 1884; also February 21, 1885; February 2, 1886; January 1 and December 10, 1887; November 10, 1888; and May 26, 1906.

18. *Commercial and Financial Chronicle*, March 20 and September 13, 1890; August 4, 11, and 18, 1894; quoted February 3, 1894; Taussig, *Tariff History of the United States*, 251–320; Nevins, *Grover Cleveland*, 563–589; Gerald Taylor White, *The United States and the Problem of Recovery after 1893* (Tuscaloosa: University of Alabama Press, 1982), 57–71; Walter LaFeber, *The New Empire: An Interpretation of American Expansion, 1860–1898* (Ithaca, NY: Cornell University Press, 1963), 159–172; Douglas Steeples and David O. Whitten, *Democracy in Desperation: The Depression of 1893* (Westport, CT: Greenwood, 1998), 111–112, 190–191, 204, n 9.

19. Quotation from *Commercial and Financial Chronicle*, December 12 1896.; Taussig, *Tariff History of the United States*, 322–360; H. Wayne Morgan, *William McKinley and His America* (Syracuse, NY: Syracuse University Press, 1963), 278; Steeples and Whitten, *Democracy in Desperation*, 191–192.

20. *Commercial and Financial Chronicle*, March 13, 20, and 27; July 17; and quoted August 7, 1909; George R. Mowry, *The Era of Theodore Roosevelt and the Birth of Modern America, 1900–1912* (New York: Harper and Row, 1958), 246–247; Taussig, *Tariff History of the United States*, 361–408.

21. For Congress and quotation, see *Commercial and Financial Chronicle*, November 28, 1896; also February 2, 1886; May 26, 1906; and February 21, 1885; Government salaries, March 8, 1873; Bureau of the Census, January 3, 1880; March 22, 1890; December 16, 1905; and May 16, 1906.

22. Quotations from Francis Wayland, *Elements of Political Economy*, 4th ed. (Boston: Gould and Lincoln, 1860), 217, 278, 287–288; see also Adam Smith, *An Inquiry into the Causes and Nature of the Wealth of Nations*, with a preface by George J. Stigler (Chicago: University of Chicago Press, 1976), 1: 26–110, 302–351.

23. For financing the Civil War, Phillip Shaw Paludan, *"A People's Contest": The Union and Civil War, 1861–1865* (New York: Harper and Row, 1988), esp. 105–126, is useful; and James Garfield Randall and David Donald, *The Civil War and Reconstruction*, 2nd ed. (Boston: D.C. Heath and Company, 1961), 285ff, 319, 340–354, remains the authoritative and most useful general one-volume account. For the debt, see Donald R. Stabile and Jeffrey J. Canton, *The Public Debt of the United States: An Historical Perspective, 1775–1990* (New York: Praeger, 1991).

24. Quotation from *Commercial and Financial Chronicle*, May 6, 1871; referring to *Hepburn v. Griswold* [First Legal Tender Case] (8 Wallace 603) 1870; and *Knox v. Lee* and *Parker v. Davis* [Second Legal Tender Cases] (12 Wallace, 457) 1871. See also, "The Legal Tender Decision and Its Effects," *Hunt's Merchants' Magazine* 57 (March 1870): 161ff.

25. *Commercial and Financial Chronicle*, March 21 and July 25, 1874.

26. *Juilliard v. Greenman* [Third Legal Tender Case] (110 U.S. 421) 1884; *Commercial and Financial Chronicle*, March 8, 1884; Paolo E. Coletta, "Greenbackers, Goldbugs, and Silverites: *Currency Reform and Policy, 1860–1897*" in *The Gilded Age: A Reappraisal*, ed. H. Wayne Morgan (Syracuse, NY: Syracuse University Press, 1963), 111–139, esp. 123; Gretchen Ritter, *Goldbugs and Greenbacks: The Antimonopoly Tradition and the Politics of Finance in America* (New York: Cambridge University Press, 1997).

27. *Commercial and Financial Chronicle*, December 27, 1873.

28. Milton Friedman and Anna Jacobson Schwartz, *A Monetary History of the United States 1867–1960* (Princeton, NJ: Princeton University Press, 1963), 50–51 and passim. Because of the leveraging properties of hand-to-hand currency, deposits, and reserves, Friedman and Schwartz term them "high-powered money." They constitute a rough equivalent to what the Federal Reserve System currently denominates as "M1."

29. *Commercial and Financial Chronicle*, quoted September 18, 1875; also see October 2, 1875.

30. *Commercial and Financial Chronicle*, October 10, 1874.

31. Dana's advocacy was typically conservative. Resumption should come but

only after a reserve had been accumulated to support it, greenbacks as a result had risen to par with gold, and provision had been made permanently to retire greenbacks from circulation. Still, assuming these things, he endorsed the maxim: "The best preparation for resumption is to resume." *Commercial and Financial Chronicle*, January 20, 1872. See also October 11, November 8, and December 13, 1873; and March 14, April 18, May 18, and October 17, 1874.

32. *Commercial and Financial Chronicle*, November 6, 1875.

33. *Commercial and Financial Chronicle*, January 8, 1878.

34. *Commercial and Financial Chronicle*, June 18, 1878.

35. Quotation from *Commercial and Financial Chronicle*, September 18, 1875. See also August 7 and 14, September 11 and October 9, 1875; July 23 and 29, August 12, September 9 and 30, and November 4, 1876; May 18, August 18, September 15, and November 4, 1876; May 18, August 18, September 15, November 10 and 24, and December 1, 1877; January 5, April 20, and June 8, 1878.

36. See Rendigs Fels, *American Business Cycles, 1865–1897* (Chapel Hill: University of North Carolina Press, 1959) 113–136; Friedman and Schwartz, *A Monetary History*, 104–116; James K. Kindahl, "Economic Factors in Specie Resumption in the United States, 1869–1879," *Journal of Political Economy* 69 (February 1961): 30–48, esp. 38.

37. Coletta, "Greenbackers, Goldbugs, and Silverites," 111–139, 260. When an international monetary conference in 1867 recommended general adoption of the gold standard, Britain had already done so. In 1871 Germany, Holland, and Spain followed. The Latin Monetary Union—Greece, Switzerland, Belgium, and France—afterward suspended the unlimited minting of silver. With the formation of the Scandinavian Monetary Confederation in 1873, Sweden, Norway, and Denmark adopted the gold standard.

38. Richard Hofstadter, *The Age of Reform: From Bryan to F. D. R.* (New York: Vintage Books, 1955), 60–93; Comer Vann Woodward, "The Populist Heritage and the Intellectual," *American Scholar* 29 (Winter 1959–1960): 55–72. The literature on agrarianism/Populism and agitation for the coinage of silver has become immense. John Donald Hicks, *The Populist Revolt: A History of the Farmers' Alliance and the People's Party* (Lincoln: University of Nebraska Press, 1961), 54ff, remains the indispensable beginning point. For silver production and prices, see United States Bureau of the Census, *Historical Statistics*, 371.

39. *Commercial and Financial Chronicle*, January 20 and June 9, 1877; January 5, 12, and 26 and February 23, 1878.

40. *Commercial and Financial Chronicle*, March 19 and quoted April 9, 1881.

41. *Commercial and Financial Chronicle*, February 18, 1882.

42. *Commercial and Financial Chronicle*, March 4ff, 1882; Steeples and Whitten, *Democracy in Desperation*, 21, 38; Davis Rich Dewey, *Financial History of the United States* (New York: Longmans, Green, 1903), 438–443.

43. *Commercial and Financial Chronicle*, quoted August 18, 1885.

44. *Commercial and Financial Chronicle*, August 31, 1889.

45. *Commercial and Financial Chronicle*, December 10, 1885; January 2 and 23, February 13 and 20, March 6, August 21, and September 11 and 25, 1886; February 4, March 3, and December 8, 1888; August 31 and December 14, 1889; January 25, March 29, July 12 and 19, August 16, and quoted December 20, 1890; April 18, May 23 and 30, July 18, and November 14, 1891; January 7 and 23, 1893. There

are two fragments of evidence hinting that as late as 1894 Dana may have remained open to international bimetallism, at least in theory. The *Commercial and Financial Chronicle* (October 13, 1894), and the article "Bimetallism and Free Silver," *Public Opinion* 17 (November 8, 1894): 763, suggest that Dana was at least still willing to debate its feasibility. However, both of these fragments stand in sharp contrast to the message that the paper was consistently conveying.

46. *Commercial and Financial Chronicle*, October 28 and November 4, 1893.

47. *Commercial and Financial Chronicle*, February 16 and quoted March 3; March 17, March 31, and April 7, 1894.

48. *Commercial and Financial Chronicle*, quoted June 22, 1895. Also July 27, August 3 and 17, and October 19, 1895.

49. *Commercial and Financial Chronicle*, November 7, 1896, and January 2 and February 13, 1897; Steeples and Whitten, *Democracy in Desperation*, 14–83 145–207; Friedman and Schwartz, *A Monetary History*, 116–120; Fels, *American Business Cycles*, 179–228; Nevins, *Grover Cleveland*, 532–548, 600–603, 686–688, and passim; James A. Barnes, *John G. Carlisle: Financial Statesman* (New York: Dodd, Mead, 1931), 226ff, 307–317, and passim.

50. For an excellent discussion, see Margaret G. Myers, *A Financial History of the United States* (New York: Columbia University Press, 1970), 124–128, 184–189; Esther Rogoff Taus, *Central Banking Functions of the United States Treasury, 1789–1941* (New York: Columbia University Press, 1941); Oliver Mitchell Wentworth Sprague, *History of Crises under the National Banking System* (Washington, DC: Government Printing Office, 1910); Stabile and Canton, *The Public Debt of the United States*; quotation from Steeples and Whitten, *Democracy in Desperation*, 177; Friedman and Schwartz *A Monetary History*, 15–18 and passim; Fritz Redlich, *The Molding of American Banking: Men and Ideas*. Part 2: *1840–1910* (New York: Hafner, 1951), 95–105.

51. William Dana, editorial reply to A. K. Shepard, "A National Currency," "Journal of Banking and Commerce," and "The National Bank Returns," respectively in *Hunt's Merchants' Magazine* 50 (January 1864): 16; 52 (April 1865): 292–296; and 63 (November 1870): 365–367.

52. *Commercial and Financial Chronicle*, February 11 and November 25, 1871.

53. *Commercial and Financial Chronicle*, October 18, 1873.

54. *Commercial and Financial Chronicle*, March 20, 1875.

55. *Commercial and Financial Chronicle*, February 28 and March 21, 1874. Dana in making this point omitted reference to the crucial role of banks' loans in creating deposit balances.

56. *Commercial and Financial Chronicle*, November 4, 1876.

57. *Commercial and Financial Chronicle*, quoted February 11, 1882; also December 10, 1881; October 2, 1886; July 19, August 23, and December 6, 1890.

58. *Commercial and Financial Chronicle*, July 11, 1891.

59. *Commercial and Financial Chronicle*, October 20, 1894, July 13 and October 19, 1895; James Laurence Laughlin, "The Baltimore Plan of Bank-Issues," *Journal of Political Economy* 3 (December 1894): 101–105.

60. For a summary discussion, see Steeples and Whitten, *Democracy in Desperation*, 179–181; full bibliographical citations, 185 n. 28–34.

61. *Commercial and Financial Chronicle*, December 5, 1896; and August 21 and quoted January 16, 1897.

62. *Commercial and Financial Chronicle*, April 17, September 18 and 25, October 2, 23, and 30, and November 6, 1897; and for Gage's speeches to the Cincinnati Commercial Club and the Maryland Bankers' Meeting as elements in the administration's efforts to build support, June 5, 1897.

63. *Commercial and Financial Chronicle*, quoted January 8, see also January 15 and 29, 1898; January 21 and 28, February 18, May 6 and 27, and June 3, 1899; December 1, 8, and 15, 1900; Morgan, *William McKinley and His America*, 281–286; Friedman and Schwartz *A Monetary History*, 135–138; James Laurence Laughlin, *The Federal Reserve Act: Its Origins and Problems* (New York: Macmillan, 1933), 3ff; Redlich, *The Molding of American Banking*, 208–209 and passim; Steeples and Whitten, *Democracy in Desperation*, 187–189, 203–204 n. 1–4.

64. *Commercial and Financial Chronicle*, February 17, March 10, and March 17, 1900.

65. *Commercial and Financial Chronicle*, quoted March 14, 1908; also October 3, 1901; February 21, July 25, September 5 and 12, and October 17, 1903; April 16 and December 24, 1904; April 14, May 5, October 6 and 27, November 3, 10, 17, and 24, and December 22, 1906; February 26 and March 2 and 9, 1907; January 11, 18, and 25, March 14, April 25, May 9 and 16, and June 6, 1908. A December 8, 1900 editorial, "THE FUNCTION OF A COUNTRY BANK," commenting on a speech about country banks seems to imply a failure to anticipate the rise of retail banking. Such a bank capitalized at $50,000 would pay 8 percent in profits, accumulate a surplus of $20,000, maintain 244 accounts with deposits of $130,000, and loans of $50,000. It would, in addition, provide improvements for the town of $10,000, currency of $2,000 in silver per month, function as a source of financial advice to the community, and manage the interests of the local college. This brief sketch suggests that account holders, and borrowers, would have been businesses and professionals, rather than ordinary townsfolk.

66. *Commercial and Financial Chronicle*, January 23, 1909; Friedman and Schwartz *A Monetary History*, 138–187; Laughlin, *The Federal Reserve Act*; Redlich, *The Molding of American Banking*, 208–209ff.

67. "Acquisitions of Territory—Russian America," *Hunt's Merchants' Magazine* 58 (January 1868): 16–23, quoted 23 and 18. For the idea of a new imperialism, see Walter LaFeber, *The New Empire*; and Thomas J. McCormick, *China Market* (Chicago: Quadrangle Books, 1967).

68. *Commercial and Financial Chronicle*, October 15, 1872; March 1 and quoted March 15, 1879.

69. *Commercial and Financial Chronicle*, July 19, 1875; June 14, 1879; quoted October 29, 1881.

70. *Commercial and Financial Chronicle*, April 13, 1878. The *Chronicle* did not even take notice of the tripartite division of Samoa, in which the United States shared, during the 1890s.

71. Germany, see *Commercial and Financial Chronicle*, July 16, 1884; the Congo and United States policy, June 3, 1885; Cuba, June 26, 1886.

72. *Commercial and Financial Chronicle*, quoted December 21, also December 7, 1895; January 2 and February 15, 1896; Nevins, *Grover Cleveland*, 641ff; "The Anglo-Venezuelan Boundary Dispute," *Public Opinion* 19 (December 26, 1895): 838–844; *New York Times*, December 18, 1895.

73. *Commercial and Financial Chronicle*, quoted February 19, March 19, April

2 and 9, and February 2–April 16; all 1898; Joseph E. Wisan, *The Cuban Crisis as Reflected in the New York Press* (New York: Columbia University Press, 1934), 21–38 and passim; Charles W. Auxier, "Middle Western Newspapers and the Spanish-American War," *Mississippi Valley Historical Review* 26 (March 1940): 525.

74. Quotations from *Commercial and Financial Chronicle*, August 20 and December 24, 1898; February 11, 1899. For a sample of the voluminous literature about the war with Spain and American expansionism in the 1890s, see LaFeber, *The New Empire*, esp. 284–406; Richard Hofstadter, *The Paranoid Style in American Politics and Other Essays* (New York: Vintage Books, 1967), 147–151; Ernest R. May, *Imperial Democracy* (New York: Harcourt, Brace and World, 1961); Frederick W. Merk, *Manifest Destiny and Mission in American History: A Reinterpretation* (New York: Alfred A. Knopf, 1963); H. Wayne Morgan, *America's Road to Empire* (New York: Wiley, 1965); Julius W. Pratt, *Expansionists of 1898* (Chicago: Quadrangle Books, 1964); Albert Katz Weinberg, *Manifest Destiny: A Study of Nationalist Expansionism in American History* (Chicago: Quadrangle Books, 1963), esp. 283–354; Harold Underwood Faulkner, *Politics, Reform, and Expansion* (New York: Harper, 1959), 235–259. Dana's revealing comments on Aguinaldo's surrender, in which he reflected that it might have been wise to attempt negotiations at the outset with this "shrewd and calculating" leader, appear in *Commercial and Financial Chronicle*, April 6, 1901.

75. Quotations for China, see *Commercial and Financial Chronicle*, February 12, August 13, and see also February 26, 1898; for Hawaii, April 1, 1899; May 12 and June 9, 1900.

76. *Commercial and Financial Chronicle*, quoted June 24, 1899; also July 25, October 24, and November 14, 1903. The treaty admitted Cuban sugar duty-free to the United States, granted the United States supervision over Cuban foreign relations and loans, and conveyed to the United States certain Cuban land for naval coaling stations.

77. Defense expenditures, see *Commercial and Financial Chronicle*, August 5, 1899; tensions, January 13, February 14 and 17, March 10, and April 7, all 1906; January 9, 1909.

78. Quotations from *Commercial and Financial Chronicle*, November 14, 1903, and January 9, 1904; see also January 2 and November 18, 1904; and William Henry Harbaugh, *The Life and Times of Theodore Roosevelt*, new rev. ed. (New York: Oxford University Press, 1975), 95, 194–196, 200–204, 374, 437.

Afterword

[In business life] as in natural history, the results of the times are inevitably produced by its needs, and that which is, is in a general sense, that which should be.

—William Buck Dana, April 28, 1906

William Dana lived a quiet, unobtrusive life. He was a very private person who believed, as did many of his social class, that one's name should appear in newspapers only three times in a lifetime: at birth, at the time of marriage, and at death. He devoted his greatest efforts to the pursuit of his business, his family, and the practical application of his religious convictions. Steadfastly nonpartisan as an editor, he eschewed any political or personal advantage that might have accrued from his role as editor-publisher of the country's most prominent business monthly, and then weekly. His correspondence contains few indications of contact with political leaders and none with the great business figures of his day, even though he was related by marriage to J. P. Morgan.[1] At first blush these circumstances appear to offer scant promise that his life and thought were worthy objects of study.

Nothing could be further from the truth. Terms such as "influence," "representativeness," and "importance" are slippery at best. They become even more so when we attempt to employ them to measure lives long since over. In Dana's case, we can come no closer than suggestions. Even these must be derived indirectly. Estimates of the circulation of the *Commercial and Financial Chronicle* offer only the merest hints, although presumably Dana's readers either agreed with his opinions or found them worth reading. Some, we know from editorial exchanges, also disagreed. That they bothered to write to the *Chronicle* to share their different views is an indication of influence, too. References to the *Chronicle* in other publications add a few more clues. The heavy reliance of the United States Bureau of the Census on business history material gleaned from it in preparing *Historical Statistics of the United States* provides further indications. The best measure, however, probably lies in a roster of its advertisers and the comprehensive character of the paper and its several supplements. By that measure, as well as the sum of all of those cited, it was peerless.[2]

We can approach the question of Dana's importance by another route, too. That is to consider *Hunt's Merchants' Magazine* and the *Chronicle* as advocates of the interests of business. We have fashioned this book to consider Dana and his publications primarily in terms of advocacy. Here, too, we find no comparable publications as to comprehensiveness and accuracy of coverage, editorial authoritativeness, and sheer breadth of interest.

Beyond these indicators lies a final, crucial fact. We have no other business publication so closely identified with the views of its editor-publisher for anything close to the half century that Dana was active. His views were indistinguishable from those printed in his publications. Nor have we a comparable figure in business journalism in terms of span of career from the moment a cash economy and canals were transforming western New York State to that when rapidly multiplying uses of electricity were reshaping national life. Dana was very much a man—a conservative but exuberantly entrepreneurial man—of his times. His advocacy of business interests took many forms. These included complicated commentaries on fine points of constitutional and commercial law. They extended to sharp criticisms of various attempts to regulate business, ameliorate labor relations through governmental action, define monetary and banking policy, and revise tariffs and other taxes. They comprehended comments on the economic significance of immigration. They even involved obituaries praising men who Dana believed represented the best in America enterprise, and the worst.[3]

Dana made a few miscalls. His condemnation of the Brooklyn Bridge, the assertion that increases in the face value of circulating money would not stimulate business, his belief that the airplane would never win commercial importance or be more than a "sort of toy," and the notion that electric street railroads would never yield place to speedier means of urban transit were cases in point. He did not even acknowledge the advent of the Model T Ford in 1909. But he was, on the whole, remarkably prescient in his grasp of the importance of new technologies and singularly attuned to his era. Better, perhaps, than any of his contemporaries he understood the potential value of Alexander Graham Bell's invention of the telephone, Thomas Alva Edison's mastery of "the difficulties which have hitherto marred the effective use of electricity for lighting purposes," the "very important . . . innovation" by which American railroads established uniform time zones in 1883, and another by which they adopted a standard track gauge three years later.[4] He immediately grasped the way in which improved communication facilitated the proliferation of securities and commodities exchanges and made possible the growth of a vibrant trade in futures.[5] As soon as they were offered he reported quotations of stocks for Edison Electric and Bell Telephone and other corporate harbingers of an emerging new order of things.[6] He similarly tracked the growth of electric power generation, and his musings on the potential of electricity during a visit to the 1881 Paris Exposition anticipated by nineteen years those of Henry Adams at another exposition in the City of Lights in 1900.[7] Whatever his skepticism about airplanes, he was sufficiently concerned about the prospect of aerial bombardment from dirigibles in wartime to express strong hopes for a successful outcome of the 1907 Hague international peace conference.[8]

That Dana used the language of his day, not ours, to express his ideas can be misleading to modern readers. In penetrating his old-fashioned mode of expression we discover that he matched his alertness to technological change with some keen, even advanced insights into the maturation and working of the American economy. His grasp of the role of fluctuations in businessmen's and investors' confidence in shaping business cycles foretold some of the later theoretical writing of John Maynard Keynes regarding the importance of expectations. So did his appreciation that investment, contrary to the teachings of classical economics, did not always equal savings.

If ideologically bound to the ideal of the open shop, he still must be credited for his advocacy of voluntary arbitration to resolve disputes between capital and labor. He understood the forces encouraging consolidation and combination in business to be the natural results of evolving business conditions. In explaining how oligopolistic and monopolistic competition worked, he in some respects anticipated John Kenneth Galbraith's conception of countervailing powers. Committed to sound money, he apprehended the principles upon which central banks operate, the fact that by the 1890s checks vastly outweighed currency as vehicles of commerce, and that credit is the crucial foundation of modern business. He very early recognized the need for elasticity in the monetary system, and he took the lead in championing ideas that in due course informed creation of the federal reserve system. All the while, he clung tenaciously to the moral premises upon which classical economic theory was based, and he achieved a reconciliation between science and the theological precepts that for millenia have been among the principal defining characteristics of Western civilization. It would be unfair not to note that in doing so he set himself apart from the self-preoccupied acolytes of sheer acquisition who coopted the term "conservativism" to serve their own selfish purposes a century later.

William Dana was singularly identified with, and a uniquely appropriate symbol of, the age of steam, steel, and electricity. He accepted a role for the United States as a colonial power hesitantly and, in truth, only after the fact. He never wavered in his advocacy for peace. His observation in 1906 that "the results of the times are inevitably produced by its needs, and that which is, is in a general sense, that which should be" reflected his enduring fidelity to the optimism of the nineteenth-century culture in which he matured. No single piece that he ever wrote better captured the essence of his advocacy and understanding than an 1895 editorial on the significance of recent changes in commerce:

We live in an age of associations. Steam, electricity, and invention have so accel- erated the pace of progress, have so re-duplicated the forces of industry and trade, that the individual has lost his place. Capital combines in corporations, not only where it is required in vast sums for railways and telegraphs, but in lumbering, mining, manufacturing and store-keeping. Labor combines both in separate in- dustries and in general federation. The educator and the scientist discover that development is so rapid that they also must form associations if they would keep step with the truth. . . . The railroad is an expression of commerce, and the iron rails, interlacing and intertwining through the States, are bonds of Union. The electric telegraph is a medium of commerce, and the wires stretching north, south, east and west keep all our peoples in daily touch with each other. The telephone is the voice of commerce. . . . [The transatlantic cable that similarly revolutionized commerce] infinitely quickened communication between the different parts of the earth and widely disseminated information. The people have benefitted in cheaper living, better homes, higher thinking, and broader education; and peace has been promoted among the nations.[9]

It is fortunate that William Dana did not live long enough to see his hopeful world destroy itself in the awful carnage of World War I. It is even more fortunate that the record of his life and thought survives as an unparalleled means of access to the era of wondrous change through which he lived, worked, observed, and advocated.

NOTES

1. See John A. Porter to William B. Dana, December 7, 1897, Dana to Porter, November 29, 1899; George B. Cortelyou to Dana, November 27, 1900; all in William McKinley papers, Library of Congress.

2. Lee Benson, "An Approach to the Scientific Study of Past Public Opinion," *Public Opinion Quarterly* 31 (Winter 1967–1968), 522–567, is still an essential start- ing point for considering this problem.

3. The obituaries of the following are representative. The date in parentheses following each name is the date of the issue of the *Commercial and Financial Chronicle* in which the obituary appears. William H. Vanderbilt (December 12, 1885); Cornelius Vanderbilt (September 16, 1899), Collis P. Huntington (August

18, 1900); Henry Villard (November 17, 1900) and Edward H. Harriman (September 11, 1909).

4. Airplanes, *Commercial and Financial Chronicle*, June 4, 1910; surface transportation, August 8, 1903; telephone and electric lighting, October 26, 1878; time zones, November 17, 1883; track gauge, May 29, 1886.

5. Exchanges, *Commercial and Financial Chronicle*, July 28, 1883; futures, June 11, 1892.

6. Edison Electric, *Commercial and Financial Chronicle*, January 6, 1883; Bell Telephone, February 3, 1883.

7. William B. Dana, unpublished diary of a trip to Europe, July 20–September 27, 1881, in Dana papers, Henry Adams, *The Education of Henry Adams* (New York: The Modern Library, 1931), 379–390. Electrical power generation, *Commercial and Financial Chronicle*, August 8, 1903, for example.

8. *Commercial and Financial Chronicle*, May 11, 1907.

9. *Commercial and Financial Chronicle*, June 1, 1895. This editorial summarized and applauded two addresses by Chauncy DePew, a leading financier of the day. DePew delivered one of the two to the Detroit Chamber of Commerce, and the other to the New York Chamber of Commerce. While Dana's comments on standing armies and the avoidance of war have been featured elsewhere, it is of interest to mention here his treatment of the Portsmouth negotiations of the summer of 1905, ending the Russo-Japanese War. See the *Commercial and Financial Chronicle*, July–August 1905 and January 6, 1906.

Select Bibliography

PRIMARY SOURCES

Bibliographies

Carman, Harry J., and Arthur W. Thompson. *A Guide to the Principal Sources for American Civilization, 1800–1900, in the City of New York*. New York: Columbia University Press, 1960.

Hamer, Philip M., ed. *A Guide to Archives and Manuscripts in the United States*. New Haven, CT: Yale University Press, 1961.

Utica (New York) Public Library. *A Bibliography of the History and Life of Utica: A Centennial Contribution*. Utica, NY: Utica Public Library, 1932.

Public or Official Documents

Adair v. U.S. 208 U.S. 191 (1908).

Addyston Pipe & Steel Co. v. U.S. 175 U.S. 211 (1899).

Book of Deeds, Oneida County, New York, 1855. Vol. 190. Office of County Clerk, Oneida County, Utica, NY.

———. *1862*. Vol. 236. Office of County Clerk, Oneida County, Utica, NY.

Chicago, Milwaukee & St. Paul R.R. Co. v. Minnesota, 134 U.S. 418 (1890).

General Index, Wills, Oneida County, New York. Office of County Clerk, Oneida County, Utica, NY.

Grantee, Index of Deeds. Bergen County, New Jersey, 1714–1962. Office of County Clerk, Bergen County, County Administration Building, Hackensack, NJ.

Hepburn v. Griswold [First Legal Tender Case]. 8 Wallace 603 (1870).

I.C.C. v. Cin., N.O. & Tex Pac. Ry. Co. 167 U.S. 479 (1897).

In re Debs. 158 U.S. 564 (1895).

Index of Deeds, 1791–1884, C–D. Oneida County, New York. Office of County Clerk, Oneida County, Utica, NY.

Index of Mortgages. Bergen County, New Jersey, 1766–1961. Office of County
    Clerk, Bergen County, County Administration Building, Hackensack, NJ.
Juilliard v. Greenman [Third Legal Tender Case]. 110 U.S. 421 (1884).
Knox v. Lee and *Parker v. Davis* [Second Legal Tender Cases]. 12 Wallace 457
    (1871).
Lochner v. New York. 198 U.S. 45 (1905).
Loewe v. Lawlor. 208 U.S. 274 (1908).
Muller v. Oregon. 208 U.S. 412 (1908).
Munn v. Illinois. 94 U.S. 113 (1877).
Northern Securities Co. v. U.S. 193 U.S. 197 (1904).
Pollock v. Farmers' Loan & Trust Co. 157 U.S. 419 (1895).
Pollock v. Farmers' Loan & Trust Co. 158 U.S. 601 (1895).
Reagan v. Farmers' Loan & Trust Co. 154 U.S. 362 (1894).
Roll of Attorneys. Office of Court Administration, Attorney Registration, State of
    New York. New York, NY.
Santa Clara Co. v. S.P.R. Co. 118 U.S. 394 (1886).
*Slaughterhouse Cases [Live Stock Dealers and Butchers Association v. Crescent City
    Livestock Landing and Slaughterhouse Co.].* 16 Wall. 36 (1873).
Surrogate Court, County of Oneida. In the Matter of the Estate of James Dana,
    Deceased [1860]. Folder No. 1099. Oneida County Court House, Utica, NY.
Surrogate Court, County of Suffolk. In the Matter of the Estate of William B.
    Dana, Deceased [December 1, 1910]. Suffolk County Court House, River-
    head, NY.
United States Bureau of the Census. *Historical Statistics of the United States:
    Colonial Times to 1957.* Washington, DC: Government Printing Office,
    1960.
United States Congress, House. *Report Submitting Resolutions Declaring Injunc-
    tion against Employees of Northern Pacific Railroad Unwarranted.* 53d
    Cong., 3d sess., 1894. House Report No. 1049.
———, House. *Sixteenth Annual Report of the Commissioner of Labor. 1901.
    Strikes and Lockouts.* 57th Cong., 1st sess., 1901. House Document 18.
———, Senate. *Report on the Chicago Strike of June–July 1894, by the United
    States Strike Commission.* 53d Cong., 3d sess., 1894. Executive Document
    No. 7.
U.S. v. E. C. Knight Company. 156 U.S. 1 (1895).
U.S. v. Trans-Missouri Freight Association. 166 U.S. 290 (1897).
Wabash, St. Louis & Pacific R.R. Co. v. Illinois. 118 U.S. 557 (1886).
Wills and Testaments, Oneida County. James Dana. March 1, 1852, codicils May
    29, 1855 and June 10, 1858. 15: 453–461. In [1860] records of Oneida County
    Surrogate Court, Utica, NY.

Books and Pamphlets

American Federation of Labor. *Proceedings of the American Federation of Labor.*
    Bloomington, IN: American Federation of Labor, 1893, 1894, 1895.
Arnott, Joseph. *The Utica City Directory for 1861–2, . . . 1862–3.* Utica, NY: Curtiss
    and White, respectively 1861, 1862.
Benham, J. H. *Benham's [New Haven, CT] City Directory and Annual Advertiser*

1847–48; 1848–49; 1849–50;1850–51. New Haven, CT: J. H. Benham, respectively 1848–1851.

Clews, Henry. *Fifty Years on Wall Street*. New York: Irving Publishing, 1908.

Cousin, Victor. *Elements of Psychology*. Translated with an introduction, notes, and additions by C. S. Henry. Hartford, CT: Cooke and Company, 1834.

Dana, William Buck. *The Commercial & Financial Register, 1870*. New York: William B. Dana and Co., n.d. [1870?].

———. *Cotton from Seed to Loom. A Handbook of Facts for the Daily use of Producer, Merchant, and Consumer*. New York: William B. Dana and Co., 1878.

———. *A Day for Rest and Worship: Its Origin, Development, and Present Day Meaning*. New York: Fleming H. Revell Company, 1911.

———. *Prices of Rail Road Stocks for 32 Years, 1854–1886*. New York: Printed at the office of the *Commercial and Financial Chronicle*, 1886.

Fowler, P. H. *A Sermon Suggested by the Death of James Dana, Esq. and Delivered in the First Presbyterian Church, Utica, N.Y., January 15, 1860, by Rev. P. H. Fowler, D.D.* Utica, NY: Curtiss and White, 1860.

Hadley, James. *Diary of James Hadley, 1843–1851*. Edited and with a foreword by Laura Hadley Mosely. New Haven, CT: Yale University Press, 1951.

Kent, James. *Commentaries on American Law*. 12th ed. 4 vols. Edited by Oliver Wendell Holmes, Jr. Boston: Little, Brown and Company, 1873.

Merrell, B. S. *The Utica City Directory for 1851–53*. Utica, NY: B. S. Merrell, 1852.

Paley, William. *Natural Theology; or, Evidences of the Existence and Attributes of the Deity. A New Edition*. 1802. Reprint, London: J. Christie, J. Richardson, R. Baynes, J. Walker, and W. Harrison, 1821.

Reid, Thomas. *Essays on the Active Powers of the Human Mind*. Introduction by Baruch A. Brody. Cambridge: M.I.T. Press, 1969.

———. *Essays on the Powers of the Human Mind*. 3 vols. Edinburgh: Bell and Bradfute, 1819.

Revised English Bible. Oxford: Oxford University Press, 1989.

Richards, S. A. & W. E. *The Utica City Directory for 1853–1854*: 1855–1856; 1856–1857. Utica, N.Y.: Published by S. A. and W. E. Richards, respectively 1854, 1855, 1856.

Smith, Adam. *An Inquiry into the Causes and Nature of the Wealth of Nations*. With a new preface by George J. Stigler. Chicago: University of Chicago Press, 1976.

Wadsworth, Olive A. [Katharine Floyd Dana]. *Bill Riggs, Jr: The Story of a City Boy*. Boston: Warren and Co., 1869.

———. *Heavenward Bound: Words of Help for Young Christians*. Philadelphia: Presbyterian Publication Committee, 1870.

———. *Kit, Fan, Tot, and the Rest of Them*. Boston: American Tract Society, 1870.

———. *Our Phil and Other Stories*. Boston: Houghton Mifflin and Co., 1888. Reprint, Freeport, NY: Books for Libraries Press, 1970.

———. *Over in the Meadow: A Counting–Out Rhyme*. San Francisco: Morgan Shepard Company, 1906. Reprint, New York: Viking Penguin, 1985.

Walker, A. H. *Atlas of Bergen County, New Jersey, 1776–1876*. Reading PA: Reading Publishing House, n.d. (In Englewood Collection, Englewood, NJ, Public Library.)

Wayland, Francis. *Elements of Political Economy*. 4th ed. Boston: Gould and Lincoln, 1860.
Woolsey, Theodore D. *An Historical Discourse Pronounced before the Graduates of Yale College, August 14 1850*. New Haven, CT: Yale College, 1850.
Yale College. *Catalog of the Officers and Students of Yale College, 1847–8; 1848–9; 1849–50; 1850–1*. Hew Haven, CT: Yale, respectively 1847, 1848, 1849, 1850.

Newspapers and Periodicals

Anonymous. "Acquisitions of Territory—Russian America." *Hunt's Merchants' Magazine* 58 (January 1868): 16–23.
———. "The Anglo–Venezuelan Boundary Dispute." *Public Opinion* 19 (December 26, 1895): 838–844.
———. "The Strikes." *Hunt's Merchants' Magazine* 55 (July 1866): 63–65.
Atlanta Constitution, 1891–1900.
The Bankers' Magazine and Statistical Register 50, new series 10: 1860–1861 through 82: 1910.
(Boise) Idaho Daily Statesman 1891–1900.
Boston Daily Advertiser 1891–1900.
Carnegie, Andrew. "Wealth." *North American Review* 168 (June 1889): 654 ff.
Chicago Daily Tribune, 1891–1900.
Cleveland Plain Dealer, 1891–1900.
Commercial and Financial Chronicle, 1865–1910, November 1, 1939.
Ely, Richard Theodore. "Natural Monopolies and the Workingman: A Programme of Social Reform." *North American Review*, 147 (March 1894): 294–303.
Englewood (New Jersey) Press, October 29, 1904, October 26, 1939.
Hunt's Merchants' Magazine, 1860–1870.
Laughlin, James Laurence. "The Baltimore Plan of Bank-Issue." *Journal of Political Economy* 3 (December 1894): 101–105.
New York Journal of Commerce, 1868–1880.
New York Times, 1865–1910.
Raleigh (North Carolina) News & Observer, 1891–1900.
(Salt Lake City) Deseret Weekly, 1891–1900.
San Francisco Chronicle, 1891–1900
Seattle Post-Intelligencer 1891–1900.
St. Louis Globe-Democrat 1893–1894.
St. Louis Post-Dispatch, 1891–1900.
Utica (New York) Daily Gazette, January 1, 1851–December 31, 1853.
Utica (New York) Daily Press, October 11, 1910.
The Yale Tomahawk, 1847–1851. New Haven, CT: Yale Archives Yeg¹A8y.

Personal Interviews and Correspondence

Allison, John (son of William O. Allison, personally knew William B. Dana). Personal interview with the author, Mastic, Long Island, New York, June 15 and September 2 and 4, 1965.

Dana, Ella Lindley (widow of William B. Dana's grandson/adoptive son). Personal interviews with the author, Mastic, Long Island, New York, June 10–11, and September 2–4, 1965. Personal letters to the author, June 15, July 22, August 26, September 1, 1965 and May 8, 1966.

Foote, Frederick (neighbor at Mastic who personally knew William B. Dana, associated with Herbert Hoover as a mining engineer). Personal interview with the author, Mastic, Long Island, New York, June 15, September 1, September 4, 1965. Personal letter to the author, July 21, 1966.

Nichols, Cornelia Floyd (Floyd descendant occupying historic family home at the William Floyd Estate, with childhood memories of William B. Dana). Personal interview with the author. Mastic, Long Island, New York, September 2 and 4, 1965.

Seibert, Claude (president, William B. Dana Company). Personal interview with the author, *Commercial and Financial Chronicle* office, New York City. March 23, 1965.

Seibert, William (treasurer, William B. Dana Company, personally acquainted as young man with William B. Dana). Personal interview with the author, *Commercial and Financial Chronicle* office, New York City. March 23, 1965.

Archival Sources

Anonymous. "Descendants of William Floyd of Mastic, Long Island, one of the Signers of the Declaration of Independence. A Family Record Brought Down to January, 1896." Unpublished manuscript at Genealogy Room of the New York Public Library, 1896.

———. "J. Wyman Jones." Unpublished manuscript in Englewood Collection, Englewood, New Jersey, Public Library, n.d.

Brothers in Unity, Yale College. "Library Circulation Records, 1850–1851." Unpublished manuscript, Yale University Archives, 1851.

Brothers in Unity, Yale College. "Secretary's Records, 24 June 1840–20 May 1851, Book 6, Unpublished manuscript, Yale University Archives. YRG 40-A-S, Box 9, Folder 41: 1851.

Brothers in Unity, Yale College. "Treasurer's Records, 1849–1863." Unpublished manuscript, Yale University Archives. YRG 40-A. Series 11 Alphabetical. Box 11, 1863.

Cleveland, [Stephen] Grover. Papers. Library of Congress.

Dana Family Photographs Folder. Oneida County Historical Society, Utica, NY.

Dana, William Buck and Katherine (Floyd). Papers. William Floyd Estate, Fire Island National Seashore, National Park Service, Patchogue [Floyd Estate, Mastic], Long Island, NY.

"Early Hand Written Credit Reporting Ledgers of the Mercantile Agency," 1841–1890. New Jersey, vol. 3: 19, 213; vol. 4: 428; New York, vol. 434; 067, a. 191, from 2,580-volume collection of unpublished, manuscript credit reports constituting the R. G. Dun & Co. Collection, Baker Library, Harvard Business School, Cambridge, MA.

Fairchild, Charles S. Papers. The New York Historical Society.

McKinley, William, Jr. Papers. Library of Congress.

Nichols, Cornelia Floyd [Mrs. John Treadwell Nichols]. "As Told by the Attic
    Letters," Part II, 43–45, 35. Unpublished manuscript, 1952. In collection of
    the Suffolk County Historical Society, Riverhead, NY.
Peal, B.J. "A Glimpse into the History of Vernon, New York." Unpublished man-
    uscript at Oneida County Historical Society, Utica, NY, 1959.
Russell Trust Association. *Catalog, 1864* [directory, Skull and Bones Society; title
    page reads "Henry P. Boyden.] Yale Archives. Yeg2R9c.
Turner, Sarah [Sadie] Floyd. "Sunny Memories of Mastic." Unpublished manu-
    script in collection of William Floyd Estate, with the William Buck and
    Katherine Floyd Dana Papers, Fire Island National Seashore, National Park
    Service. Undated, with notation: "Written in about 1889."

SECONDARY SOURCES

Books and Pamphlets

Ahlstrom, Sydney E. *A Religious History of the American People.* New Haven,
    CT: Yale University Press, 1972.
Atherton, Lewis. *Main Street on the Middle Border.* Bloomington: Indiana Uni-
    versity Press, 1954.
Bagg, Moses M. *Memorial History of Utica, N.Y.: From Its Settlement to the Present
    Time.* Syracuse, NY: D. Mason and Co., 1892.
————. *The Pioneers of Utica: Being Sketches of Its Inhabitants and Its Institutions,
    with the Civil History of the Place, from the Earliest Settlement to the Year
    1825.* Utica, NY: Curtiss and Childs, 1877.
Bailyn, Bernard. *Education in the Forming of American Society: Needs and Op-
    portunities for Study.* Chapel Hill: University of North Carolina Press, 1960.
Barnett, Paul. *Business Cycle Theory in the United States, 1860–1900.* Chicago:
    University of Chicago Press, 1941.
Boorstin, Daniel J. *The Americans: The Democratic Experience.* New York: Vin-
    tage Books, 1974.
Brand, H. W. *T.R.: The Last Romantic.* New York: Basic Books, 1997.
Bruchey, Stuart. *Enterprise: The Dynamic Economy of a Free People.* Cambridge:
    Harvard University Press, 1990.
Buder, Stanley. *Pullman: An Experiment in Industrial Order and Community Plan-
    ning, 1880–1930.* New York: Oxford University Press, 1967.
Burns, James McGregor. *Roosevelt: The Lion and the Fox.* New York: Harvest
    Books, 1962.
Campbell, Ballard C. *The Growth of American Government: Governance from the
    Cleveland Era to the Present.* Bloomington: Indiana University Press, 1995.
Campbell, Edward Gross. *Reorganization of the American Railroad System, 1893–
    1900.* New York: Columbia University Press, 1938.
Carosso, Vincent P. *Investment Banking in America.* Cambridge: Harvard Univer-
    sity Press, 1970.
Chandler, Alfred D., Jr. *Giant Enterprise: Ford, General Motors, and the Auto-
    mobile Industry.* New York: Harcourt, Brace and World, 1964.
————. *Scale and Scope: The Dynamics of Industrial Capitalism.* Cambridge, MA:
    Harvard University Press, 1990.

——. *Strategy and Structure: Chapters in the History of the Industrial Enterprise.* Cambridge: MIT Press, 1962.

——. *The Visible Hand: The Managerial Revolution in American Business.* Cambridge: Harvard University Press, 1977.

Chernow, Ron. *The House of Morgan: An American Banking Dynasty and the Rise of Modern Finance.* New York: Simon and Schuster, 1990.

——. *Titan: The Life of John D. Rockefeller, Sr.* New York: Random House, 1998.

Clark, T. Wood. *Utica: For a Century and a Half.* Utica, NY: The Widtman Press, 1952.

Clark, Victor S. *History of Manufactures in the United States.* 3 vols. New York: McGraw-Hill, 1929.

Cochran, Thomas Childs, and William Miller. *The Age of Enterprise: A Social History of Industrial America.* New York: Macmillan, 1941. Rev. ed. Harper and Brothers, 1961.

Colby, Frank, M. A. Moore, and Allen Leon Churchill. *The New International Year Book: A Compendium of the World's Progress for the Year 1910.* New York: Dodd, Mead and Company, 1911.

Commons, John Rogers, et al. *The History of Labour in the United States.* Vol. 2. New York: Macmillan, 1918: 2.

Comparato, Frank E. *Chronicles of Genius and Folly: R. Hoe & Company and the Printing Press as a Service to Democracy.* Culver City, CA: Labyrinthos, 1979.

Cookingham, Henry J. *History of Oneida County, New York: From 1700 to the Present Time.* 2 vols. Chicago: S. J. Clark Publishing, 1912.

Cowles, Alfred A., III, et al. *Common Stock Indexes, 1871–1937.* Bloomington, IN: Principia Press, 1938.

Cross, Whitney. *The Burned Over District: The Social and Intellectual History of Enthusiastic Religion in Western New York.* Ithaca, NY: Cornell University Press, 1950.

Dana, Elizabeth Ellery. *The Dana Family in America.* Cambridge, MA: Wright and Potter Printing, 1956.

Dana, John Jay. *Memoranda of Some of the Descendants of Richard Dana.* Boston: Wm. H. Chandler and Co., 1865.

David, Henry. *The History of the Haymarket Affair: A Study in the American Social–Revolutionary Labor Movement.* New York: Farrar and Rinehart, 1936.

Degler, Carl. *The Age of the Economic Revolution, 1876–1900.* 2d ed. Glenview, IL: Scott, Foresman, 1967.

Demos, John. *A Little Commonwealth: Family Life in Plymouth Colony.* New York: Oxford University Press, 1970.

Dewey, Davis Rich. *Financial History of the United States.* New York: Longmans, Green, 1903.

Dexter, Frank Bowditch. *Sketch of the History of Yale University.* New York: Henry Holt and Company, 1887.

Dobson, John. *Reticent Expansionism: The Foreign Policy of William McKinley.* Pittsburgh, PA: Duquesne University Press, 1988.

Dorfman, Joseph Harry. *The Economic Mind in American Civilization*. 5 vols. New York: Viking, 1949.

Ekirch, Arthur Alphonse Jr. *The Idea of Progress in America, 1815–1860*. New York: Columbia University Press, 1954.

Faulkner, Harold Underwood. *The Decline of Laissez Faire: 1897–1917*. New York: Holt, Rinehart and Winston, 1961.

———. *Politics, Reform, and Expansion, 1890–1900*. New York: Harper, 1959.

Fels, Rendigs. *American Business Cycles, 1865–1897*. Chapel Hill: University of North Carolina Press, 1959.

Fogel, Robert William. *Railroads and American Economic Growth: Essays in Econometric History*. Baltimore: Johns Hopkins Press, 1964.

Fones-Wolf, Elizabeth A. *Selling Free Enterprise: The Business Assault on Labor and Liberalism, 1945–1960*. Urbana: University of Illinois Press, 1994.

Foreman, Sally Griffith. *Home Town News: William Allen White and the Emporia Gazette*. New York: Oxford University Press, 1989.

Forsyth, David P. *The Business Press in America, 1750–1865*. Philadelphia: Chilton Books, 1964.

Friedman, Milton, and Anna Jacobson Schwartz. *A Monetary History of the United States 1867–1960*. Princeton, NJ: Princeton University Press, 1963.

Gabriel, Ralph Henry. *The Course of American Democratic Thought: An Intellectual History since 1815*. New York: Ronald Press, 1940.

———. *Religion and Learning at Yale: The Church of Christ in the College and University, 1757–1957*. New Haven, CT: Yale University Press, 1958.

Galbraith, John Kenneth. *American Capitalism: The Concept of Countervailing Power*. Rev. ed. Boston: Houghton Mifflin, 1956.

———. *The Great Crash: 1929*. Boston: Houghton Mifflin [Sentry], 1960.

Gall, Gilbert J. *The Politics of the Right to Work: The Labor Federations as Special Interests, 1943–1979*. New York: Greenwood, 1988.

Garraty, John A. *The New Commonwealth, 1877–1900*. New York: Harper and Row, 1968.

Gioia, Dana. *Can Poetry Matter? Essays on Poetry and American Culture*. St. Paul, MN: Graywolf Press, 1992.

Grant, H. Roger. *Self-Help in the 1890s Depression*. Ames: Iowa State University Press, 1983.

Greco, James. *The Story of Englewood Cliffs*. Englewood Cliffs, NJ: Tercentenary Committee, 1964.

Griffith, Sally Foreman. *Home Town News: William Allen White and the Emporia Gazette*. New York: Oxford University Press, 1990.

Harbaugh, William Henry. *The Life and Times of Theodore Roosevelt*. New rev. ed. New York: Oxford University Press, 1975.

Hicks, John Donald. *The Populist Revolt: A History of the Farmers' Alliance and the People's Party*. Lincoln: University of Nebraska Press, 1961.

Hidy, Ralph W., and Muriel E. Hidy. *Pioneering in Big Business, 1882–1911*. Vol. 1 of *History of Standard Oil Company*. New York: Harper, 1955.

Higgs, Robert. *The Transformation of the American Economy, 1865–1914*. New York: Wiley, 1971.

Himmelberg, Robert F. *The Rise of Big Business and the Beginnings of Antitrust and Railroad Regulation, 1870–1900*. New York: Garland, 1994.

Hislop, Codman. *The Mohawk*. New York: Rinehart and Company, 1948.

Hoffman, Charles. *The Depression of the Nineties: An Economic History*. Westport, CT: Greenwood, 1970.

Hofstadter, Richard. *The Age of Reform: From Bryan to F.D.R*. New York: Vintage Books, 1955.

———. *The Paranoid Style in American Politics and Other Essays*. New York: Vintage Books, 1967.

Horseman, Reginald. *The Frontier in the Formative Years, 1783–1815*. New York: Holt, Rinehart and Winston, 1970.

Humphrey, Jeffrey A. *Englewood: Its Annals and Reminiscences*. New York: J.S. Ogilvie Publishing Company, 1899.

Hurd, Richard M. *A History of Yale Athletics, 1840–1888*. New Haven, CT: R.M. Hurd, 1888.

Huss, Richard E. *The Development of Printers' Mechanical Typesetting Methods, 1822–1925*. Charlottesville: University Press of Virginia, 1973.

Hyman, Harold M., and William M. Wiecek. *Equal Justice under the Law: Constitutional Development 1835–1875*. New York: Harper Torchbooks, 1982.

Jones, Pomroy. *Annals and Recollections of Oneida County*. Rome: Author, 1851.

Kelley, Brooks Mather. *Yale: A History*. New Haven, CT: Yale University Press, 1974.

Keynes, John Maynard. *The Economic Consequences of the Peace*. New York: Harcourt Brace and Company, 1920.

———. *The General Theory of Employment, Interest, and Money*. New York: Harcourt, Brace and World, 1936.

———. *Treatise on Money*. 2 vols. New York: Harcourt, Brace and Company, 1930.

Kingsley, William Lathrop. *Yale College: A Sketch of Its History*. 2 vols. New York: Henry Holt and Company, 1879.

Kirkland, Edward Chase. *Dream and Thought in the Business Community, 1860–1890*. Ithaca, NY: Cornell University Press, 1956.

———. *Industry Comes of Age: Business, Labor, and Public Policy, 1860–1897*. New York: Holt, Rinehart and Winston, 1961.

Kolko, Gabriel. *Railroads and Regulation, 1877–1916*. Princeton, NJ: Princeton University Press, 1965.

Kovaleff, Theodore P. *The Antitrust Impulse: An Economic, Historical, and Legal Analysis*. 2 vols. Armonk, NY: M.E. Sharpe, 1994.

Krause, Paul. *The Battle for Homestead, 1880–1892: Politics, Culture, and Steel*. Pittsburgh, PA: University of Pittsburgh Press, 1992.

LaFeber, Walter. *The New Empire: An Interpretation of American Expansion, 1860–1898*. Ithaca, NY: Cornell University Press, 1963.

Lamoreaux, Naomi R. *The Great Merger Movement in American Business, 1895–1904*. New York: Cambridge University Press, 1985.

Lattimer, John K. *This Was Early Englewood: From the Big Bang to the George Washington Bridge*. Fairview, NJ: Englewood Historical Society, 1990.

Laughlin, James Laurence. *The Federal Reserve Act: Its Origin and Problems*. New York: Macmillan, 1933.

———. *Report of the Monetary Commission of the Indianapolis Convention*. Indianapolis, IN: Hollenbeck Press, 1900.

Letwin, William. *Law and Economic Policy in America: The Evolution of the Sherman Antitrust Act*. New York: Random House, 1965.

Lindsey, Almont. *The Pullman Strike: The Story of a Unique Experiment and of a Great Labor Upheaval*. Chicago: University of Chicago Press, 1942, 1964.

Lydecker, Robert C., comp. *Lydecker Descendants: Ryck Lydecker, 1650*. Short Hills, NJ: Lydecker, 1987. Bergen County Historical Society Collection, Johnson Free Library, Hackensack, NJ.

Mandel, Bernard. *Samuel Gompers: A Biography*. Yellow Springs, OH: Antioch Press, 1963.

Marty, Martin. *Pilgrims in Their Own Land: 500 Years of Religion in America*. Boston: Little, Brown and Company, 1984.

May, Ernest R. *Imperial Democracy*. New York: Harcourt, Brace and World, 1961.

May, Henry Farnham. *Protestant Churches and Industrial America*. New York: Harper and Brothers, 1949.

McClellan, Elisabeth. *History of American Costume, 1607–1870*. New York: George W. Jacobs and Company, 1904. Reprint, New York: Taylor Publishing, 1937.

McCormick, Thomas J. *China Market*. Chicago: Quadrangle Books, 1967.

Merk, Frederick W. *Manifest Destiny and Mission in American History: A Reinterpretation*. New York: Alfred A. Knopf, 1963.

Mitchell, Broadus. *Depression Decade: From New Era through New Deal, 1929–1941*. New York: Holt, Rinehart and Winston, 1961.

Moody, John. *The Truth About the Trusts*. New York: Moody, 1904.

Moore, Doris Langley. *Fashion through Plates, 1771–1970*. New York: Clarkson N. Potter, 1971.

Morgan, H. Wayne. *America's Road to Empire*. New York: Wiley, 1965.

———. *William McKinley and his America*. Syracuse, NY: Syracuse University Press, 1963.

———, ed. *The Gilded Age: A Reappraisal*. Syracuse, NY: Syracuse University Press, 1963.

Mott, Frank Luther. *A History of American Magazines*. 5 vols. Cambridge: Harvard University Press, 1938–1957. 1.

———. *A History of Newspapers in the United States through 260 Years, 1690–1950*. Rev. ed. New York: Macmillan, 1950.

Mowry, George R. *The Era of Theodore Roosevelt and the Birth of Modern America, 1900–1912*. New York: Harper and Row, 1958.

Nelson, Daniel. *Shifting Fortunes: The Rise and Decline of American Labor from the 1820s to the Present*. Chicago: Ivan R. Dee, 1997.

Nelson, Ralph L. *Merger Movements in American History, 1865–1916*. Princeton, NJ: Princeton University Press, 1959.

Niebuhr, H. Richard. *The Kingdom of God in America*. 1937. Reprint, New York: Harper and Brothers, reprint Harper Torchbooks, 1959.

Ong, Father Walter J. *Orality and Literacy: The Technologizing of the Word*. New York: Methuen, 1982.

Paludan, Phillip Shaw. *"A People's Contest": The Union and Civil War, 1861–1865*. New York: Harper and Row, 1988.

Paul, Arnold M. *Conservative Crisis and the Rule of Law: Attitudes of Bar and Bench, 1887–1895*. Ithaca, NY: Cornell University Press, 1960.

Persons, Stow. *American Minds: A History of Ideas.* New York: Henry Holt and Company, 1958.

Pieper, Joseph. *Leisure: The Basis of Culture.* Translated by Alexander Dru. New York: A Mentor Book, 1963.

Pratt, Julius W. *Expansionists of 1898.* Chicago: Quadrangle Books, 1964.

Randall, James Garfield, and David Donald. *The Civil War and Reconstruction.* 2nd ed. Boston: D.C. Heath and Company, 1961.

Redford, Emmette S. *American Government and the Economy.* New York: Macmillan, 1965.

Redlich, Fritz. *The Molding of American Banking: Men and Ideas.* Part 2: *1840–1910.* New York: Hafner, 1951.

Rischin, Moses, ed. *The American Gospel of Success: Individualism and Beyond.* Chicago: Quadrangle Books, 1965.

Ritter, Gretchen. *Goldbugs and Greenbacks: The Antimonopoly Tradition and the Politics of Finance in America.* New York: Cambridge University Press, 1997.

Roberts, Ellis Henry. *New York: The Planting and the Growth of the Empire State.* 2 vols. New York: Houghton Mifflin, 1887.

Rossiter, Clinton. *Conservatism in America: The Thankless Persuasion.* 2d ed. Rev. New York: Random House, 1962.

Rudolph, Frederick. *The American College and University: A History.* New York: Vintage Books, 1965.

———. *Curriculum: A History of the American Undergraduate Course of Study since 1636.* San Francisco: Jossey-Bass, 1978.

Ryan, Mary P. *Cradle of the Middle Class: The Family in Oneida County, New York, 1790–1865.* Cambridge: Cambridge University Press, 1981.

Schwantes, Carlos A. *Coxey's Army: An American Odyssey.* Lincoln: University of Nebraska Press, 1985.

Sinclair, Upton. *The Jungle.* New York: Doubleday and Page, 1906.

Sosin, Jack B. *The Revolutionary Frontier, 1783–1815.* New York: Holt, Rinehart and Winston, 1967.

Soule, George. *From War to Depression, 1919–1929.* New York: Holt, Rinehart and Winston, 1961.

Spicher, Craig R. *The Practice of Presswork.* Pittsburgh, PA: N.p., 1919.

Sprague, Oliver Mitchell Wentworth. *History of Crises under the National Banking System.* Washington, DC: Government Printing Office, 1910.

Stabile, Donald R., and Jeffrey A. Canton. *The Public Debt of the United States: An Historical Perspective, 1775–1990.* New York: Praeger, 1991.

Steele, Janet L. *The Sun Shines for All.* Syracuse, NY: Syracuse University Press, 1993.

Steeples, Douglas, and David O. Whitten. *Democracy in Desperation: The Depression of 1893.* Westport, CT: Greenwood, 1998.

Steigerwalt, Albert Kleckner. *The National Association of Manufacturers, 1895–1914: A Study in Business Leadership.* Ann Arbor: University of Michigan Press, 1964.

Sterling, Adaline W. *The Book of Englewood.* Englewood, NJ: City of Englewood, 1922.

Stokes, Anson Phelps. *Memorials of Eminent Yale Men.* 2 vols. New Haven, CT: Yale University Press, 1914.

Stone, William L. *In Memoriam: William Johnson Bacon.* Utica, NY: n.p. n.d. [1889?].

Sutton, Antony C. *America's Secret Establishment: An Introduction to the Order of Skull and Bones.* Billings, MT: Liberty House Press, 1986.

Taus, Esther Rogoff. *Central Banking Functions of the United States Treasury, 1789–1941.* New York: Columbia University Press, 1941.

Taussig, Frank W. *Tariff History of the United States.* 7th ed. New York: G. P. Putnam's Sons, 1923.

Taylor, George Rogers. *The Transportation Revolution, 1815–1860.* New York: Holt, Rinehart and Winston, 1962.

Tebbel, John, and Mary Ellen Zuckerman. *The Magazine in America, 1741–1990.* New York: Oxford University Press, 1991.

Thelen, David F. *The New Citizenship: Origins of Progressivism, 1895–1900.* New York: Columbia University Press, 1972.

Thorelli, Hans Birger. *The Federal Anti-Trust Policy.* Baltimore: Johns Hopkins University Press, 1955.

Ullmer, Melville J. *Trends and Cycles in Capital Formation by United States Railroads, 1870–1950.* New York: National Bureau of Economic Research, 1954.

Veysey, Laurence. *The Emergence of the American University.* Chicago: University of Chicago Press, 1967.

Voss, Kim. *The Making of American Exceptionalism: The Knights of Labor and Class Formation in the Nineteenth Century.* Ithaca, NY: Cornell University Press, 1993.

Wager, Daniel E., ed. *Our County and Its People: A Descriptive Work on Oneida County, New York.* Boston: Boston History Company, 1896.

Wall, Joseph Frazier. *Andrew Carnegie.* New York: Oxford University Press, 1974.

Walsh, Margaret. *The Rise of the Midwestern Meat Packing Industry.* Lexington: University of Kentucky Press, 1982.

Warren, Charles. *Bankruptcy in American History.* Cambridge: Harvard University Press, 1935.

Weinberg, Albert Katz. *Manifest Destiny: A Study of Nationalist Expansionism in American History.* Chicago: Quadrangle Books, 1963.

Weir, Robert E. *Beyond Labor's Veil: The Culture of the Knights of Labor.* University Park: Pennsylvania State University Press, 1996.

Weisberger, Bernard A. *The American Newspaperman.* Chicago: University of Chicago Press, 1961.

———. *They Gathered at the River: The Story of the Great Revivalists and Their Impact upon Religion in America.* Chicago: Quadrangle Books, 1966.

Whitten, David O. *The Emergence of Giant Enterprise, 1860–1914: American Commercial Enterprise and Extractive Industries.* Westport, CT: Greenwood, 1983.

Wiebe, Robert H. *The Search for Order, 1877–1920.* New York Hill and Wang, 1967.

———. *Self-Rule: A Cultural History of American Democracy.* Chicago: University of Chicago Press, 1995.

Wisan, Joseph E. *The Cuban Crisis as Reflected in the New York Press.* New York: Columbia University Press, 1934.

Wyllie, Irvin G. *The Self-Made Man in America.* New Brunswick, NJ: Rutgers University Press, 1954.

Woodward, Comer Vann. *Origins of the New South, 1877–1913.* Baton Rouge: Louisiana State University Press, 1951.

Yeager, Mary. *Competition and Regulation: The Development of Oligopoly in the Meat-Packing Industry.* Greenwich, CT: JAI Press, 1981.

Periodicals and Chapters

Anonymous. "Reid, Thomas." *The New Encyclopaedia Britannica.* 32 vols. Chicago: Encyclopaedia Britannica, 1985. *Micropaedia,* 9:1007.

———. "Freeman Hunt." *Memorial Biographies of the New England Historic Genealogical Society,* 3:200–207. N.P., 1856–1859.

Auxier, Charles W. "Middle Western Newspapers and the Spanish-American War." *Mississippi Valley Historical Review* 26 (March 1940): 525.

Barnett, George E. "The Introduction of the Linotype." *Yale Review* 12 (November 1904): 251–273.

Benson, Lee. "An Approach to the Scientific Study of Past Public Opinion." *Public Opinion Quarterly* 31 (Winter 1967–1968): 522–567.

Boas, George. "Cousin, Victor." *The Encyclopedia of Philosophy.* 8 vols. 2:248. New York: Macmillan and The Free Press, 1967.

Chandler, Alfred D. Jr. "The Beginnings of 'Big Business' in American History." *Business History Review* 33 (Spring 1959): 1–31.

———. "Henry Varnum Poor: Philosopher of Management, 1812–1905." In *Men in Business: Essays on the Historical Role of the Entrepreneur,* edited by William Miller, 254–285. Cambridge: Harvard University Press, 1951. Reprint, New York: Harper and Row, 1962.

Cleveland, Frederick A. "The Final Report of the Monetary Commission." *Annals of the American Academy of Political and Social Science* 13 (January 1899): 31–56.

Coletta, Paolo E. "Greenbackers, Goldbugs, and Silverites: *Currency Reform and Policy, 1860–1897.*" In *The Gilded Age: A Reappraisal,* edited by H. Wayne Morgan, 111–139. Syracuse, NY: Syracuse University Press, 1963.

Conant, Luther, Jr. "Business Consolidations in the United States." *Quarterly Publications of the American Statistical Association* 8 (March 1900): 207, 226.

Grave, S.A. "Reid, Thomas." *The Encyclopedia of Philosophy.* 8 vols. New York: Macmillan and The Free Press, 1967, 7:118–121.

Gregory, Frances W. and Irene D. Neu. "The American Industrial Elite in the 1870s: *Their Social Origins.*" In *Men in Business: Essays on the Historical Role of the Enterpreneur,* edited by William Miller, 193–211. New York: Harper and Row, 1962.

Hafen, LeRoy R. "Butterfield, John." *Dictionary of American Biography.* 20 vols., edited by Allen Johnson and Dumas Malone, 2: 374. New York: Charles Scribner's Sons, 1928–1937.

Heald, Morrell. "Business Attitudes toward European Immigration, 1890–1900. *Journal of Economic History* 31 (Summer 1953): 291–304.

Hoffman, Charles. "The Depression of the Nineties." *Journal of Economic History* 16 (June, 1956), 137–164.

Kindahl, James K. "Economic Factors in Specie Resumption in the United States, 1865–1879." *Journal of Political Economy* 69 (February 1961): 30–48.

Lebergott, Stanley. "Wage Trends, 1800–1900." In *Trends in the American Economy, in the Nineteenth Century*, 449–499. Princeton, NJ: Princeton University Press, 1960.

Merrill, George P. "Dana, James Dwight." *Dictionary of American Biography*. 20 vols., edited by Allen Johnson and Dumas Malone, 5:55–56. New York: Charles Scribner's Sons, 1928–1937.

Miller, William. "American Historians and the Business Elite." In *Men in Business: Essays on the Historical Role of the Enterpreneurs*, edited by William Miller, 309–328. New York: Harper and Row, 1962.

———. "The Recruitment of the American Business Elite." In *Men in Business: Essays on the Historical Role of the Enterpreneurs*, edited by William Miller, 329–338. New York: Harper and Row, 1962.

Nerlove, Marc. "Railroads and Economic Growth." *Journal of Economic History* 26 (March 1966): 109–115.

Peterson, A. Everett. "Hunt, Freeman." *Dictionary of American Biography*. 20 vols., edited by Allen Johnson and Dumas Malone, 9:384–385. New York: Charles Scribner's Sons, 1928–1937.

Rezneck, Samuel S. "Distress, Relief, and Discontent in the United States during the Depression of 1873–1878." *Journal of Political Economy* 38 (December 1950): 494–512.

———. "Patterns of Thought and Action in an American Depression, 1882–1886." *American Historical Review* 61 (January 1956): 284–307.

———. "Unemployment, Unrest and Relief in the United States during the Depression of 1893–1897." *Journal of Political Economy* 61 (August 1953): 324–345.

Sprague, Elmer. "Paley, William." *The Encyclopedia of Philosophy*. 8 vols. New York: Macmillan Company and The Free Press, 1967, 6:19–20.

Steele, Janet L. "The 19th Century *World* versus the *Sun*: Promoting Consumption (Rather than the Working Man)." *Journalism Quarterly* 67 (Autumn, 1990): 592–600.

Steeples, Douglas. "DANA, William Buck." *American National Biography*. 20 vols., edited by John A. Garraty and Mark C. Carnes, 6:69–70. New York: Oxford University Press, 1999.

Tufano, Peter. "Business Failure, Judicial Intervention, and Financial Innovation: Restructuring U.S. Railroads in the Nineteenth Century." *Business History Review* 71 (Spring 1997): 1–40.

White, Robert A. "Mass Communication and Culture: Transition to a New Paradigm." *Journal of Communication* 33 (Summer 1983): 279–301.

Woodward, Comer Vann. "The Populist Heritage and the Intellectual." *American Scholar* 29 (Winter 1959): 55–72.

Personal Correspondence and Interviews

Brookes, Barbara. Reference Librarian. Utica (New York) Public Library. Personal letter to the author, December 17, 1991.

Butler, Dr. Howard, Vernon, NY. Personal interview with the author, March 17, 1992.

Dixon, Patricia. Librarian. Vernon, NY. Personal interview with the author, March 17, 1992.

Dodge, Alice C. Reference Librarian. Utica (New York) Public Library. Personal letter to the author, February 3, 1966.

Ellison, Miriam T. Alumni Secretary, Yale University. Personal letter to the author, January 12, 1965.

Folts, James D. New York State Archives. Personal letter to the author, June 17, 1992.

Forsyth, David P. (historian of the business press in America). Personal letter to the author, July 7, 1965.

Gehl., P.F. Custodian, The John M. Wing Foundation on the History of Printing. Personal letters to the author, July 27 and August 31, 1992.

Griffith, Alice B. Research Volunteer. Oneida County Historical Society, Utica, NY. Personal letter to the author, August 17, 1989.

Schiff, Judith Ann. Chief Research Archivist. Yale University Libraries. Personal letter to the author, July 22, 1991.

Sforza, A.J. Personal interview with the author, March 17, 1992.

Sharpe, Beverly. Director of Records Management. Oneida County, Utica, NY. Personal letter to the author, July 17, 1991.

Unpublished Manuscripts

Berkhofer, Robert Frederick, Jr. "The Industrial History of Oneida County, New York, to 1850." Master's thesis, Cornell University, 1955.

Everett, George. "The Linotype and U.S. Daily Newspaper Journalism in the 1890s: Analysis of a Relationship." Ph.D. diss., University of Iowa, 1972.

Peal, B.J. "A Glimpse into the History of Vernon, New York." Utica, New York: Oneida County Historical Society, 1959.

Index

About the Author

DOUGLAS STEEPLES is Professor of History Emeritus and formerly Dean at Mercer University. His primary research interests are the American West and U.S. Business History. His recent books include *Treasure from the Painted Hills* (Greenwood, 1999) and *Democracy in Desperation* (Greenwood, 1998).